A FUNDRAISING Guide

for Nonprofit Board Members

The AFP Fund Development Series

The AFP Fund Development Series is intended to provide fund development professionals and volunteers, including board members (and others interested in the nonprofit sector), with top-quality publications that help advance philanthropy as voluntary action for the public good. Our goal is to provide practical, timely guidance and information on fundraising, charitable giving, and related subjects. The Association of Fundraising Professionals (AFP) and Wiley each bring to this innovative collaboration unique and important resources that result in a whole greater than the sum of its parts. For information on other books in the series, please visit:

http://www.afpnet.org

The Association of Fundraising Professionals

The Association of Fundraising Professionals (AFP) represents over 30,000 members in more than 207 chapters throughout the United States, Canada, Mexico, and China, working to advance philanthropy through advocacy, research, education, and certification programs.

The association fosters development and growth of fundraising professionals and promotes high ethical standards in the fundraising rofession. For more information or to join the world's largest association of fundraising professionals, visit www.afpnet.org.

2011-2012 AFP Publishing Advisory Committee

Steven Miller, CFRE

Director of Individual Giving, American Kidney Fund

Benjamin T. Mohler, CFRE

Director of Development, UNC Charlotte

Robert J. Mueller, CFRE

Vice President, Gift Planning, Hospice Foundation of Louisville

Maria-Elena Noriega

Director, Noriega Malo y Asociados. S.C.

Timothy J. Willard, Ph.D., CFRE

Vice President of Development, Ranken Technical College

AFP Staff:

Rhonda Starr

Vice President, Education and Training

Reed Stockman

AFP Staff Support

Chris Griffin

Professional Advancement Coordinator

Jacklyn P. Boice

Editor-in-Chief, Advancing Philanthropy

John Wiley & Sons, Inc.:

Susan McDermott

Senior Editor (Professional/Trade Division)

A FUNDRAISING Guide

for Nonprofit Board Members

Julia Ingraham Walker

WILEY

John Wiley & Sons, Inc.

Published by John Wiley & Sons, Inc., Hoboken, New Jersey.

Published simultaneously in Canada.

For general information on our other products and services or for technical support, please contact our Customer Care Department within the United States at (800) 762-2974, outside the United States at (317) 572-3993 or fax (317) 572-4002.

Wiley also publishes its books in a variety of electronic formats. Some content that appears in print may not be available in electronic books. For more information about Wiley products, visit our web site at www.wiley.com.

Library of Congress Cataloging-in-Publication Data:

Walker, Julia Ingraham.
   A fundraising guide for nonprofit board members/Julia Ingraham Walker.
      p. cm. -- (The AFP fund development series; 198)
   Includes index.
   ISBN 978-1-118-07356-8 (hardback);   ISBN 978-1-118-22249-2 (ebk);   ISBN 978-1-118-23643-7 (ebk);
   ISBN 978-1-118-23732-8 (ebk)
   1. Fund raising. 2.   Nonprofit organizations.   I. Title.
   HG177.W344 2009
   658.15'224--dc23

                                                                          2011039740

Printed in the United States of America

10 9 8 7 6 5 4 3 2 1

With grateful appreciation to all the nonprofit board members who give so much of their time, energy, and resources to help improve life for all of us. I have been fortunate to have worked with many wonderful and knowledgeable board members, and I have learned everything I know about fundraising from them. May this book be seen as my effort to pass this knowledge along so that others can make a similar impact on behalf of the organizations and causes that they so passionately support.

Contents

Contents

Contents

Preface

We in the nonprofit sector find ourselves caught up in the world of that famous Chinese proverb, "May you live in interesting times." Our nonprofit organizations and the services they provide are more important than ever before, but we are under immense pressure to find more resources to sustain these activities.

The basic thesis of this book is that raising more money in an increasingly competitive environment requires tapping the energy and enthusiasm of every one of our nonprofit board members. This book aims to help your board develop from playing a passive role receiving fundraising reports into an active fundraising board that is ready and able to tap into all the philanthropic resources available.

And there definitely are philanthropic resources available. Even given some recent blips and dips (including threats to the charitable deduction), the spirit of private philanthropy is alive and well in the United States today. Estimated charitable giving in the United States totaled over $290 billion in 2010. Over 73 percent of that total came from individuals.[1]

You and your fellow board members can play a leadership role in securing these resources for your nonprofit. In the process, you will learn some new things, develop some new skills, and hopefully have a little fun. We hope that you will discover how rewarding it can be to raise money for a cause you believe in.

---

[1]*Giving USA 2011: The Annual Report on Philanthropy for 2010*, published by Giving USA Foundation, researched and written by the Center on Philanthropy at Indiana University, 2011.

An Introductory Note to Board Members

Leadership and learning are indispensable to each other.

—John F. Kennedy[2]

You already know that times are tough for most nonprofits in this challenging economy. For many, revenues are down and requirements for services are up. Your nonprofit may be squeaking by or perhaps is trying to retool for growth. Where will your organization turn for the increased financial support it needs to meet its mission?

The key to providing concrete, measurable improvements in fundraising productivity lies with you and your fellow board members. It is time to embrace your role as an active member of the fundraising team.

Your role must evolve so that you and your colleagues view the development of resources as a coherent and integral part of your basic function on the board. The purpose of this book is to help you on that journey.

This book is designed to help you improve your own personal fundraising skills as well as to serve as a guide for you, your board, and your organization's executive leadership on ways to improve overall board performance in fundraising. Once that improvement kicks in, your organization will experience greater fundraising activity, improve donor satisfaction, and reach higher fundraising goals.

You can expect to see your own role delineated in the sections titled "Your Role as a Board Member." As you will see, many of the concepts and techniques presented here will also require development and implementation by others in the organization. You are part of a team and should expect support from the other members of the team.

Your role is a key one. You can demonstrate the leadership, commitment, and passion for your cause that will attract additional financial support. But you must also educate yourself—about your organization, about the fundraising

---

[2]All epigraphs and quotes throughout are from brainyquote.com.

process, and about how to ask for and close a gift. This book will be one resource along that educational path.

Your board leaders, your executive director, and the members of your organization's advancement staff all have their own roles to play. Introducing you to their responsibilities is meant to help you see how your work fits into the big picture.

You will need to learn more about the components of the broader team effort and how the advancement team can support your work. You can help advocate for these additional staffing and programmatic resources if they aren't available in your organization.

If your organization has limited staff and resources, your role as a board member may expand into areas more commonly reserved for the executive director or for advancement staff. Chapter Four, for instance, delineates fundraising activities for board members based on several different models of advancement staff support.

Boards and organizations don't change overnight. Add patience to your list of virtues and take small steps toward the goals you seek. As you and your colleagues begin to experience success, the path will become smoother.

There is incredible power and energy in a board that exhibits fundraising leadership. Implemented successfully, this effort will enhance your board service, build your own personal skill set, and provide personal satisfaction as your organization moves forward confidently with the resources it needs to meet its mission.

An Introductory Note to the Executive Director/CEO

A leader is best when people barely know he exists, not so good when people obey and acclaim him, worst when they despise him. But of a good leader, who talks little, when his work is done, his aim fulfilled, they will say, "We did this ourselves."

—Laozi

It's time to take a fresh look at how to empower and support board leadership in fundraising. The old mantra of "give or get" must be replaced with defining a more active fundraising role for board members. You know that you need help in securing more resources for your organization. This book is meant to help you find new ways to motivate, engage, and team up with your board members to find those resources.

There are many threats to the nonprofit sector looming in the current economic and political climate. Dropping or changing the charitable deduction, once viewed as an untouchable pillar of the tax code, is under discussion. The volatility of the stock market is making donors wary of large gifts and long-term commitments. Global recession (and the fear of recession) provides an ongoing threat. Fiscal policy is being restructured in dramatic ways at both the federal and the state level.

All of these larger issues, most of them out of your control, affect your organization's ability to maintain and grow revenues and to provide the services to meet your mission.

This backdrop of uncertainty makes your job of ensuring the financial sustainability of your organization much more difficult. Why not mobilize all of the resources at your disposal to build additional support? Harnessing the energy, commitment, enthusiasm, personal connections, and giving of your board has never been more important to the future of your organization.

The most recent national survey of board effectiveness, the BoardSource *Nonprofit Government Index 2010*, reports that fundraising is the area most in need of improvement. Nonprofit CEOs in the survey rated fundraising as the worst area of board performance on a report card of 10 basic board responsibilities. Board fundraising received the lowest grade, a D+, from chief executives and only a C+ (still the lowest grade) from board members.[3]

You can help to reverse this poor performance record! The purpose of this book is to give you some insight into how your organization can build the appropriate structures, staffing, and programs to support board leadership in fundraising. From holding a board retreat to preparing a campaign table of needs, you will learn how to board buy-in and ownership of your organization's resource development activities.

Change can be difficult, and your board members are not going to embrace fundraising overnight. Think of your work in this area as an investment in building long term support for your mission. Your encouragement, support, leadership, and patience will all be required. As a board member quoted in the BoardSource survey noted, "The board's effectiveness is directly related to the level of the chief executive's engagement with the board."[4]

Successful fundraising depends on arming yourself with new strategies and techniques that have proven to be effective. Learn what works for other boards and their executive directors. Develop a more productive fundraising team by having your advancement staff integrate their efforts with those of your board members. Improve board fundraising skills through training and mentoring programs. Be an effective teacher and leader: Raise expectations, set goals, hold people accountable, report on results, and praise success.

The stakes are high and the timing is crucial. Find ways to harness the passion, energy, and skills of your board members in the search for additional resources. The alternative is too ugly to contemplate—that your nonprofit will wither, lose momentum, and perhaps die on the vine. Take steps now to engage your board in the development arena and your fundraising results will soar. This book will give you the tools to make this happen.

---

[3] *BoardSource*, p. 7.

[4] *BoardSource*, p. 7.

How This Book Is Set Up and How to Use It

This book is comprised of 10 chapters and appendix material, as well as a companion web site, with the goal of providing a guide for nonprofit board members on how to take an active leadership role in fundraising.

The material is arranged in a manner that initially introduces the reader to the main components of major fundraising programs common to all nonprofits, so that board members become educated about basic fundraising topics. Exhibits and ancillary material, including real-world examples, are used to educate readers about strategic elements and to suggest applications of each program to their own needs. Every chapter includes a section that focuses on the specific role of board members and advice on how the board can implement programs and strategies that will improve their organization's fundraising results.

Chapter 1 starts with a look at board fundraising leadership: what it is, and what steps to take to build an active fundraising board. Chapter 1 also explains how the board's fiduciary role has undergone a transition in recent years and how that role applies to fundraising. Chapter 2 covers key aspects of board giving and how board members can prepare for the expanded role they will play in fundraising.

In Chapter 3, board members learn about using strategic planning to identify organizational needs. This chapter includes recommended board committee structures and training options for improving board fundraising skills. Practical issues such as development staffing and budgets, hiring fundraising consultants, and the role of board members vs. the role of advancement staff are featured in Chapter 4.

Chapter 5, on the annual fund, is all about how to raise more money for operations. It includes a plan for putting in place a leadership annual fund program to raise annual gifts of $1,000+. Major gifts and prospect identification are the focal points of Chapter 6, which includes a section on how to find transformational gifts of $5 million and up. These chapters show board members how to focus their time and energy on fundraising programs that provide a strong return on their investment.

Chapter 7, titled "How to Ask for and Close a Gift," provides a step-by-step guide to how to make a successful solicitation call for a major gift. Chapter 7 is augmented by material posted on the book's companion web site, found at www.wiley.com/go/boardfundraising, which includes materials for a board retreat on fundraising, a training exercise on how to ask for major gifts, and a related PowerPoint presentation on The 5 Elements of the Successful Ask.

Chapters 8 and 9 focus on fundraising campaigns: How to prepare for them, how to set realistic goals, elements of campaign structure, recognition and pricing, as well as campaign leadership and volunteer structure. Campaigns are still the most efficient method of raising money for capital projects and endowment, and they require substantial board engagement to reach their goals.

Chapter 10 introduces board members to corporate and foundation giving, a step beyond fundraising from individuals. Chapter 10 also introduces fundamentals of planned giving and the elements of good donor stewardship. Familiarity with these elements of fundraising gives board members a broader understanding of how to develop and maintain relationships with donors to support the organization over the longer term.

The Appendix includes materials for a board retreat on fundraising and related materials to use for board training. This book has a companion web site at www.wiley.com/go/boardfundraising, where readers can go to download the materials that appear in the Appendix. These materials are available on the web site so that you or your staff can download them and edit them to fit your organization's needs. Included exclusively on the web site is the PowerPoint presentation, "The 5 Elements of the Successful Ask."

These materials include:

- Materials for a Board Retreat on Fundraising
  - Preparation
  - Sample Board Retreat Agenda
  - Sample Board Retreat Agenda with Discussion Points

- Next Steps: After the Retreat
- Attachments to Use in Board Retreat
- Materials for a Board Training Exercise on Fundraising
  - PowerPoint Presentation: The 5 Elements of the Successful Ask
  - Role-Play Exercise
  - Three Sample Role-Playing Scripts

Acknowledgments

My thanks go to my family, especially to Cedric, my sweet and long-suffering husband and companion; and to my sons Jake, who served as my first editor, and Ben, who designed my first web site. Along with them I am very grateful to my former colleague Eva Martinez, who provided the insight of an informed reader at an early stage in the development of this book.

Thanks also go to Susan McDermott, Jennifer MacDonald, Melissa Lopez, and the rest of the team at John Wiley and Sons, my publishers, along with the AFP Publishing Advisory Committee that approved my proposal for this book. You are the real pros in this field and I feel lucky to have worked with all of you.

To my clients and longtime friends in the advancement profession: You deserve a special acknowledgement for teaching me so much. I depend on each one of you to keep me in touch with the reality of what works in fundraising.

Finally, many thanks to the generous donors who make meeting our goals possible, and whose philanthropy we count on to make our nonprofits succeed. We couldn't make a dent on improving this troubled world of ours without your incredible and uplifting support. May your giving natures be blessed and your charitable tax deductions be secure forever.

About the Author

Julia Ingraham Walker holds a BA and an MA in English from Tulane University and an MBA from Rollins College in Florida. Her initial marketing expertise was gained during 10 years as a professional in college admissions, first at Tulane and then as Director of Admissions at Rollins. In 1985, she returned to New Orleans and began a career in fundraising that has spanned more than 25 years and numerous positions ranging from annual funds to major gifts.

In 1990, Ms. Walker was appointed Vice President for Institutional Advancement at her alma mater, Tulane, where she served until 1998. In this position she directed the university's successful $250 million capital campaign. At Tulane she helped to raise over $100 million for the school's endowment and secured resources for the construction or major renovation of eight campus buildings. In 1994, Ms. Walker was named Outstanding Fundraising Executive by her peers in the New Orleans chapter of AFP, the Association of Fundraising Professionals.

Ms. Walker has been active as an independent fundraising consultant since 1998 and has conducted and advised campaigns that raised a total of more than $1 billion. Her clients include a wide range of nonprofits, from museums and schools to grassroots community organizations. A resident of New Orleans, she returned to the city post–Katrina to repair her home and has been working with nonprofits in the region since then as they reopened, recovered, and rebuilt.

As an independent fundraising consultant, Ms. Walker has worked with clients in the fields of religion, health care, the arts, historic preservation, low-income housing, K-12 education, higher education, museums, and a community foundation. Her areas of expertise include campaign planning and nonprofit management, including building and training nonprofit boards for fundraising leadership.

Ms. Walker is a member of AFP and has participated in numerous national conferences and workshops on fundraising topics. She has published three prior fundraising books with John Wiley & Sons in the Nonprofit Essentials series: *The Capital Campaign*, *Major Gifts*, and *Jump-Starting the Stalled Fundraising Campaign*. Ms. Walker can be reached through her web site, www.walkercapitalcampaigns.com, or by email at julia.i.walker@gmail.com. She would welcome any comments or suggestions from readers of this book.

CHAPTER 1

Board Leadership in Fundraising

Act as if what you do makes a difference. It does.

—William James

After reading this chapter, you will be able to:

- Take a leadership role in fundraising.
- Build an effective fundraising board.
- Understand the board's fiduciary role.

A Challenging Economic Environment

There are many financial challenges facing the nonprofit sector today.

It is getting harder to predict where to find the resources that organizations need to sustain their operations and to grow. An ongoing environment of economic uncertainty has increased the demand for new sources of revenue. Financial planning, modeled on what used to be regular and predictable annual growth, has proven less and less reliable. Volatility is affecting markets and service providers.

For many nonprofits, almost every source of revenue is getting more difficult to maintain. There are perils in depending on earned revenue, which can decline in bad times, when the organization needs the money the most.

Endowments, meant to be a savings account for a rainy day, dropped with the falling markets a few years ago and are only slowly regaining their former value. Government grants, whether local, state, or federal, have dried up. Congressional earmarks have become unworkable in the current political environment of budget deficits and spending cuts.

There are even growing concerns that private philanthropy has been affected, perhaps over the long term, by the uncertain economic conditions.

The reports of weakness keep rolling in. In an article under the headline "Corporate Giving Slow to Recover as Economy Remains Shaky," a survey of 180 companies from *The Chronicle of Philanthropy* finds that corporate gifts will remain flat in the coming year because of the bad economy.[1]

Yet in the face of all of these financial challenges, nonprofit leaders report that their boards are not doing a good job in fundraising. (See the national survey results reported in the *In the Real World* box nearby.) Fundraising at the board level is the area *most in need of improvement* according to both executives and trustees.

The Board's Leadership Role in Fundraising

It seems clear that nonprofit institutions must become more effective and more efficient at raising private funds to face the financial challenges ahead. But what is the best way to make an organization's fundraising efforts more productive?

There are a number of actions that an organization could take in an attempt to improve fundraising results. Adding more advancement staff is a common response. The hope is that by hiring the best, most experienced fundraisers, the organization can implement new programs and find new donors.

---

[1]Eric Frazier and Marisa Lopez-Rivera, in *The Chronicle of Philanthropy*, July 24, 2011.

This solution could work to a certain degree, but new fundraising staff often lacks the entrée to potential donors provided by board members. Staff are often more limited in their ability to influence wealthy donors to invest in a program or project than their peers or associates, who often have personal connections to those donors and who have made their own commitment to the organization.

IN THE REAL WORLD

Fundraising Needs the Most Improvement

A recent national survey showed that both executive directors and board members rated fundraising as the area most in need of improvement among all the responsibilities that board members are asked to take on.

The survey comes from *The 2010 Nonprofit Governance Index*, an annual report produced by BoardSouce, an organization based in Washington, DC, that focuses on improving nonprofit boards.

The survey reports that 53 percent of executive directors see fundraising as the number one most important area for board improvement. Board members surveyed felt just as strongly—54 percent of board members rated fundraising as the area most in need of improvement.

As reported in Eric Frazier, "Trustees Don't Do Well in Fundraising or Promoting Diversity, CEO's Say," *The Chronicle of Philanthropy*, November 1, 2010.

Another option often pursued by boards is to delegate all the responsibility for fundraising to the board's development committee, increasing the pressure on a few board members to do all the work. Exerting more pressure on the executive director to get out and raise money is also a common response.

Both of these alternatives increase the risk of burnout for board members and CEOs, leading to blame for poor results being placed on a small number of overwhelmed individuals. And implementing these options will only provide a partial solution to the need for enhanced resources.

The best way to increase productivity in fundraising is to build an outstanding fundraising team that involves every board member in the important work of resource development.

TALES FROM THE BOARDROOM

A board member called on a wealthy widow to ask her to name the new museum wing after her second husband, who had been a major donor to the art museum before his untimely death. She admired the pretty color rendering, looked back at the board member, and replied, "I like it, but can I name it after my first husband instead?"

Beyond "Give or Get"

Effective fundraising requires an effective team. The strong team includes three components: board, executive leadership, and fundraising staff (referred to here as *advancement staff or development staff*).

The role of the board is the most critical because the board by definition provides leadership for the organization. All the members of the board, in coordination with the executive director/CEO and the advancement staff, must develop into a strong, well-coordinated team for the nonprofit to excel at fundraising.

Board members traditionally have been told to "give or get," which means they either make their own gifts or help to solicit others. The strongest fundraising boards, however, are those that encourage their members to do more than just give and get. There are many ways that board members can participate in and provide leadership for fundraising efforts.

RULES OF THE ROAD

The key to more productive fundraising is for the entire board to commit to taking on an active, leadership role in fundraising.

There are four key strategic reasons why all board members should commit to taking on an active, leadership role in fundraising:

1. ***The board has fiduciary responsibility for the organization.***

   The board is ultimately responsible for seeing that the organization has the resources it needs to meet its mission. In the great majority of non-profits, this means that the organization must raise additional funds from outside sources to ensure that the appropriate resources are available. The board must be actively involved as part of the team to identify those resources and help to secure them.

2. ***The board has oversight of all fundraising programs and operations.***

   Board members, whether through the development committee or as members of the full board, must approve fundraising projects, goals, and time lines; they must ensure that fundraising dollars are raised in an ethical and responsible manner; and they must see that the financial goals of the organization are synchronized with its overall mission and goals.

3. ***The board sets the pace for fundraising through their own giving.***

   Board members show their commitment to the organization by making their own gifts first. Board members should give at a level that is consistent with their financial capability. Many funders, especially foundations, ask for participation rates and levels of giving from the entire board when making their decision about whether to support a nonprofit. A strong commitment from the board in giving helps to convince other donors that the leadership group is committed to the organization's mission and to success in reaching its goals.

4. ***The board sets the tone for the broader community's view of the nonprofit.***

   Board members' level of commitment, engagement in, and passion for the work of the organization are major factors in attracting others who have the means to support the organization. One of the most visible ways for board members to show their support is to make their own gift, then participate in asking others to give. The level of passion for the cause shown by board members exerts a powerful influence on other donors across the community.

The chair of the board, the executive board leadership, and the relevant committee chairs must all commit to excellence and participation in fundraising and call for the entire board to do the same. This commitment should start with the board chair and the executive committee and be transmitted out to the full board. A call for commitment from the chief advancement officer (CAO) does not carry the same weight.

When the entire board, the executive director, and the advancement staff are operating at peak performance, incredible things can happen. Goals that seemed unreachable can be met. External roadblocks, including a weak economy, can be overcome. The services provided by the nonprofit can experience tremendous leaps forward.

Ultimately, it is the clients, users, patients, students, and visitors—those who make use of the organization's services—who will be the beneficiaries of great board fundraising leadership. (See Exhibit 1.1.)

EXHIBIT 1.1

Rating Your Board's Fundraising Leadership Quotient: Does Your Board Have It?

Take this test to determine your board's fundraising leadership quotient. Answer each question with a number from 1 to 3 based on the following scale:

3 = Yes, everyone, always

2 = Maybe, some people, sometimes

1 = Not really, not many people, not often

1. Do you think it is your role as a board member to help the organization secure the resources it needs to meet its mission?
2. Does your board have a policy that everyone must make an annual gift?
3. Does your organization explain giving expectations and fundraising responsibilities to new board members when they are being recruited?

---

4. Does your board play an active role in setting fundraising goals, selecting projects for fundraising, and meeting fundraising goals and timelines?

5. Does your organization have a board solicitation plan in which board members ask fellow board members to make their gifts (peers asking peers)?

6. Have you and your fellow board members been asked to make a gift to the organization's current campaign (over and above an annual fund gift)?

7. Have you and all your fellow board members been asked to review prospect lists and help open doors for fundraising calls?

8. Are you as a board member offered training in how to present the case for giving to a potential donor?

9. Do you and your fellow board members make calls on prospects to solicit gifts (either individually or as members of a team)?

If you scored from 24 to 27 . . . Your board has an A to A+ Fundraising Leadership Quotient! Keep it up!

If you scored from 20 to 23 . . . Your board has a B to B+ Fundraising Leadership Quotient. There is more work to do to get everyone on your board to embrace their true fundraising potential, but you are on the right path.

If you scored from 15 to 19 . . . Your board has a C to C+ Fundraising Leadership Quotient. Your board needs a serious discussion about its role in furthering the goals of the organization. Consider bringing in a consultant to help with benchmarking and to provide an outside perspective.

If you scored 14 or below . . . Your board has a D or F for its Fundraising Leadership Quotient. It's time to reconsider how your board approaches resource development. Reform may be needed across the board, from the nominations process to committee structure. You can be a catalyst in reorganizing and reenergizing your board through your own leadership and involvement.

Board leadership in fundraising is not an outcome that can be mandated through an executive order. It is the product of a combination of factors, from education to individual commitment, that all work together to create a successful model. Not surprisingly, it starts with building a board whose members are ready to accept their new role.

Building a Fundraising Board

The first rule of board leadership in fundraising is to make sure that all board members understand and accept the concept that resource development is the responsibility of each and every member of the board.

Don't delegate all the responsibility to the usual suspects: the advancement staff, the executive director/CEO, the members of the development committee, or various fundraising committees and their chairs.

The advancement staff is there to provide structure, expertise, support, and to implement fundraising programs, but the board is there to lead, and it is their leadership that will inspire others to give.

In order to build an active fundraising board, the board leadership, the nominating committee, the executive director, and the staff who prepare the recruitment and orientation materials for new board members must be committed to this principle. It is not enough for the executive director (or even worse, the chief advancement officer) to get up at a board meeting and ask every board member to help out in development.

A real commitment to outreach and fundraising efforts must be clearly identified in the selection of new board nominees, in the job description for board members, in the discussion that takes place during board recruitment, and in the training that new members experience as they prepare to join the board.

Realize that not all board members are going to be equal in the fundraising arena. Not all board members are ready, willing, or even appropriate to send on a call to ask for a million dollars. But everyone can do something, and a positive attitude toward the development effort should be encouraged from the beginning of board service.

It is important to set an appropriate board policy on giving and fundraising. (See Exhibit 1.2.) The leaders of the board and of the nominating committee should support this policy in three ways: It should be discussed in the nominating committee process as a factor in the selection of potential board members; it should be discussed with the potential member during the recruitment process; and it should be delineated in writing as a responsibility of all board members in

EXHIBIT 1.2

Sample of Board Policy on Giving and Fundraising

All board members are expected to support the institution financially to the best of their ability, first through an annual gift, and if the organization is in a capital campaign, through a gift to the campaign. (Some nonprofits set a minimum gift level—this will depend on each board's culture and membership constituencies.)

All board members are expected to assist in identifying potential sources of financial support, opening the door to introduce the institution to these prospective donors, and assisting with the solicitation of those sources to the extent that they are able.

All board members are expected to support the organization's fundraising efforts by attending fundraising events, participating in fundraising programs, and assisting with community outreach to broaden the base of support for the organization across the community.

board orientation materials and reviewed with new members during their orientation to the board.

Recruiting the Fundraising Board

There are many reasons for including specific individuals on a board, and some of them trump fundraising skills. Professional knowledge, familiarity with legal or financial issues, community representation, service in a governmental or private capacity that can be effective in furthering the mission of the organization; these are all good reasons to recruit and to keep board members who may not have a lot to offer in the development arena.

The members of the nominating committee should make a conscious decision, however, to include individuals who offer personal qualities or skill sets that would be useful in the development sector. These are some of the qualities to look for:

- Prior experience as a volunteer in asking for gifts.

- Knowledge of fundraising campaigns.

- Access to a specific industry (e.g., mining, banking, or telecommunications).

- Access to a specific social or religious group.

- History of philanthropic giving (outside of this nonprofit).

- History of giving to this nonprofit.

- Passion and commitment to the cause (and ability to articulate this to others).

- Ability and willingness to tap new resources for giving.

- Willingness to expend time and energy on behalf of the organization.

Finding and recruiting board members with strong development skills has become a challenge for many nonprofits as volunteers have become less eager to give up their free time. See the nearby *Tips and Techniques* for some suggestions on ways to identify good people to build a strong fundraising board.

TIPS AND TECHNIQUES

Ideas for recruiting new members to help build a strong fundraising board:

- *Review the list of current donors* who have made a substantial commitment to your organization. Donors are often eager to join a board where they are already invested, and board participation may encourage them to give more.

- *Identify names of family foundation trustees and community foundation board members* who can either help secure gifts or who know those who are philanthropic in your community.

- *Look for representatives from key industries* in your community who can help introduce your organization to professional colleagues; examples might include industries like oil and gas, banking, tourism, or mining.

- *Be open to the next generation*: Invite younger people who show signs of potential leadership to join your board before they are tapped by others. Young people can bring new energy and new ideas to your board. They might even understand social networking and how to use it on behalf of your organization.

- **Identify skilled fundraisers** in your community and ask them to join your board after they have completed their commitment to another project.
- **Identify volunteers** already working in your nonprofit (or in organizations that work in the same issues), especially those who volunteer in fundraising. Annual fund volunteers, for instance, can become strong board members who understand the need for fundraising and have already developed the requisite skills.

The past several decades have brought positive changes to board selection policies as boards have expanded their ideas about who should belong. Many boards have diversified to include young people, seniors, people of all races and ethnic backgrounds, and people of all wealth categories. An incredibly diverse array of nonprofits requires an incredibly diverse array of board members to provide oversight, hire professional leadership, ensure strategic planning, and execute fiduciary responsibility for their nonprofit of choice.

There are many considerations in developing a truly diverse board. Diversity in board recruitment affects fundraising because board members often make the case for support to their colleagues and peers in the community. A strong fundraising board is diverse in racial and ethnic background, but also considers geographic distribution, age, gender, religious affiliation, social circles, economic background, differing skills, and differing political viewpoints.

A truly heterogeneous board will operate more effectively in decision making and will be more successful in reaching out into the community on behalf of the organization than a board that is more homogeneous. This is particularly important in fundraising, where board members' social and business networks are often the basis for community outreach and fundraising efforts. A diverse board will be more able to tap diverse sources of support, whatever the actual fundraising skills a specific board member might offer.

Recruiting to build a strong fundraising board requires long-term efforts at board development. Your organization may want to think about ways to try out potential members to evaluate their skills and develop their enthusiasm for your organization's cause. One common method of trying out future board members is to ask them to join a committee, where they can contribute right away to the organization's activities. Another method is to create an advisory council, where potential future board members can become more educated about the organization and demonstrate their commitment.

TALES FROM THE BOARDROOM

What board members say about the donor who always wants to have the building named after him: He has an edifice complex.

The Fiduciary Role of the Nonprofit Board

This book seeks to engage you in your role as a board member in the development of resources for a cause that you already feel is important. This section is meant to help you become better informed about your legal and ethical role as a board member as it applies to fundraising.

Board service can be fun, thoughtful, demanding, productive, and rewarding, as well as time-consuming and exasperating. In recent years nonprofit board service has become more focused on legal and ethical concerns and how to improve transparency and accountability. Thus board membership has become both more productive and more challenging, especially when it comes to financial issues.

The Handbook of Nonprofit Governance,[2] a comprehensive resource published by BoardSource, identifies three primary roles for the board as a whole:

- Setting organizational direction, including ensuring effective planning.
- Ensuring the necessary resources, both financial and human.
- Providing oversight of the chief executive, assets, and programs and services.

---

[2]BoardSource, *The Handbook of Nonprofit Governance* (San Francisco: Jossey-Bass, 2010), p. 31; emphasis added.

Since nonprofits seldom generate enough money from revenues associated with their programs to meet their needs, most organizations find it necessary to seek charitable contributions. Thus fundraising becomes a board role when, in order to ensure the necessary resources, the organization must turn to fundraising to meet its needs.

The New Role of Boards in Ensuring Accountability

Board members are being asked to take on increased fiduciary responsibilities in response to an increased demand for accountability and transparency in the nonprofit world.

The Sarbanes-Oxley Act, passed by the U.S. Congress in 2002, was created in an attempt to curb practices in the business world that were seen as abusive. While most of the provisions of the act are not directly applicable to nonprofits, there are several exceptions,[3] and some states have drawn up related regulations for nonprofits (e.g., the California Nonprofit Integrity Act of 2004).

The Handbook of Nonprofit Governance outlines some of the basic financial practices set out by Sarbanes-Oxley that many nonprofits now observe:

- "Having an audit committee of the board, preferably separate from the finance committee.

- Having at least one financial expert on the audit committee.

- Making the audit committee completely responsible for the relationship with the outside auditor (if one is used).

- Having both the chief financial officer and the chief executive publicly attest to the adequacy and effectiveness of the organization's internal controls and the fairness of the presentation of its financial statements."[4]

---

[3]Exceptions include "prohibition of retaliation against whistle-blowers and prohibition of the alteration or destruction of documents that are relevant to a lawsuit or regulatory proceeding." *Handbook of Nonprofit Governance,* p. 152.

[4]*Handbook of Nonprofit Governance,* p. 153.

Sarbanes-Oxley has proven influential in the nonprofit sector, mainly because so many members of the for-profit business sector sit on nonprofit boards. There have also been a number of congressional hearings, many of them spearheaded by "watchdogs" such as Senator Grassley of Iowa, which have brought to light various inappropriate uses of funds by nonprofits.

Through these recurring scandals, issues of transparency and accountability in nonprofits have been elevated to the headlines of the national news media. The nonprofit sector's use (or misuse) of funds has become a thread of common concern across society. See, for example, the report on the Fiesta Bowl in the box *In the Real World* nearby.

IN THE REAL WORLD

Hanky Panky at the Fiesta Bowl

An investigative report showed that Fiesta Bowl money was misspent on personal parties, outrageous gifts to staff, and trips to strip joints, while employees were reimbursed for making political contributions with sham bonus payments.

(The Fiesta Bowl, like many sports events, including football bowl games, the PGA Tour and Tour events, and the NFL, is set up as a 501(c) (3) entity, meaning that donations are tax-deductible, and the organization is not allowed to lobby the government.)

The scandal resulted in the firing of the bowl organization's long time president. The Board released a statement claiming that although there had been rules and regulations forbidding many of the actions that took place, "there was a lack of enforcement." The Board also noted that the actions taken "were effectively hidden from the Board of Directors."

Stronger board oversight might have helped to prevent this embarrassment. "Boards are legally expected to have their fingers on the pulse of the organization's operations," notes Michael Peregrine, a partner in the Chicago office of McDermott Will & Emery, a legal services firm, in commenting on the Fiesta Bowl situation.

Among his suggestions for cleaning up the finances:

- Board members must establish guidelines to set out levels of authority to handle matters that require board approval and review.

- Ensure that information is distributed in such a way that potential problems get the attention of board members.
- Put policies in place in areas that may be "prone to mischief, such as lobbying and campaign expenditures, discretionary expenditures, gifts, and travel expenses."

From the *Chronicle Board Report for Nonprofit Organizations* (May/June 2011) and the Fiesta Bowl public statement at http://www.fiestabowl.org/_documents/reports/Q_A.pdf.

Fiduciary responsibility means much more than just reviewing the budget and signing off on the financial statements. (See Exhibit 1.3.) The board that is "vigilant" must ask questions, review progress toward goals, and monitor any changes to financial performance.

In the current nonprofit environment, where fiscal solvency depends so heavily on outside financial support from both public and private sources, providing this oversight means gaining a true view and a deep understanding of the fundraising programs, goals, and challenges of the organization.

EXHIBIT 1.3

Defining Fiduciary Responsibility

The principal financial role of board members is to act as fiduciaries for the organization. This role entails securing organizational viability through planning and assessing the effectiveness of the plan. The board oversees the overall financial activity of the organization and ensures that appropriate internal controls are in place. The board approves the budget and must receive timely and accurate reports from staff to be able to survey the financial development and achievement of the fiscal goals. Setting financial indicators, asking pertinent questions, and staying vigilant about environmental factors that might affect the financial performance of the organization all allow the board to stay on top of its oversight responsibilities.

Source: BoardSource, *The Handbook of Nonprofit Governance.* San Francisco: Jossey-Bass, 2010 (pp. 153–154).

One way to ensure that everyone follows appropriate policy and procedures in fundraising is to conduct a fundraising audit. This could mean an informal review of policy by a fundraising expert from a similar organization, or the organization could hire an experienced fundraising consultant to make sure that all the appropriate legal and ethical standards are being met.

Conducting a regular annual audit of financial records will also help to determine whether donors' funds are being used in the manner and for the purpose that they were donated, whether pledges have been recorded accurately, and whether donors' financial records are being kept properly.

It is important for board members, as part of their fiduciary responsibility to the organization, to know what is happening to the money they help to raise.

★ OVERCOMING COMMON BARRIERS TO SUCCESS

There are a number of reasons why nonprofits don't develop strong leadership in board fundraising. You will find some common roadblocks identified at the end of each chapter of this book with suggestions on ways to resolve them. Here are two that can be particularly insidious.

CONFLICTS OF INTEREST

Avoiding conflicts of interest is a basic requirement of good board management. Like most bad news stories, conflicts of interest usually have a way of coming out in the most embarrassing and public way, and they can sap the energy and enthusiasm of board members while creating an environment of cynicism and a sense of unfairness.

Conflicts of interest often involve business with, or favors granted to, companies and entities associated with board members. While not all of these activities pose legal challenges, they do cross ethical boundaries. Board members should not derive personal or professional profit from their association with a nonprofit.

Examples of conflicts of interest include:

- Requiring that a nonprofit move all its accounts to a bank run by a member of the board.
- Requiring the nonprofit to use goods or services from a board member's company in return for gifts.
- Awarding a contract that delivers a profit to a board member's company.

EXHIBIT 1.4

Example of a Conflict of Interest Policy

Each individual board member should be committed to avoiding conflicts of interest by committing to:

- Serving the organization as a whole rather than any special interest group or constituency.

- Avoiding even the appearance of a conflict of interest that might embarrass the board or the organization; disclosing any possible conflicts to the board in a timely fashion.

- Maintaining independence and objectivity and doing what a sense of fairness, ethics, and personal integrity dictate.

- Never accepting (or offering) favors or gifts from (or to) anyone who does business with the organization.

Source: Handbook of Nonprofit Governance, p. 47.

Boards should develop a conflict of interest policy and take clear action if it appears to have been breached. See Exhibit 1.4.

BOARD BURNOUT

Board burnout is a common theme in complaints from board members who feel they have expended too much personal time and energy on a nonprofit. Burnout is a factor of too much effort being expended by too few people. It occurs when the full board delegates its duties (either formally or, more often, informally) to a few "worker bees" who are willing to shoulder the day-to-day tasks required to keep the organization going.

Burnout is an especially common problem in board fundraising efforts, because fundraising is often viewed (erroneously) as specialized work for a few volunteers, and so many board members are happy to step back and let one or two talented members take on the burden of major fundraising efforts.

There are many techniques that can be used to avoid board burnout (see **Tips and Techniques** nearby) but little that can be done once burnout is experienced—so be prepared! Make plans ahead of burnout time to spread the leadership and responsibility to a broader group of your fellow board members.

Ways to Avoid Board Burnout

- Rotate the chairs of key working committees, such as campaign committees or development committees, every year or two years.
- Limit campaign chair terms to two years, even during a longer campaign, to bring in fresh leadership and fresh energy.
- Actively seek ways to delegate tasks to newer and younger board members to bring them into the mix, so that the older and more experienced members of the board aren't always leading the charge.
- Create a Young Leadership group that reaches out to younger donors.
- Ask new board members to "shadow" chairs of board committees to learn the work of that committee.
- Create succession plans for board leaders by identifying and training new leadership as an ongoing strategy.
- Encourage open discussion and welcome challenging questions from board members who are not part of the inner circle to support broader board participation and involvement.

Creative Solutions to Board Burnout

The fundraising staff at Horizons for Homeless Children in Boston created a game as a fundraising challenge to motivate board members who felt that the organization was asking them to take on too much responsibility for fundraising.

The charity's chief development officer, Meryl Sheriden, and her staff created a competition they call the "Board Game," a system in which all board members compete to gain points for specific fundraising actions, such as giving the organization a prospect's name (one point) or bringing a potential donor to the site for a tour (25 points). The winning team is given a dinner by a board member. As Ms. Sheriden points out, "these are successful, highly competitive people, and the game is a fun way of capitalizing on that."

As told in the *Chronicle Board Report for Nonprofit Organizations* (May/June 2011).

Summary

There are many good reasons why every board member should take a leadership role in fundraising. A primary one is that the development of resources to meet the organization's mission is part of the fiduciary responsibility of being a board member. In these challenging economic times it is more important than ever to have skilled, active, and strong board leadership on the fundraising team.

The executive staff and leaders of the board should develop policies, procedures, and orientation materials that support fundraising involvement by every board member. When recruiting new members, nominating committees should consider qualities like fundraising experience, giving capability, and access to community donors in order to help build a strong fundraising board.

In a changing regulatory and legal environment, it is the board's fiduciary responsibility to ensure that the organization operates with transparency and accountability. Even the appearance of conflicts of interest should be avoided. Donors should be able to depend on the board to make sure that their gifts are used in a manner that is legal, ethical, appropriate, and for the purposes they have been donated.

CHAPTER 2

Setting the Pace with Board Giving

A rich man without charity is a rogue; and perhaps it would be no difficult matter to prove that he is also a fool.

—Henry Fielding

After reading this chapter, you will be able to:

- Set the pace for fundraising with board giving.
- Develop a plan for board giving.
- Prepare for your role as a fundraiser.

Giving and Asking at the Board Level

As a board member, you can expect to be asked to support your nonprofit financially with a charitable gift. You know that your gift will help to set the pace for other donors in the community. But what is the right level for your gift? How should board members be solicited? And how can you encourage your fellow board members to respond generously?

There are a variety of ways to approach giving and asking at the board level. Finding the right approach for each board may involve some trial and error.

There are, however, some basic rules to follow that will help the board to achieve success in this area:

1. Because board members differ in their capacity to give, they should be approached individually and personally (face to face) for a gift based on their giving history, interest, and potential.

2. Board members should be asked to give by other board members, preferably by someone who has already made his or her own commitment.

3. Executive directors and advancement staff members are crucial members of the team. Involve them in making the board giving plan, have them join the team to make the ask, and use them for follow-up after solicitations have taken place.

RULES OF THE ROAD

Set a basic policy that every member of the board must make an annual gift to show his or her commitment to the goals and direction of the organization.

Achieving 100 percent participation in annual giving should be the first goal of board giving. This is not only important for meeting the organization's financial goals, it is increasingly important for convincing other prospective donors to give. Many individual donors and foundations now routinely ask how much a board has given, or what percentage of the board has given, when they are approached for a gift.

Some community organizations want to emphasize participation over dollars, and they feel comfortable setting a target of 100 percent board giving as their goal without adding additional pressure to give at a certain level. For board members of modest means, a gift of $25 a month for several months may be a generous level of giving. Board members should be made to feel comfortable with whatever their situation allows them to give. Focus on the fact that many donors and foundations will want to see 100 percent board participation as an indicator of the board's commitment to the enterprise.

Setting a Minimum Gift Level

Not all boards are content with setting just a participation goal. Some set a minimum required gift level for all board members. Charitable giving is a highly personalized decision and depends on a variety of individualized factors, so you must take the composition and history of your board into account when making these decisions.

Some experienced board leaders say making a "stretch gift" is the key to successful board giving. A stretch gift is one that other board members will recognize as a generous gift, one made to the fullest extent of your means. A stretch gift should be one that makes your peers sit up and say, "Wow! She really does support this mission!" Setting a minimum goal can undermine the stretch gift concept by focusing on the minimum dollar level to give, rather than emphasizing the maximum possible gift level.

TALES FROM THE BOARDROOM

The chair of the board made a call on a wealthy widow. "Please consider endowing the new education program," he asked. She looked regretful as she responded, "Oh, I couldn't possibly do that. I'm down to my last $20 million."

Stretch gifts are hard to define, however, and fit better into a campaign setting, where larger gifts are important to meet higher goals. At the annual fund level, many organizations do find it helpful to set a minimum or recommended gift level for each board member, which leads to setting a dollar goal for total board giving.

Often this requirement is imposed by boards that have already achieved 100 percent giving among board members. Setting a specific dollar giving level requires a more sophisticated and mature fundraising culture than just emphasizing participation. The amount selected depends on the organization's history and culture, the level of wealth among the membership, the preferences of the board leaders, and the state of the economy.

A useful standard is to ask board members to join one of the leadership donor recognition groups offered through the organization's annual fund, usually set at $1,000 or $1500. High-profile boards with more prominent individuals who are wealthy might ask for more; $10,000 or $25,000 is appropriate as an annual gift level for board members of national museums, universities, and hospitals. It might be useful to benchmark board giving levels by checking with peer institutions to see what they have set for their required levels of board giving.

IN THE REAL WORLD

One Board's Giving Plan

A prominent national museum board set a policy that requires all board members to make a minimum annual gift of $10,000. They exempt one category of board membership—their young leadership members—from this giving level, but ask these younger members to participate at a lower level. With 30 board members, they set a goal of $250,000 for board annual giving, a significant portion of their entire annual goal for fundraising for operations.

Board fundraising is led by the development committee. At the beginning of the fiscal year, a letter goes out to every board member to ask for the annual gift over the development committee chair's signature. Individual calls on each board member are made by the development committee chair and his committee members. Some calls are face to face (new members, recalcitrant members, and those who will respond well to the attention). Some calls are made by phone.

The board volunteers are supported by a staff member who provides giving records, prepares materials, makes appointments, and handles follow-up calls. Donors are recognized at board meetings by name. Laggards are called on privately by the chair of the board or by the executive director. Their goal of $250,000 was reached by the middle of the fiscal year.

This museum is also in a capital campaign. Their board agreed on a policy where all members would make a gift to the capital campaign in addition to the $10,000 annual gift. Board members are approached individually by members of the capital campaign committee for a separate ask for the campaign based on their means. Capital campaign gifts are pledged over a series of years, so at any one time most board members are paying on their campaign pledge at the same time they are being asked to make a leadership annual gift.

Thus far over 40 percent of the campaign funds have been raised from board members or entities associated with board members, such as corporations and foundations. This strong example of board commitment has encouraged other, nonboard members to invest in the project. This board has set the pace for giving!

Decisions about whether to require giving and how much giving to require should be made by the board's executive committee with input from the development committee, the executive director/CEO, and the chief advancement officer. Be sure that all potential board members understand the rules and present them in writing during the recruitment and orientation process for new board members. It can be embarrassing to deal with new board members who feel they have been "hoodwinked" or misinformed about giving requirements.

Special circumstances can always be dealt with on an individual basis. Every board member can give something, even if it is as little as $50. Or it may be appropriate to exclude certain members from giving requirements, such as those who aren't selected through the normal nomination process, including ex officio members and religious, political, or honorary members.

The goal isn't to create an inflexible rule, but rather to create an environment on the board where annual giving is seen as important, a basic responsibility, and a key function of the organization's leadership.

Often board members will be asked to give an additional gift beyond support for annual operations. Major gifts, program needs, capital campaigns, endowment, planned gifts—the options for giving are boundless. The board leadership needs to decide what areas of support are crucial to the success of the organization and communicate those needs clearly to all board members.

Capital Campaign Giving

If your organization is mounting a capital or endowment campaign, the board should accept responsibility for giving a certain percentage of the goal. The goal often used as a benchmark for board giving in a capital campaign is in the range of 30 percent to 50 percent of the total campaign goal. Of course some boards give more, and many give less. This is not a hard-and-fast percentage, but rather a guideline. The board goal for a capital campaign will need to be set knowing the circumstances and capacity of each board member.

RULES OF THE ROAD

A common benchmark for board giving in a capital campaign is in the range of 30 percent to 50 percent of the total campaign goal.

There are many organizations whose boards are not wealthy enough to provide such a high percentage of the campaign goal. In such cases, it is preferable to develop a capital campaign committee that has membership well beyond the members of the board (see Chapter 9). Even if the board giving falls short of the suggested percentages, the board should be expected to provide leadership, including leadership gifts, in support of the campaign objectives.

Remember that no matter what goal your board sets for board giving, other donors will look to what you and your fellow board members have given as a measure of the potential success of your campaign.

TIPS AND TECHNIQUES

How Much Should You Give?

Here are some hints for how to determine the right level for your gifts as a board member:

For an annual unrestricted gift:

- Don't give just the bare minimum if you can afford more; you are a leader, so make a gift to the extent of your means.

- If you aren't wealthy, your gift is important at whatever level you can afford; participation is the basic requirement of all board giving.
- Annual participation means you are making a new gift each year.
- If you have the financial means, plan to give at one of the leadership recognition levels for annual donors.
- Ask your board to recommend a specific dollar level for annual giving for all members if the organization's experience and culture support this.
- Make use of monthly payment programs if that suits your needs.
- Make use of any matching gift programs you are eligible for and ask your organization to count these gifts toward your annual giving level.

For a capital campaign or major gift:

- Take your time to get to know the organization and decide which program or area you want to support.
- Ask for additional information, talk to program leaders, and make a site visit to make your decision an informed one.
- Terms of a gift can be negotiated, but once they are agreed upon, be sure to put them in writing to avoid future disagreements.
- Use multiyear pledges to make a stretch gift, one that maximizes your giving potential.
- Assess the impact you want your gift to have on the future of the organization and give accordingly.
- Board giving is often an important early component of campaign giving; find out the timeline for your campaign, so that your giving will have the maximum positive effect on your campaign.
- Review planned giving options to see if there are deferred giving strategies that might benefit you and your family.
- Ask about the recognition or naming opportunities that come with each level of giving (if recognition is important to you).
- Ask for anonymity if you don't want your gift to be announced publicly.
- Board giving in a campaign tends to cluster around a specific dollar range; you can wait to see what others do, or you can lead by setting your own pace.

YOUR ROLE AS A BOARD MEMBER

Start with your own commitment to make an annual gift. Know what your board requires for giving, relative to both annual gifts and campaign gifts, and plan to support the goals of the organization with a gift that will help set the pace for giving from others.

If you are a member of the development committee, you should become engaged in the solicitation of your colleagues on the board. This requires developing a plan for board giving, which is introduced in the following section.

Develop a Plan for Board Giving

Board members should be solicited respectfully and carefully, as part of an individualized plan for board giving. In order to plan the solicitation of the board, create a team comprised of the executive director/CEO, the board chair, the development committee and/or campaign committee chair, the chief advancement officer, and relevant staff. This group should meet at the beginning of the fiscal year to plan board level annual fund solicitations and at the beginning of a campaign to plan board level capital campaign solicitations.

Many boards use their development committees as the core team for making board solicitations. If your development committee is unable or unwilling to take on this task, consider providing training in solicitation techniques using either a staff member or a consultant. Don't forget that volunteers who ask should make their own gifts first. Some boards prefer to have the development committee chair, or some group of executive committee members, make the board asks. The best decision for your organization will probably be a mix of history, or what has worked in the past, and pragmatism, defined as how to get the job done.

How to Solicit Board Members

First, develop an individualized giving plan for each board member. The plan should include the following considerations:

- Review how much the board member has given in the past (look at a five-year giving history).

- Determine this board member's capacity to make a gift.

- Discuss this board member's interests and commitment level to the organization.

- Set an annual ask amount at a specific level based on previous giving history, board requirements, and financial capability.

- Set a capital or endowment ask amount based on giving history, capacity, area of interest, and organizational needs.

- Determine the best person or the best team to call on this board member (include at least one fellow board member on every team).

Most board members will respond best (i.e., make their best gift) to a solicitation by another board member. It is common to include the executive director/CEO and high-level staff (such as the chief advancement officer) as members of the team. The advancement staff can provide follow-up to board asks and nudge tardy donors. Exhibit 2.1 reviews how to establish an

EXHIBIT 2.1

Components of a Board Giving Program

- Develop an individualized giving plan with a specific ask level for each board member.

- Set a timetable for board solicitations.

- Establish whether the annual ask and capital ask will be made together or separately.

- Identify and train a small cadre of board solicitors and give them their assignments (this is a good task for the development committee).

- Set a timetable for all board solicitations to take place.

- Send out a letter from the board chair or campaign chair letting the board know that they will be called on for a gift.

- Set a timetable for the donors to respond.

- Make face-to-face calls on each board member using a team approach; pair a board member with an advancement staff member, or pair board members with the executive director to ensure effective calls are made with every board member.

overall board giving program based on face-to-face solicitation of every board member.

Once solicitations have taken place, provide a follow-up plan for laggard donors. Options include a call from the chair, a follow-up e-mail, or calls from staff members. While you should do what it takes to engage each member of the board, there comes a point when additional calls become fruitless. It's best to stop short of angering your fellow board members. Three reminders are probably enough in most instances.

TALES FROM THE BOARDROOM

The wealthy board member staggered out of a meeting where he had just been solicited for a seven-figure campaign gift. The team making the call included the chair of the board, the chair of the executive committee, the chair of the development committee, the chair of the campaign, the executive director, and the chief advancement officer. No one wanted to be left out, but the group had too many heavyweights for the occasion.

"I felt ganged up on," he reported later. "They were all looking at me and I could hardly move—I felt boxed into a corner. I ended up giving only about half of what I had been thinking about doing just to get out of there."

While the board solicitations are being made, keep up the discussion about giving during board meetings. Ask the staff or the development committee chair to provide ongoing reports about the need for funds, the uses of funds raised, and the progress toward goals.

Like all donors, board members enjoy being thanked for their gifts. Both the board leaders and the executive leadership should emphasize recognition, provide praise, and thank both solicitors and donors by name, especially at board meetings. Some boards have a board member or committee chair call donors to thank them for their gifts. Continue to emphasize the importance of leadership giving by the board in public forums and especially at board meetings.

The hardest part of a board giving plan is to determine the consequences for those who won't or don't give. The working team—board chair, development committee chair, advancement chief, and executive leadership—should all agree on a range of actions to use when repeated appeals fail. These tactics could range from decapitation (kicking them off the board) to public shaming (embarrassing them by naming all the other donors at a board meeting).

There are softer tactics to use with holdouts, of course; many boards arrange for a quiet talk with the board chair on the side. Decide what will work best in your culture and with your organizational needs. Balance your organization's priorities and use good common sense. On the one hand, it's not fair to press everyone to give and then let certain people off the hook. On the other hand, it's not a good idea to kick off the board the person who could be your largest donor a few years from now. Patience and judiciousness should rule the day.

How to Increase Board Giving

A consultant can be useful in working with the board leadership to provide additional perspective on board giving, provide benchmarks, raise sights, and set goals, especially in the context of a capital or endowment campaign. Some boards may respond well to a challenge gift from one of their own. Board leaders might agree to work to reach a specific goal by a targeted date. The goal is to find the best way for all board members to participate at a leadership giving level in both annual and capital campaign giving.

IN THE REAL WORLD

Using a Board Challenge

Board challenges can be an effective way to encourage board participation in a special campaign. At an independent school, a board member made a $500,000 pledge to the endowment campaign and challenged three of his fellow board members to match that amount. The resulting $2 million in early gifts built the momentum needed to get the campaign off to a strong start.

For a different challenge at another organization, a group of four board members pooled their resources to create a $2 million "board challenge," then asked the remainder of the board to give until a second $2 million was raised. With their new total of $4 million in hand, the board was able to go out to their community and raise an additional $8M. They set the pace for their campaign.

Make sure that all new board members know what they are getting into when joining the board. If all members are going to be solicited for a capital campaign gift in addition to making an annual gift at a certain level, this should be discussed and established as a board policy, then included in the recruitment and orientation of new members. It is considered bad form to recruit new board members into an ongoing capital campaign without making their obligations clear. For this reason, it is preferable to add members to your board before the commencement of a campaign or special fundraising drive.

See the nearby *Tips and Techniques* for a summary of ways to maximize the board's giving commitment. While some of these tips should be implemented by the executive director or the chief advancement officer working with the board, many of these ideas can be put in place through the work of the board development committee or other board members who are leading the fundraising effort.

TIPS AND TECHNIQUES

Ways to Increase Board Giving

- Set a minimum annual gift level for all board members. Make sure that new board members are told about any expected gift levels when they are recruited.
- Educate board members on the reasons the nonprofit needs the money and how it will be used. Report often on progress toward goals.
- Practice transparency and accountability; make sure the board has access to financial information and understands where the money is coming from and where it is going.
- Identify a few respected leaders on the board and ask them to make the first gifts.
- Ask these first donors to "set the pace" by making gifts that others will view as a "stretch gift" in terms of their capacity.
- Create excitement about the projects and programs you are fundraising for: Use architectural renderings, models, videos, marketing materials, and presentations to help the board feel informed and engaged.

- Develop donor giving levels, benefits, and naming opportunities for various gift levels. Circulate them to your board members and talk about recognition.
- Ask board members who have made early commitments to solicit members who haven't given yet.
- Set a board goal or challenge the board to reach a certain level of total giving.
- Recognize board gifts in front of the whole board and thank board donors promptly, publicly (get their permission first!), and often.

Prepare for Your Fundraising Role

You will want to start preparing for the components of your board service beyond making your own gift. The key to strong preparation is in building your depth of knowledge about your own nonprofit. Start by reviewing the areas identified in Exhibit 2.2 to see if you need to shore up any weak points.

The time and effort you need to spend in each of these areas will vary based on the specific needs of your nonprofit, the depth of your knowledge and experience, and the type of fundraising that you are preparing to take on.

EXHIBIT 2.2

Seven Ways to Prepare for Your Role in Fundraising

1. Become educated about the programs and services provided by your organization.
2. Help spread the good word by talking about your nonprofit in the community.
3. Understand the big financial picture and how fundraising fits into it.
4. Become familiar with the fundraising operation and programs.
5. Start thinking about whom you know who could provide new sources of funds.
6. Assist the development operation in ways beyond giving money.
7. Practice and ensure ethical behavior.

A more detailed discussion follows that covers each of the areas identified in Exhibit 2.2.

Become Educated About the Programs and Services Provided by the Organization

You probably joined this organization's board because you have a strong interest in or sympathy with their mission. As a board member, now it's time to learn as much as you can about the ways in which that mission is realized.

Educate yourself about the programs, goals, and services provided. If you can, volunteer in one of the service areas, so that you become familiar with the way the organization works, how it provides services, and how it treats volunteers.

Don't shy away from asking questions about program services, outcomes, and effectiveness—your work as a board member will be enhanced if you have the knowledge and capability to answer tough questions. If you can answer basic questions about the services provided, you can provide the correct information to others when they have jumped to the wrong conclusions or are repeating rumors or misinformation.

Questions to ask for you to become familiar with the organization's programs:

- What are the main services offered?
- What problems are the service providers trying to solve?
- Who are the clients/users of these services?
- Are there measurements of effectiveness for these programs in place?
- Are requests for services increasing or decreasing, and why?

Keep up with major changes in the organization. Nonprofits are always subject to change, often positive change, but sometimes change is controversial. Programs can change, or perhaps management takes a new path.

Make sure you understand the nature of the changes, how they affect the community, the services provided, and the budgetary consequences so that you can speak about them effectively when the topic comes up in general conversation. You are a leader and a representative of your organization—your peers will look to you for answers.

Spread the Good Word About Your Organization Throughout the Community

One of your major responsibilities as a board member is to speak positively and knowledgeably about the organization to your friends, family, and colleagues. Your friends will assume that you know the inside scoop, so become educated, especially about measures and programs that affect the public. Your excitement, interest, passion, and commitment will rub off, so speak well and speak often to share your feelings with others.

First order of business: Make sure you do no harm! See the **Tips and Techniques** nearby for the basic rules on how to spread the word on behalf of your organization.

TIPS AND TECHNIQUES

Spreading the Word: Dos and Don'ts for Board Members

- Do talk to friends and family about the great things that your organization is doing.
- Do share your own enthusiasm and commitment to the cause.
- Do help to correct misconceptions about the organization.
- Do educate yourself to be able to speak knowledgeably about the goals and services of the organization.
- Do stand up for the organization in times of controversy.
- Don't spread rumors or bad news indiscriminately; always check sources!
- Don't speak to news sources on behalf of the organization unless you are the designated speaker.
- Don't get bogged down in board politics or participate in power plays.

Understand the Big Financial Picture and How Fundraising Fits In

Fundraising is only one factor in the larger financial health of the organization. You will be more effective as a fundraiser and as a board member if you understand the overall financial picture of your organization and can explain it to others.

You should become familiar with the broader context of the organization's finances, but you do not need to learn all the details of the annual budget, unless you are on the finance committee. Sample questions to ask about the finances:

- How does the organization make its money (basic sources of revenue)?
- What does the organization spends its money on (major expenditures)?
- Is the budget balanced?
- What financial threats and/or opportunities exist?
- How has the organization addressed its long-term capital needs? Is there any debt? How is that debt being paid off?
- Is there an endowment? How big is the endowment and how much annual income does it generate for the nonprofit?

If you are not offered this information in a board orientation or sent it before a board meeting, ask your chief financial officer for a quick "tutorial" on organizational finances. This is both your responsibility and your prerogative. It is in everyone's best interests for you to become an educated and engaged board member. In your fiduciary role, you and every one of your fellow board members are responsible for overseeing the financial health of the organization.

Now that you have a snapshot of the bigger financial picture, you are ready to move on to take a closer look at the fundraising operation, methods, and goals.

Become Familiar with the Fundraising Operation and Programs

Review the fundraising history for the past couple of years and learn more about the way funds are raised at this organization. Either attend a meeting of the development committee, or ask for some time with the chief advancement officer. Your knowledge of the main activities of the development operation will help you to become a more capable fundraiser as a board member.

Learn the answers to basic questions, such as these:

- What are the organization's fundraising goals?
- Are there multiple goals for annual, capital, program, and endowment?
- Have the goals been met over the past several years?

- How does the fundraising for this year look?

- What percentage of the annual budget comes from fundraising?

- Is the organization currently in a campaign or planning a campaign?

- How large is the development staff and what can you expect from them in terms of support for your fundraising efforts on the board?

- How much is spent to raise a dollar?

- Is the donor base for the organization growing or shrinking?

Get to the know the chief advancement officer and key advancement staff members. They can help to make your fundraising efforts as a board member successful. They will be part of your team as you take the steps to secure more resources for your organization.

Ask to see the fundraising materials that are used to solicit funds for the organization. Note how the services are described, what the money is solicited for, and the recognition that is promised.

Consider how the organization "makes its case," which means how it presents its need for financial support to a prospective donor. You will want to be able build a case for giving when you make calls, so think carefully about what areas of the organization's work appeal to you the most and how to present them to donors.

If you are a member of a board for an organization where there are no fund-raisers on staff, there may be little you can learn about fundraising operations in a formal way. Try to find out from other board members or from the executive director what kind of fundraising efforts have been developed in the past and how successful they have been. Check with the CFO to see if gifts have been coming in over the transom, without having been solicited. Often these unsolicited gifts provide an important starting point for planning a new or enhanced fundraising initiative.

Start Thinking About Who You Know

Every nonprofit has to nurture a combination of new donors and repeat donors. Board members are expected to help by opening the doors to new sources of funding. You don't have to be on the development committee or a campaign committee to assist with the securing of new resources. All board members should become advocates for the needs of the nonprofit and should be prepared to bring new donors to the table.

How to find new donors? Your personal contact list, whether it's in your iPhone or an old rolodex system, can be an important resource for expanding the organization's fundraising reach.

Think about whom you know. Many people don't truly appreciate how extensive their circle of contacts really is. If you include family, friends, business acquaintances, clients, colleagues, and those who serve on other boards that you are affiliated with, you probably have access to hundreds of people. It is likely that a number of these contacts would support your organization if they knew more about it.

As you look at your array of contacts, focus on those whose interests are most likely to parallel the mission and services of the nonprofit. This could mean selecting people of a certain age, those who share a passion for education (or whatever the cause may be), or someone who has access to a source of funds that the organization could tap, such as a foundation board member or a corporate executive.

Bring the names you have identified to the attention of the chief advancement officer of your organization. A savvy CAO will meet with each new board member to learn more about the contacts and resources that member can provide. If your organization has no advancement staff, identify one board member who will organize prospect names—it could be the chair of the development committee, for instance.

Follow up with how the organization is going to contact the people whose names you provide. You can stay involved to help open the door and to provide an introduction. Consider, for instance, bringing potential donors whom you know to make a site visit, invite them to join you at an event held by the organization, or provide an opportunity for your friends to volunteer with the nonprofit. Your role in opening the door and engaging new prospects with the organization is a valuable one.

Assist the Development Operation in Ways Beyond Giving Money

There are many ways that you can help to further the goals of a nonprofit beyond just giving money or getting money. You have many skills; find ways to put them to good use for the organizations you support.

Board members can volunteer for a variety of tasks that will help the organization move forward. Examples include providing architectural planning, space planning, and program support; providing services like printing or PR; and offering (free or at cost) professional advice in areas like finance, marketing, and management. Be sure to follow any conflict of interest policies that your board has developed if you are providing services for which you receive payment.

In many cases, having these tasks done by volunteers will save the organization time, money, and headaches. The board member who serves in these ways is also making a gift, although all board members should also make a financial contribution. You may feel inspired to give more than just money, and you may find it personally rewarding to provide a service. It is wise, however, to check with the executive director/CEO or department heads before you offer your services to make sure that they are needed and appropriate.

Practice and Ensure Ethical Behavior

Unhappily, in recent years, financial abuses, conflicts of interest, and misuse of funds have all been known to rear their ugly heads in nonprofit circles.

Scandal is not helpful to the long-term health of a nonprofit organization. Most nonprofits live and die on their reputation for good governance, financial transparency, and making good use of the funds they raise. Board members should be especially careful to keep the reputation of the organization they serve squeaky clean.

Appearances do count. From riding in limos to excessive expenditures on fundraising events, realize that your decisions will be judged by others and will ultimately reflect on the organization you help to lead.

IN THE REAL WORLD

The National Public Radio Scandal

Supporters and critics all over the world watched the scandal unfold at NPR as their chief fundraiser's inappropriate comments, made to a political operative posing as a donor, were caught on video.

The NPR fundraiser was caught making negative comments about Jews, Republicans, and the Tea Party to a (fake) prospective Muslim donor. He also volunteered that NPR didn't need federal funding to continue its programming at a time when the station was seeking renewed federal funding. An assistant was taped making promises to the (fake) donor about concealing their gift from the IRS, a clear violation of both law and NPR policy.

Although in this case it quickly became apparent that there were political enemies who lured this man to his doom, the incident makes a strong case for taking care and practicing ethical behavior in all donor contacts. The staff members were seduced into this unethical behavior by the possibility of a $5 million gift, a large gift by the standards of any nonprofit.

The board responded quickly by cleaning house, firing the fundraisers and the executive director. Because the board took quick action, the damage was limited. But it's a good lesson to remember that whether you are a board member or a staff member, what you say and what you do as a representative of your nonprofit will circle back to affect the organization you serve.

Always take the high road and demand strong ethical behavior from yourself, your colleagues, and the staff at your organization. Here are a few examples of areas in fundraising where ethical behavior can be a problem:

- Avoid conflicts of interest or the appearance of conflicts of interest.
- Preserve the privacy of donor-related information.
- Ensure that funds are used for the purpose designated by the donor.
- Avoid exploitation of a donor or staff relationship.

RULES OF THE ROAD

Don't do anything on behalf of the organization that you wouldn't want to see on the front page of your local newspaper (or on YouTube!)

OVERCOMING COMMON BARRIERS TO SUCCESS

SETTING BOARD GIVING REQUIREMENTS

Achieving 100 percent board participation is a sign of good board leadership. Here are some good reasons why board giving is essential:

- Board giving shows that the leadership supports the direction the nonprofit is taking.

- Board giving provides a core level of financial support that the nonprofit can count on from year to year.

- Board giving is a sign of board engagement and commitment to the mission.

- Board giving sets an example for others who are less involved.

- Board giving is often a factor in funding decisions from foundations.

Board giving levels can be set at a dollar level, such as $100, $1000, $10,000, or more if board members are willing to impose a giving requirement. This level should be set at a dollar amount that is realistic given the board membership. Allowing younger members to opt out or give at a "junior level" might be an option.

If your board balks about setting dollar-giving-level requirements, it may be wise to back off temporarily. Concentrate on meeting the 100 percent board participation goal for annual and capital gifts. You can always come back in a year and reopen the discussion.

If you are having difficulty with your board on setting a policy for board giving, consider engaging a consultant who can bring in an outside perspective about best practices for boards and benchmark the giving practices at other nonprofits in your community. Sometimes the message is clearer when it comes from an outsider.

GIVING MORE THAN MONEY

There are lots of ways you can help your organization succeed in resource development beyond giving and getting gifts. Here are some examples of assistance beyond donations that you and your board colleagues can provide to support development and marketing efforts. (Check with your nonprofit's executive director and department heads first to make sure that your offer of support is needed and appropriate.)

- Offer PR and/or marketing advice and support.
- Donate ad space or billboards.

- Print or design materials at cost.
- Offer to help build a social network or develop the web site.
- Provide professional services for free or at cost (legal, accounting, architectural, etc.).
- Serve as a focus group member or take part in a feasibility study.
- Help prepare fundraising materials, marketing materials, and communications outreach materials, such as newsletters.
- Help to plan and staff events and sell tables for events.
- Call donors to thank them for their gifts.
- Provide items for auctions or other fundraising events.
- Volunteer to help clean up data, prepare lists, do mailings, and other behind the scenes development tasks.

Summary

Board members set the pace for giving with their own gifts. You should make an annual gift at a level you can afford and support any campaigns with a stretch gift according to your means.

You can help to set new policies for board giving and create a plan to solicit your peers on the board. Board members should be solicited by fellow board members. The plan for board solicitation should include specific goals, a timetable, and personal calls. The development committee should play a lead role in soliciting the board for annual gifts.

There are a number of ways that you as a board member can prepare to contribute in your service to the organization. Educate yourself about your organization, including its programs and services, its financial practices and fundraising programs. Be prepared to talk about your organization with your friends and colleagues.

Find ways to help beyond fundraising and think about whom you know who could become a donor. Remember that what you say, what you give, your level of passion, and how you represent your nonprofit will influence others to become involved and to give.

CHAPTER 3

Getting Ready to Fundraise

Anticipate charity by preventing poverty.

—Maimonides

After reading this chapter, you will be able to:

- Define organizational needs and priorities.
- Get organized for fundraising: development committees and campaign committees.
- Build board buy-in for fundraising.

Define Organizational Needs

Fundraising doesn't occur on demand. The organization's leaders can't just get up in the morning and say, "We need more money." (Well, they can say that, but it won't happen without a lot of additional work and planning!) The leadership, on the executive side as well as on the board, has to develop a well-thought-out plan for where the organization is headed and how to fund its needs over the long term.

Many nonprofits lurch from crisis to crisis, looking to fundraising as a stop-gap measure to meet the deficits and patch up budget holes. This is not a productive way to operate on a long-term basis. It burns out both fundraisers and donors, who feel they are always under the gun to bail out the organization. It also turns off board members, who don't feel their efforts are going to provide a long-term solution to the problems the organization is trying to address.

It is far more efficient to take the time to work together to define organizational needs and priorities, set longer-term goals, develop a plan of action, and bring the nonprofit's constituencies together to help meet those goals.

What Is Your Organization Raising Money For?

The role of defining organizational needs and priorities falls to the executive director/CEO working hand in hand with the board. The board looks to the executive director for leadership to craft and articulate the vision for the future role of the organization. It is then up to the board leadership and the executive staff working together to plan the steps toward the implementation of the vision.

Implementation of the vision includes defining the path toward meeting the vision, assessing the resources that will be required to get there, and articulating the vision broadly across a range of stakeholders (both internal and external constituencies) to gain their support.

TALES FROM THE BOARDROOM

The board member came back from a call on a big donor. "How did it go?" asked the executive director. "Not bad," reported the board member. "She agreed to do $1,000,000 but we had to promise not to tell her kids about it."

Many organizations determine their future needs and direction through a strategic planning process. Such a process, often undertaken before a major fundraising campaign, can help to determine what assets are needed by the organization to grow, maintain its position, or move in a new direction. Often consultants are brought in to help with strategic planning, and they can provide a valuable outside perspective.

Strategic Planning and the Board

The board or representatives from the board should play a major role in strategic planning, since these decisions will determine the direction of the organization for years to come.

Tougher economic times may call for tough responses in defining the organization's role. Nothing should be off the table: expansion, dissolving or merging with another nonprofit, cutting services, shifting resources to new programs, closing buildings, adding buildings, or renovating buildings to offer more or different services. Any of these could end up being an appropriate response to a challenging economic and political environment.

When conducting a strategic planning exercise, start with defining the vision for the organization; then define how that vision can be realized; then consider the costs of the plan and how the money can be raised.

RULES OF THE ROAD

Fundraising goals are derived from the strategic planning process, not the other way around. Fundraising is the tool that the organization will use to pay for the buildings, staff, and programs that have been defined by the strategic plan.

While the development committee and the chief advancement officer should be involved in shaping the strategic direction, don't put the cart before the horse—the organization needs to decide on its basic direction, identify what its needs will be to move in that direction, and then assess the costs of those needs. Those costs will form the basis for the fundraising plan.

Simply identifying needs doesn't mean that raising the money to meet those needs is achievable. There are ways to test the market before embarking on a big campaign (see Chapter 8). Consider conducting a feasibility study, for instance, and be prepared to scale back goals if necessary. Reality must guide the organization's dreams.

Without a strategic plan, however, and lacking an understanding of what is strategically best for a given organization within a given timeframe and in a given market, the nonprofit is just flying by the seat of its pants. And that is not a good way to get others to invest and to make an impact on your community!

The organization should develop a 3- to 5-year time frame in doing its planning. Consultants used to advise undertaking strategic planning for a 7- to 10-year framework, but the uncertainty of the economic climate, pending cutbacks in local, state, and federal funding, along with proposed changes in the tax code argue for a shorter planning time frame. (See Exhibit 3.1.)

If your plan calls for a new facility, be warned that many nonprofits underestimate the full range of costs that will be incurred in a new or expanded facility. Be sure that all capital needs are factored into the plan, including

---

EXHIBIT 3.1

Basic Components of the Strategic Plan

- What services does your nonprofit currently provide to meet its mission?

- Who else is offering those services in the markets you compete in and how does your organization differ from the competition?

- The changing nature of your markets: Are they growing or declining?

- What opportunities and needs are there to enhance, cut back, or combine services in the current markets?

- What opportunities are there to expand to new markets?

- What services will be provided based on these opportunities?

- What will the costs of providing those services be? (Include capital costs like new facilities, renovations, equipment; make sure to also include operating costs, like new staff, new programs, and additional overhead.)

- Identify any new revenues that can be attached to new services.

- Determine what additional resources will be needed to make these services available and sustainable.

construction, renovation, maintenance, lease costs, depreciation, debt structure, and equipment costs.

Then consider the costs of operating the new facility. In addition to the costs of overhead, maintenance, and depreciation, don't underestimate the human side of the equation: Will you need to add staff to provide new programs? Are there changes required to attract new people, such as enhanced retirement funding, moving expenses, improved health care benefits, training, new offices, new program space, new program support?

In most nonprofits the responsibility for budgeting, whether it is money for operating, capital, program, or benefits, starts with the executive staff leadership, most notably from the CEO and/or the CFO. It is the board's role to review and approve policy, usually through the committee structure, for example, the finance committee, personnel committee, and development committee.

While it is the norm for the annual budgeting process to be staff driven, what is called for here is an enhanced board role in long-term strategic planning. The engagement and excitement of the board in the planning process up front leads to board ownership and buy-in for the plan. The strategic planning results are used to drive the goals for the fundraising that will take place. Board buy-in and ownership lead to the board's commitment to undertake the fundraising activity required to implement the plan. Without active board participation in the planning process, the goals are simply one more assignment for busy board members.

YOUR ROLE AS A BOARD MEMBER

As a board member you should participate in strategic planning opportunities and expect all planning to be conducted in a professional and constructive manner. Many organizations create a new plan every three to five years. Changing circumstances, such as major changes in market conditions for the services your organization offers, may require new planning on a faster timetable.

As an active board member, you will want to explore how you can get involved. This could mean joining a strategic planning committee, taking part in a planning retreat, being interviewed to give your input, or meeting with a consultant hired by the organization. The executive staff should help to lead the process to provide insight into key plan elements such as programs, markets, competition for services provided, and financial planning.

With participation and leadership in the planning process, you and your fellow board members will help to build the fundraising plan from day one. This provides for the "buy-in" and "ownership" of the goals that is so often missing from nonprofit board activity. There is a qualitative difference between hearing a report on the organizational needs and playing a major role in creating that report. Your active participation and leadership at the board level in planning will lead directly to your active participation in fundraising to meet the long-term goals of the organization.

TALES FROM THE BOARDROOM

The cantankerous old donor attended the dedication for the new Art Center named after his family. He looked around at the contemporary art exhibit in the main gallery and harrumphed to his friend on the board. "What is all this stuff?" he growled. "I thought we were naming a new Heart Center."

Fundraising for Current Operations

Almost all nonprofits have to fundraise to support current operations. Ideally the CFO should prepare and have the board review a five-year projected operating budget. Annual fund goals (fundraising for current operations) should be identified as one of the revenue components of the operating budget. Annual fund goals can usually be projected fairly accurately at least one or two years in advance, but they need to be adjusted if there are substantial changes in economic conditions or drops in other sources of revenue for the organization.

An example of a change in revenue would be a substantial cut in the organization's federal or state funding level. If that happens, then the need to make up the missing revenue requires either raising more outside money or cutting back on program and personnel. The first fallback position is usually to raise the annual fund goal to meet the burden of that additional fundraising.

If the strategic planning process produces a plan for expansion or major changes to the organization's programs and facilities, make sure that the CFO has included the additional operating costs that these projected changes in program will entail. Annual operating costs usually rise when new buildings and new programs come online, and often the annual fund goal must be increased to meet these new costs.

Setting Annual Fund Goals

Most organizations use some version of the "gap" method in determining annual fund goals. The gap is the difference between the total projected annual revenues for the nonprofit and the total projected expenditures. For details on this method and some variances see the annual fund discussion in Chapter 5.

Unexpected volatility in operating budgets or large gaps in revenue often translate into large increases in annual fund goals. Beware of simply making knee-jerk decisions to increase the annual fund goal. There is no evidence to show that enhanced needs can be met through fundraising without the organization making a substantial investment in the fundraising operation, producing additional overhead.

Increases on the order of 10 percent, 15 percent, and 20 percent in annual operating budgets are problematic unless there is an identified source of revenue attached to them. Boards and development staff members are going to have a hard time meeting big jumps in the goal for the annual fund unless substantial resources are plowed into the development operation.

In general, given a flat or depressed fundraising environment, annual fund goals should be increased by small increments, if they are increased at all. A goal that includes an increase of 3 to 5 percent on top of the amount raised over the previous year is probably achievable in most markets, but even small incremental increases have been difficult to sustain in recent years. The truth is that many organizations are just trying to hang on to their donors and keep giving from declining.

Many organizations are trying to decrease their dependence on annual fundraising for operations. There are some good reasons for this approach:

- Unrestricted fundraising is the hardest kind of money to raise because many donors prefer to make gifts that are restricted to capital or program.

- The annual fund is usually derived from a broad base of donors from all wealth levels, so it can be more vulnerable to broad shifts in the economy.

- Funds raised to balance the budget cannot be counted on to cover huge gaps, such as cuts in government funding.

Alternatives to annual funding often take time to develop, but your organization can begin planning some solutions that will bring future budget relief. The most effective, long-term way to relieve annual budgetary needs is to build a strong endowment. Many capital campaigns include an endowment component for this reason.

Even if annual fundraising remains strong, it may be preferable for the organization to try to grow its fundraising through efforts that enhance specific improvements to facility, program, or endowment. These areas of restricted giving, which generally attract major gifts, often form the basis of a campaign effort.

YOUR ROLE AS A BOARD MEMBER

As a board member, you will want to take a thorough look at how the annual fund is faring, in terms of both donors and dollars. While reviewing annual fund results is often the purview of the development committee, the health of the annual fund is crucial to your fiduciary responsibility as a board member. Remember that it is usually the annual fund that closes the budget gap.

Learn how annual fund goals are set in your organization. Make sure that your organization considers other ways of increasing revenues, such as raising prices for services provided, cutting costs, and increasing endowment fundraising, before automatically increasing annual fund goals.

IN THE REAL WORLD

One institution counted all its bequests as annual fund gifts in the year in which they were realized. The problem was that the CFO automatically raised the annual fund goal each year by 5 percent over the amount raised the year before. When there was a year with a big bequest, the annual fund went up. But there was no basis for assuming that the organization could raise the same amount, and certainly not a 5 percent increase on that amount, in the following year. The result was that the goals became totally unrealistic and had to be completely realigned.

Moral: Don't count one-time gifts in the same total as recurring gifts. It leads to bad assumptions.

YOUR ROLE AS A BOARD MEMBER

You have an additional role to play as a donor and solicitor. As discussed in Chapter 2, every board member should be an annual fund donor, preferably at a leadership giving level. You should also be prepared to assist with raising gifts from your fellow board members. These leadership gifts are needed to meet annual fund goals.

Some organizations have very structured annual fund campaigns with tiers of giving, phone call banks, trained volunteers, and personal call assignments. These programs are often staff driven. In this type of program, your involvement may be limited to joining an annual fund committee, making phone calls, and writing thank-you notes. These activities, while considered routine, are crucial to meeting the annual budget and need to be taken seriously. Your involvement demonstrates leadership from the board to those volunteers and staff who are down in the trenches.

As a board member you can play a more important role in the annual fund campaign by helping to increase the top levels of annual giving. Many organizations have found that they can increase annual giving substantially by building donor societies for donors of annual gifts of $1,000, $5,000, $10,000, and more. Building up to these higher gift levels almost always requires a small cadre of board members to take the initiative. You and your peers can lead this program by making the initial gifts, developing the call list, making the calls, and thanking the donors. This topic will be covered in more detail in Chapter 5, which focuses on annual fundraising.

Planning for Comprehensive Campaigns

If your organization conducts a strategic planning exercise, the resulting plan is likely to call for long-term resource development. Even without a formal strategic plan, it is normal for a nonprofit to find that it requires resources beyond those provided by annual fund drives. These funding needs might be related to the operating budget, for example, increasing endowment to provide budget relief, or they might be comprehensive, like building a new building, hiring new staff, and creating new programs.

The most efficient way to bring in more money on a comprehensive basis is through mounting a campaign.

Campaigns can be short or long (less than one year to five years); they can be for one purpose (endowment) or comprehensive (annual fund, program, endowment, and/or capital); they can be local or national; volunteer driven or staff driven; big or little. What they all share is this: Campaigns are a coordinated effort on behalf of the organization to achieve an established set of funding goals within a specific time frame.

If you are a board member of a nonprofit that is undertaking a campaign or planning for a campaign, your knowledge, leadership, participation, and giving to that campaign is crucial to its success.

Defining a Table of Needs

The table of needs is the list of things that your organization has identified that it wants to raise money for. You might call it the organization's approved "wish list." The table of needs forms the backbone of your campaign. If your organization has completed a strategic planning exercise, the strategic plan should drive the list of priority needs that will form the basis of your fundraising efforts.

If no long-term planning has been done, your organization still must under-take some kind of process, even if it's the chair writing a list of needs on a paper napkin, to decide what it will raise money for.

IN THE REAL WORLD

Setting Goals

One small independent school thought that it would set a capital campaign goal based on what its peer institutions were raising. The headmaster polled several bigger, successful schools in its market and decided that his school needed to raise $100 million to be just like them. When he told the board they were going to raise $100 million, they balked. The largest campaign they had ever completed was for $25 million. Where were they going to find four times that amount?

The school brought in a consultant to conduct a feasibility study. Discussions with potential donors and board members took over six months, but the final result was a recommendation to develop a $75 million campaign in three phases. The first phase was for $25 million to build a new science center, the second phase of $25 million would be for faculty salaries and program needs, and the third phase was for $25 million for scholarships and endow-ment. In this way the board agreed to most of the aims of the headmaster but focused on a realistic set of needs and a time line that could be met.

The planning process, whatever it looks like, should result in a three- to five-year table of needs (over and above annual operating fund goals). This list of specific needs should have the costs attached, so that the board and develop-ment staff can make it the basis for their shopping list for fundraising. The list should be prioritized so that as potential donors are identified, the projects that are most important to the organization get funded first.

In the sample table of needs illustrated in Exhibit 3.2, this organization has identified capital needs, both short-term and long-term, that will result in a new facility by year 5. Then they developed a plan that splits funding for one new staff member and related program needs between endowment fundraising and new sources of revenue. Note that this plan relieves the annual fund of picking up the additional annual cost of a new staff member, a method commonly used to fund new staff, which creates more pressure on fundraising for operations.

It is also useful to have a "wish list" of big-ticket items held back in reserve in case the right funder appears. The nonprofit in Exhibit 3.2 has identified several high-impact gift scenarios for expansion or merger with another organization that are not included in its basic strategic plan for the next five years. If they find a donor who wants to effect major change in the organization, these ideas are ready for further development and investment.

The organization in Exhibit 3.2 is now ready to plan for a comprehensive fundraising campaign. Their table of needs covers capital, endowment, program, and staffing goals over the next five years. And, if they are fortunate enough to find a "high-impact" gift of $2 million to $3 million in addition to the priorities they have identified, they have some big ideas to explore for expanding their services.

For a small nonprofit with no history of major gift fundraising there are major financial and staffing implications to planning a comprehensive fundraising

---

EXHIBIT 3.2

Sample Table of Needs

In this example, the nonprofit has developed a set of needs that are derived from a five-year strategic plan that supports an expansion of the organization's services.

The plan calls for first renovating the current facility, then building a new facility; adding one new staff member to run a new program; and raising endowed funds to cover the costs of the additional overhead for the new staff member. Most of these needs will have to be funded by year 5, with the exception of the renovation, which is a year 2 goal.

While funding for the new staff person will be covered by endowment, funding for the new program will need to be raised annually; alternatively, a new source of revenue can be identified as part of the expansion of services to help pay for the new program costs. Note that the needs are prioritized and subdivided into capital, program, and endowment goals.

Priority #1: Capital needs

—Renovation of current facility (by year 2):	$ 150,000
—Construction of new facility (by year 5):	$ 1,500,000
Total capital needs:	$ 1,650,000

Priority #2: Program and staffing needs

—New programs for new facility (starting year 5):	$ 56,000/year
—New staff person for new facility (starting year 5):	$ 70,000/year
Total program and staffing needs (starting year 5):	$126,000/year

Priority #3: Endowment needs

Endowment to be raised by year 5:	$ 1,400,000

(Note: An endowment of $1.4 million at an annual payout of 5% will produce $70,000/year, enough to pay the salary of the new staff person.)

Total to be raised over 5 years: **$ 3,106,000**

Priority #4: High-impact gift—what would it take to make the greatest impact on our ability to expand our programs and services?

—Expand services in a new location:	$ 3,000,000
—Expand serves provided at current center:	$ 2,000,000
—Merge with an organization that provides similar services:	$ 1,000,000+

(Note: Merger costs to be determined when potential partner is identified.)

campaign to meet the needs outlined in Exhibit 3.2. It will take energy and resources well beyond those available on the board for this nonprofit to succeed. All of the nonprofit's board members must be willing and able to devote their energy and resources to the enterprise, as well as help to seek additional resources, to reach the fundraising levels required by a plan such as this one.

The executive committee, along with all the appropriate board committees, will need to be involved in the effort. Integrated planning must be conducted by the finance committee, the facilities committee, the development committee, and operations. The CFO and CEO should bring appropriate materials to each committee in a timely and transparent fashion so that the entire board can understand, accept, and support the plan.

YOUR ROLE AS A BOARD MEMBER

Before your board approves a campaign of any size or duration, additional information should be gathered to show that the organization has the fundraising capability to meet these enhanced goals. Not all needs can be funded, especially in these times of economic constraint. Hiring an outside consultant to conduct a campaign feasibility study is one accepted method used to provide information to the board when these key decisions are being made (more about consultants and studies in Chapter 4).

A comprehensive multiyear, multimillion-dollar fundraising campaign built around a table of needs should not be entered into lightly. It requires a long-term commitment from the entire board, the executive leadership, and the staff, as well as from the donors who will provide the resources.

As a board member, make sure that you and your peers fully understand what kinds of funds the organization is seeking, how they fit into the long-term needs of the organization, and the timetable for raising them. Then delve into the organization and structure required to put together a campaign of this size and complexity.

Getting Organized for Fundraising

Board buy-in and ownership of the fundraising activity and goals are the key ingredients to successful nonprofit fundraising. The goal is to harness the full strength of the board to leverage funding results. No matter how large or small your board may be, the sum total of the outreach efforts provided by you plus every other board member is going to be needed to meet the goals for funds raised.

If your board wants to expand or strengthen its fundraising role, one option is to make the full board the "development committee as a whole." This means that all board members carry the responsibility for seeing that the organization gets its resources met and that fundraising is a part of every board member's responsibility. Spreading the responsibility across the entire board can help to ensure that annual budgets are balanced and that long-term capital and program plans are funded in a timely manner.

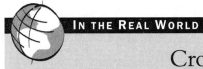

IN THE REAL WORLD

Crossed Signals

The university president walked out of the elevator and into the office of the president of a major oil and gas company in Houston, whose son had just enrolled that fall in the university's business school. The university president was making his first call on what could be a major benefactor. His goal was to ask for the company to sponsor an important scientific effort, a project that could lead to millions in research funding.

The business leader greeted his university colleague warmly. "I'm so glad you came today," he said. "I was just meeting with the dean of your business school this morning, and he was talking about our doing an internship fund with the B-school. I committed to $25,000 and hope it goes well. Junior just loves it there."

It's possible that this university just lost out on the potential for millions in return for a $25,000 gift. Make sure all parties with access to the donor talk to each other!

In the "development committee as a whole" scenario, all annual fund and campaign reports are given to the full board, all board members are asked to participate in fundraising events and activities, and all board members become involved in prospect identification and cultivation. All board members are also asked to make a gift within their means.

Organizing and staffing all this activity is a task that can be delegated to staff, to volunteer campaign committees, or to some combination of the two.

As a board member, don't assume that you should be able to pick up the phone, make calls, and start raising money without communicating with the campaign leadership and/or the advancement staff. Establish a central clearinghouse for donor assignments and activities. This can be either a staff or a volunteer function, as long as it is implemented well and adhered to.

Big problems can arise when board members go out on their own to raise money without first checking in. You want your donors to be approached with the best ask for the highest priority of the organization. You don't want three board members to approach the same prospect separately all at the same time. Communication and respect for one another are paramount to running a good fundraising program at the board level.

See Exhibit 3.3 for some pointers on how your board can prepare for a fundraising campaign.

EXHIBIT 3.3

Before the Fundraising Starts

As a board member, you will want to . . .

1. Understand both short-term and long-term fundraising goals and how they fit into the needs and plans of the organization.

2. Participate in a strategic planning exercise to help determine future needs.

3. Attend a training session provided for fundraising at the board level; if none is provided, ask for a session with the staff and/or a consultant.

4. Assign resource development as a function of the "committee of the whole," rather than keeping it the sole purview of the development committee, so that all board members have fundraising in their portfolio.

5. Consider joining the campaign or development committees if you want to help set fundraising policy and measure fundraising success.

6. Sign up to open the door with prospects or make calls on potential donors with whom you think you can be effective.

7. Plan your own gift to the organization in a way that meets both your own interests and the organization's greatest needs.

8. Expect to communicate with either staff or a board volunteer before making calls and asking for money.

9. Attend a board retreat to take part in setting the strategy and timeline for meeting fundraising needs.

Development Committees

The most common board fundraising committee structure is the development committee, which should focus its work on policy review and accountability. (See Exhibit 3.4 for a sample list of development committee responsibilities.)

Even if the entire board takes ownership of the fundraising effort, there are still activities that are best undertaken at the smaller committee level because it is more efficient. Service on the development committee provides a core group

---

EXHIBIT 3.4

Sample Charge to the Development Committee

1. Take responsibility for the solicitation of all board members for their annual and/or capital gift as established by board rules and procedures.

2. Review all policy related to the solicitation and acceptance of gifts to ensure that donors and their gifts are treated in an ethical and legal manner.

3. Recommend fundraising goals for approval to the full board; set achievable goals and develop accountability measures to ensure that goals are being met in a timely manner.

4. Review development staffing, organizational structure, and budgets. Review cost of funds raised in order to ensure that this cost is within peer and industry standards.

5. Assist with hiring of key development staff, especially the chief advancement officer and the fundraising consultant.

6. Review all materials, electronic and print, that present the fundraising case; not to design by committee, but to ensure that the organization, its mission, and its goals are fairly and accurately represented to potential donors.

7. Oversee standards for gift accounting, gift receipts, thank-yous, and donor stewardship to ensure that donors are being treated fairly and that funds are deposited efficiently and meet the wishes of the donor.

8. Provide opportunities for training for all board members so that fundraising leadership can be exercised by the board as a whole.

9. Actively lead in identifying prospects, opening doors, asking for money, and expanding the reach of the organization to develop new resources.

of board members who are more experienced in fundraising, and the best fundraisers on the board often gravitate to this committee.

The development committee is usually a standing committee of the board with a chair and members who are appointed to serve as one of the assignments of their board service. Development committee terms can range from one year to five years, depending on board governance. Longstanding knowledge of the organization and its donors is useful, so longer service is often preferable on this committee.

It is useful for the development committee chair to have served on the committee prior to taking on the leadership so that knowledge of fundraising policy and procedure is already present. Committee size should be limited to 10 to 12 members, even on large boards, so that meetings can proceed in a timely and efficient manner. Smaller committees are fine if the work gets done without being too onerous for committee members.

The development committee should bear the responsibility for seeing that each board member is solicited for his or her annual gift, and if appropriate, for a capital gift. Often this solicitation process takes place on a set fiscal year calendar, and thus the calls on other board members become standard operating procedure for a certain time of the year (for example, at the start of the new fiscal year, all board members are asked for their annual gift). The solicitation of board members should be made on a personal basis as discussed in Chapter 2.

Some development committee chairs prefer to write a personal letter to each board member, outlining the need for funds, and then assign follow-up calls to committee members to bring the gifts in. This works well with a national board, where travel and calendar issues can delay face-to-face meetings.

Beyond ensuring giving across the board, the development committee charge is to review policy and procedures for all fundraising programs. Setting goals, measuring progress against goals, reviewing policies for giving, ensuring the appropriate use of funds donated, and assisting with the development of the case and related materials are all development committee functions.

Annual Fund and Capital Campaign Committees

Annual fund committees and capital campaign committees are usually ad hoc committees, established for a specific purpose and lasting for the duration of a specific fundraising campaign.

Annual fund and capital campaign committees, unlike development committees, often recruit nonboard members for their work. It is preferable that the membership of these committees include a broad range of volunteers since the committee members are the workers who will actually raise the funds needed. These committees should be placed under the jurisdiction of a standing board committee, such as the development committee, to ensure that appropriate policy is followed. In this manner, the development committee provides oversight for all fundraising activities.

Annual fund committees may operate year round, but most have a period of several months when their activity is at a peak. Annual fund drives are often led by a group of lower-level volunteers who are willing to make many contacts for small annual gifts. These annual drives may be supported by direct mail, phone banks, and personal calls. See Exhibit 3.5 for suggested activities for annual fund committee members.

RULES OF THE ROAD

Have annual fund and campaign committees report to the development committee or to another standing board committee so that the board retains control of all major fundraising efforts.

Capital campaigns usually have a set timetable and goal, so the campaign committee is charged with meeting those goals within the time frame established, and the committee may run for several years. Capital campaign chairs and co-chairs do not have to be board members; however, it is best to have some overlap in membership between the campaign committee and the development committee for reporting and review. The campaign committee should function according to the goals, procedures, and policies set by the board, so that the board retains control of major fundraising efforts.

EXHIBIT 3.5

Activities for Annual Fund Committee Members

1. Identify potential annual fund donors by looking at lists, e.g., prior donors, past board members, vendors, and families of people who use your organization's services.

2. Make calls to lower-level donors to "bump up" their giving to a new higher level.

3. Use social networking to increase the number of young supporters.

4. Write and sign annual fund letters with a personal handwritten note.

5. Help to build systems to support the annual fund, such as volunteer committees and delineated giving levels.

6. Investigate the potential of programs (like giving societies) that provide more recognition and benefits for annual donors.

7. Create a competition between groups to raise more money for the annual fund, using classes, cities, or other categories to build teams.

8. Promote and develop a plan to raise leadership-level gifts to the annual fund (recurring annual gifts of $1,000, $5,000, and $10,000).

Capital campaign committees should be populated with volunteers who can play a specific role in the success of the campaign. This is not an honorary position, but rather a working position. The members of the committee should be able to provide access to the kind of prospects that the organization will approach for campaign gifts. Include members who can approach corporations and foundations, for instance, as well as members who are able to open the door to the major philanthropists in your community.

Training Board Members to Fundraise

There are several different ways to prepare and train board members to fundraise. Conducting a board session on how to raise money, led by either advancement staff or a consultant, is a popular technique. These sessions will probably run from one to two hours and can be offered independently, as one component of a board meeting, or integrated into a board retreat.

A complete step-by-step guide on "The Five Elements of the Successful Ask" is featured in Chapter 7. An agenda and materials for a board retreat on fundraising are included in the Appendix to this book. See the companion web site for this book at www.wiley.com/go/boardfundraising for more board retreat materials and a PowerPoint presentation on this topic that can be downloaded and individualized for your organization.

Experience shows that anyone who is willing to learn can become a good fundraiser. The problem comes with those who aren't willing or who have made up their minds that they can't ask for money. Overcoming anxiety is a key element in the training process, which is why role playing and other interactive strategies are often used in workshops.

Often the best way to train a hesitant fundraiser is to take him or her along on a real call with a real donor. Role playing only goes so far in re-creating the give-and-take rhythm of a real solicitation call. Pairing up teams, with the experienced board member taking a neophyte under his or her wing on calls, is a great training exercise.

TALES FROM THE BOARDROOM

The chair of the development committee and her spouse took the visiting VIP from the national foundation to dinner after a day spent touring their facility. The restaurant was a famous one, but it was noisy and the group had to practically shout to hear one another. The board member made an impassioned appeal for support for her organization, and then leaned forward to hear the foundation person's response.

"We really like what we saw today," was the encouraging opening from the big funder. "We think we are ready to do mmmmmmm," and the number was lost in the crowd noise.

The board member responded with a nod but had no idea what was said. When the dinner was over, and the group was out on the sidewalk, she had to ask, "What were you thinking of doing again?"

The foundation person responded, "I think we can do a million."

Motivating people to fundraise who are resistant to making the ask is like getting people to exercise who don't like to work out—it takes a little bit of psychology, a dose of technique, and some peer pressure, accompanied by lots of encouragement, early success, and a good example to keep them going strong.

Flexibility of assignments is another key to success with volunteers. There is always something that every board member can do well in fundraising, even if they are reluctant to ask. This is why solicitation teams are so successful; each volunteer can play the role that is best suited to his or her skill set. Opening the door to the prospect, making the case for the organization, providing a tour of the site—all of these activities are crucial to the fundraising process and can contribute to the ultimate goal of closing the gift.

Special Training Options

Board members might also benefit from more specialized training options to update their fundraising techniques. The development committee can help to sponsor training updates or small workshops for those who need a brush-up on their skills.

Consider bringing in an estate planning expert, for instance, to talk about planned giving. This is an area that is often underutilized as a giving resource at many nonprofits, and providing training can give board members the confidence to bring up planned giving options with prospective donors (as well as teach them what they can and cannot say legally).

There are a couple of areas where specific techniques can be learned to help solicitors ask for and successfully close a gift. Workshop presentations can be keyed to teach targeted skills, such as "overcoming objections" and "how to close a gift." In general, board members will be more willing and confident in their fundraising work if they have been trained in established fundraising techniques. All of these techniques are used to provide additional tools to support board members in their fundraising efforts.

While training can build skills and help board members to overcome their reluctance to ask for money, the enthusiasm and energy of the active board must be carefully nurtured. Here are some steps to follow to encourage board owner-ship and buy-in for fundraising activity.

Build Board Buy-In for Fundraising

Building board ownership of fundraising goals requires a unique combination of staff and volunteer efforts. Here are seven elements your board should consider:

1. *Education is key.*

   All board members must understand how much money is needed, how to make the case with a donor, how the organization will use the money, and why their help is essential.

2. *Clarify expectations.*

   Make it clear from the initial recruitment phase going forward that on this board, members are expected to learn how to fundraise and to help with the development of resources.

3. *Provide tools: Build confidence through providing good techniques.*

   Fundraising is not an intuitive skill for most people. Attend a training ses-sion; learn through role playing, use videos, write scripts, assign roles, deal with objections, and make the work fun. Learn techniques for how to close a gift, how to overcome objections, and how to talk about planned giving.

4. *Start with easy assignments and build on success.*

   Assign less experienced volunteers to prospects who will say yes. Hold back the harder cases for the seasoned veterans. Begin with annual fund asks with your fellow board members. Make thank-you calls. Get com-fortable talking about real money with real donors.

5. *Assign a mentor and create donor solicitation teams.*

   If you are a hesitant or inexperienced board member, pair up with an experienced solicitor who really loves the work. Watching the techniques and learning the ropes from an experienced solicitor is an invaluable exer-cise. It will help you gain confidence to develop your own skills.

6. *Find ways to contribute other than asking for money.*

There are many other ways you can contribute beyond asking for money. Volunteers are important to every organization and can contribute on many fronts. In the fundraising area, board volunteers can review and advise on materials, identify and rate potential donors, open the door to potential donors, and make an introductory call or write a letter to acquaint the donor with your organization.

7. *Provide plenty of practice and plenty of praise.*

Like most skills, fundraising skills improve with practice. Keep the momentum up with calls because even the best volunteers get rusty without practice. Provide regular board-level fundraising reports that go beyond the dollars raised to highlight the assistance that active board members are providing to the fundraising effort. Make sure that everyone involved with a gift gets praise when the gift is closed.

OVERCOMING COMMON BARRIERS TO SUCCESS
OUR BOARD ISN'T COMFORTABLE WITH ASKING

This is a common problem that results from anxiety about talking about money and fear of being turned down. Try demystifying fundraising through discussion, training, and practice. View fundraising as a process that can be learned, a process that requires a skill set that can be improved with practice. See the following *Tips and Techniques* for some helpful ideas.

OUR BOARD DELEGATES THE FUNDRAISING TO THE DEVELOPMENT COMMITTEE

The proper role of the development committee is to set policy, provide oversight for all fundraising activities, and lead the solicitation of the rest of the board. The development committee should be prepared to do some fundraising, but successful fundraising requires a commitment from every board member to help secure resources.

A strong development committee chair can take the lead in involving other board members in fundraising activities. If the development committee chair doesn't want to end up doing all the work herself, she needs to work with the other board leaders in getting not just the committee, but the entire board, involved with fundraising activities.

Planning a training session for board members, leading a board retreat on fundraising, or bringing in an expert in a specialized area, like planned giving, are examples of activities where the development committee can take initiative. The development chair can improve board communications on fundraising programs and results. Development efforts should be front and center in all board reports and updates.

The development committee should be a catalyst for fundraising, the core group responsible for organizing, training, and motivating the entire board in its fiduciary role. Because the development committee is charged with the responsibility to see that goals are met in a timely manner, the members can play a key role in developing an environment where the entire board assists in the fundraising effort.

TIPS AND TECHNIQUES

Ways to Build Confidence in Asking

- Provide training for all board members on how to ask and how to close a gift.

- Pair up board members to make calls, using a more experienced solicitor to make calls with a less experienced peer.

- Provide a more experienced "mentor" for a board member who hesitates to raise money (this could be a donor, a development staff member, the executive director/CEO, or another board member).

- Start by assigning a new volunteer the smaller, easier calls, like annual fund calls on donors who give every year.

- Don't start by making the board member ask for money. Have board volunteers join in on a solicitation call to open the door to the prospect or to talk about their passion for the organization. Bring along another volunteer or staff member to make the ask. Just being in the room when an ask is made provides training.

- Order the solicitation calls so that the hesitant board member has success early on and gains confidence.

- Prepare board members well for solicitation calls; use a script, assign roles, and role play the call ahead of time if necessary.

- Make sure that the organization provides good staffing support; talk through possible objections, brainstorm solutions, and praise success.

Summary

Weak board level fundraising is a common issue for boards across the nonprofit sector. Your board doesn't have to follow suit. Be sure that your organization has done the strategic planning necessary to identify reasonable and achievable goals. Have the board share responsibility in the planning so that the final goals are based on a vision and set of needs that are understood and supported by the entire board.

Your organization should develop a table of needs that will drive the fundraising for the next three to five years. Make sure that the board buys in to the needs, the costs, and the timetable. Factor in operating costs and find ways to relieve pressure on the annual fund. Creating board buy-in for goals is a key step in getting the board to accept responsibility for fundraising.

Good fundraising requires good organization, including creating strong development committees and campaign committees. Board training in fundraising can help to relieve the fear many people have of asking for money. Consider holding a board retreat to review fundraising goals, build enthusiasm, provide training, and create an environment where the entire board becomes engaged in the fundraising effort.

CHAPTER 4

Building the Team

When I was young I thought that money was the most important thing in life; now that I am old I know that it is.

—Oscar Wilde

After reading this chapter, you will be able to:

- Define fundraising roles for the board and staff.
- Build the advancement team.
- Hire a fundraising consultant to meet your needs.

Who Is on the Team?

Fundraising requires a team effort. Many nonprofits can't afford to hire an extensive fundraising staff, and there is a wide range of services provided, so you will find three different scenarios here: one for the organization with no development staff, one for the organization with a single person in the development office, and finally, for the larger organizations, the comprehensive fundraising staff that offers "full-service" support.

Nonprofits with No Professional Fundraising Staff

If your organization falls into this category, don't think that you are alone—there are thousands of nonprofits that raise money without a full-time staff member.

A nonprofit organization should be raising about $250,000 to $300,000 minimum per year before the program is productive enough to pay for a full-time development person. You don't want your organization raising just enough funds to pay for the development staff—that is a demotivating scenario for donors, who expect their gifts to support programs that actually contribute to the organization's mission.

One option for getting started on a new fundraising initiative without staff is to bring in a consultant who can advise, train, and guide the board on initial outreach efforts. If the consultant is a good match for the nonprofit, this is usually a productive and efficient use of scarce resources.

Another option for start-up fundraising is to begin with a part-time development professional, or to share one with another nonprofit, and build the program until it becomes successful enough to produce the funds to pay for both a full-time staff member and provide support for the organization.

In nonprofits with no professional fundraising staff, volunteers (often board members) must pick up the slack. The organization and structure of the fundraising effort must be developed without staff support. In many cases, the development committee takes the lead with organization and planning. Often, one or two board members who are more experienced step forward to lead the fundraising efforts as volunteers in the absence of more formal staff or programs.

As in most group efforts, it is a good idea to put in place a plan, a timetable, and a leadership structure, and to delegate the tasks involved to make the fundraising efforts more productive. With no staff to provide support, board members and other volunteers must take responsibility for a wide range of basic fundraising activities (see the nearby *Tips and Techniques* for a list).

TIPS AND TECHNIQUES

Basic Fundraising Activities
(No Staff Support Provided)

Select an experienced board member, use the development committee, or hire a consultant to accomplish these steps:

- Set fundraising goals.
- Identify prospects.
- Prepare solicitation materials.
- Identify and recruit a small cadre of fellow board members to help.
- Assign calls to volunteers (which may include other board members).
- Solicit every member of the board.
- Report back to the board on results.
- Maintain oversight of financial recording, gift accounting, and gift receipts.
- Thank donors (ask fellow board members to call or write donors).

These activities can be very time consuming, to say the least! If the organization can afford to devote a portion of the time of a staff administrative assistant to the effort, it can improve fundraising productivity, allowing the board and volunteers to focus more on the top tier of activities: setting goals, identifying prospects, assigning calls, and soliciting gifts.

Some nonprofits without fundraising staff focus all their volunteer efforts on a single annual fundraising event. Events are not the most efficient way to raise money. Like social networking, events draw attention to the cause, keep people engaged, and provide a basis for communicating with supporters. However, unless they are very carefully planned, event costs can eat up the proceeds.

TALES FROM THE BOARDROOM

The donor was an architect whose business was designing parking garages. After he passed away, his foundation made a gift to name the new parking garage at the hospital. The board of the hospital saved the first parking space and marked it with a plaque in his honor, so that it would be perpetually open to receive him, should he ever choose to visit.

The lack of professional staff to support fundraising doesn't need to hamper the focus of board members on the development effort. In fact, sometimes the board is more engaged in fundraising without staff support. The time to add staff is when the complexity of the goals and the operational needs outweigh the time and ability of the volunteers on the board to handle all the work.

YOUR ROLE AS A BOARD MEMBER

You must take the place of staff and work with your colleagues to create a fundraising plan. Set a reasonable goal and develop a team of fellow volunteers to help you get there. Pool your resources on the board to figure out who has the best contacts with top prospects in your community. Use local prospect research resources, often available through your community foundation, to identify the biggest philanthropists, the companies that provide the most sponsorships, and the foundations that might support your cause.

Assign three or four prospects to each member of your group, review the case for giving, and take off! The enthusiasm and sincerity of your approach will cover for a few faux pas made by green volunteers. Don't be afraid to ask if you are convinced your program is using its money wisely. You are asking for resources for something you believe in, not for yourself.

When it comes time to bring a staff person on board, let them know the history of the gifts and contacts you have uncovered. There is nothing worse than having to recreate records from a haphazard development program—be sure to record the names of those whom you approached, what they said, what gifts were promised, and who made them.

RULES OF THE ROAD

Adding professional staff should not be seen as taking the place of the board's fundraising efforts, but rather as providing organizational support and structure to help make the board's efforts more productive.

The One-Person Development Shop

The one-person development shop represents the majority of development operations at nonprofits across the sector. You might think that a one-person shop would be inherently focused on fundraising; however, that focus often becomes diluted because so many additional duties are thrown into the mix.

Additional responsibilities that can distract from fundraising include public relations, board staffing and management, special event management, program oversight, volunteer management, and various other duties that end up at the development office door. The key to good fundraising is the ability to focus, so try to develop a job description that gives the development person room to achieve his or her assigned fundraising goals.

Hiring a development staff person allows the board to rely on a professional to provide support for the board's fundraising role. Examples of the kinds of activities that could be assigned to a development staff person are listed in Exhibit 4.1. Note that no single person can adequately perform all of these tasks without assistance from volunteers and staff.

EXHIBIT 4.1

Role of the Development Staff Person in a One-Person Shop

Note: These activities are listed to provide an example of the types of activities an advancement staff person can provide. Each nonprofit will want to develop its own job description and determine what activities it needs most from a solo fundraising staff member. No single development officer can manage all of these activities without additional support from volunteers or staff. Types of activities for the advancement staff member in a one-person office:

- Assist in the development and presentation of fundraising goals to the board.

- Create a timetable for all development activities.

- Provide training and support for board fundraising activities.

- Develop and implement a plan to engage the board in fundraising activities.

- Prospect identification: Review lists, names, giving histories, and background information on potential prospects with board members and other volunteers.

- Prospect rating: Work with the board to determine who can give, at what level, and where the donor's interests lie.

- Assign prospects to board and volunteers in an organized fashion.

(continued)

EXHIBIT 4.1

Role of the Development Staff Person in a One-Person Shop (Continued)

- Provide appropriate materials to use for calls on prospects.

- Assist in providing cultivation activities, such as site visits, events, and small group gatherings.

- Make his or her own calls on a selected group of prospects and ask for gifts as appropriate.

- Support calls made by board members: This might include appointment setting, research, script preparation for the call, and joining the team making the call.

- Follow-up activity after calls: Produce proposals, letters, pledge forms, gift agreements, and track follow-up activity.

- Oversee or conduct gift recording and gift accounting.

- Provide thank-you letters and gift receipts in a timely fashion.

- Create and implement a basic stewardship plan to keep donors satisfied and informed about their giving to the organization.

YOUR ROLE AS A BOARD MEMBER

It is very important to see the staff fundraiser as a professional supporting your efforts, not as a professional replacing your efforts.

The best way to think of the professional fundraiser is as a team member who can organize and provide support for your own fundraising work as a board member. The staffer is best suited to provide the structure, planning, integration with other efforts, and back-office work to make the fundraising program more efficient and effective. These are all areas where staff is more efficient than the board.

Your role as a board member is to do those things for which the staff is least well suited. These areas include providing new names of prospects, opening the door to prospects, helping to strategize calls, rating prospects, identifying the interests of prospects, participating in cultivation activities, taking prospect assignments, making calls, asking for money, providing follow-up to close gifts, thanking donors, making your own gift, and taking the responsibility to see that other board members make their gifts.

Depending on the nature of your fundraising program, even with a development staff member on board, you might also be engaged in hosting events, selling tickets or tables, attending events, taking part in prospect cultivation activities, bringing donors to the site, spreading the word, and generally doing whatever you can think of to expand the reach of your organization further into your community.

IN THE REAL WORLD

The One-Person Shop

The development director of a small nonprofit had no staff to help with support work, so she often spent time on administrative tasks and other time-consuming work not directly related to her fundraising duties. At the end of the fiscal year, the development operation had only succeeded in raising $80,000, barely enough to cover her salary and a few equipment items.

The development director was called on the carpet by the executive director for poor performance. "Where is the money?" asked the distraught executive. The development director had been keeping a record of her time spent on various projects, and she shared it with her boss. Some examples: printing, addressing, and mailing holiday cards, two weeks; preparing gift receipts and gift accounting, 25 percent of her time; preparing reports on fundraising (or lack thereof) for the board, 10 percent of her time; comparing monthly financial reports with the CFO, 10 percent of her time. She was very busy, but she did not have time for any outreach in the community, had made no contact with prospects, and was unable to find the time to encourage and lead active board participation in fundraising.

The solution? The development director hired a part-time data-entry clerk to take gift recording off her list. She found volunteers to take over the holiday card assignment. She hired a systems consultant and developed a report generator to make financial reporting more efficient. She began to work closely with members of the board to make calls on real prospects. She even found time to develop some prospects on her own.

The result? She spent more—development added about $40,000 more to its overhead. But she raised $250,000 the next year instead of $80,000.

Moral of the story: It takes a focus on prospects to raise the money. Spending a little more to make that happen can improve returns dramatically.

Staffing Larger and More Complex Organizations

Universities, hospitals, independent schools, larger museums, and many other kinds of larger nonprofit organizations eventually reach the point where additional development staff assets are required to pursue loftier goals. Professional development operations that run multimillion- and multibillion-dollar campaigns can grow to include hundreds of staff persons working at many sites. Usually these large organizations grow up over time and require good coordination just to work well together without stepping on one another's toes.

TALES FROM THE BOARDROOM

The college kept on its old and ineffective alumni director because he had a special relationship with their most important donor, the scion of a wealthy old family, who had already endowed their art museum and the science complex. Board members complained about the $60,000 a year it cost to pay the alumni director—after all, what did the guy do besides play golf? Then the donor passed away and the college received a $100 million bequest from his estate. It turned out that the investment of $60,000 a year for the alumni director brought a great return for the college.

In a larger, more complex development operation, staff members are hired with specific areas of expertise, such as prospect research, foundation relations, or event management. Development professionals can make an entire career out of one specialization, or they can move from one area to another as their career unfolds. Some people offer a combination of skills and can meet more than one need. Your organization may have some or all of these areas of staff specialization—ask for a development organizational chart to see what positions are filled and by whom.

YOUR ROLE AS A BOARD MEMBER

A large development shop should reflect the high professional standards of the staff involved. Part of their work is to serve you, the board member, and make your time and efforts in the fundraising arena count for a lot. Exhibit 4.2 outlines the kinds of services that a large

EXHIBIT 4.2

Examples of Activities in Support of Board Fundraising Efforts that could be Provided by an Advancement Office with a Larger Professional Staff

Note: These activities are listed to provide an example of the types of support that a larger professional advancement staff can provide for board fundraising efforts. Each nonprofit will want to develop its own staffing plan, job descriptions, and determine what activities it needs most from fundraising staff members. There will be other activities not listed here, that are not directly related to board fundraising, that the advancement staff carries out.

Types of activities that could be provided by the advancement staff in an office with a larger professional staff:

- An organized plan and timetable for board fundraising efforts.

- Good, up-to-date research and information about prospects.

- High-quality written, printed, and electronic materials to support board and volunteer asks.

- Prospect lists that are accurate, timely, well targeted, and prequalified as to the prospect's interest in the organization.

- A focus on pairing each board member with higher-level prospects who are a good match, and creating appropriate teams for prospect cultivation and solicitation.

- Training and updates on current fundraising strategies, including planned giving.

- An organized effort to assist board members in developing prospect strategy and providing cultivation resources for high-level prospects.

- Event support (catering, invitations, program, site selection, etc.) for any fundraising events that board members are involved with.

- Clear ongoing communication on prospect tracking, activities, giving, and follow-up so board members know where things stand and what they are expected to do next.

- Appropriate recognition and thanks for volunteer efforts.

- Appropriate stewardship for donors and gifts of all levels.

professional development staff can provide. Note that each nonprofit will want to set its own priorities for staff job descriptions and goals, so not all of these activities will be provided in every advancement office.

Even with the largest of development operations, it is very important that you and your colleagues on the board continue to identify prospects, open doors, provide cultivation, attend and host events, and thank donors. In fact, the larger the organization, the more special it becomes for a board member to call on a donor. This doesn't mean that staff members can't identify prospects, make a call, or ask for money; they do all of that. It just means that your time becomes a more valuable commodity and should be targeted to the most important prospective donors.

How to Hire: What to Look for in a Chief Advancement Officer

As a board member, you may be asked to participate in the search for a chief advancement officer (CAO). This is a very important position for the organization, but it is also an important position in terms of your ability to succeed as a fundraiser on the board. So get involved and help to identify a great addition to the executive staff!

There are different levels of complexity and experience required for the position, depending on what the goals are and how large a staff the person will be overseeing. There are several traits, however, that tend to augur success in the position. Meet the candidates (or at least the top two or three finalists) in more than one setting to get a more balanced and nuanced view of their strengths and weaknesses.

Here are the main qualities to look for in the CAO position:

- *Commitment to the mission.*

  Passion and commitment to the cause can cover for a lot of other things that can be learned on the job.

- *Nonprofit fundraising experience.*

  Preferably with a similar-sized organization or perhaps one in the same service area.

- *Knowledge of fundraising*.

  Ability to meet goals, manage programs, familiarity with fundraising techniques, track record of getting the job done.

- *Knowledge of the community*.

  You and your fellow board members can provide this if it is missing, but a fundraiser who knows the major players in the community can hit the ground running rather than take years to develop relationships.

- *Good relationship-building skills*.

  Relationships are at the core of good fundraising. Evaluate the candidate based not only on your own gut reaction but on his or her ability to get along with your peers. Do you see good communication skills? Is the person able to connect well with the board and organizational leaders?

- *A good fit with the organization*.

  Is there a good fit with the style and approach the organization takes? Can you imagine sending this person to see your top donor? Will he or she be a good representative for your cause?

- *Management experience and style*.

  If the CAO is going to manage others on the development staff, then his or her ability to motivate, direct, and delegate work to others is a key ingredient for success. Many great fundraisers, elevated from the major gifts staff, bomb when they have to supervise others. Make sure your candidate is prepared to manage others who can bring in gifts, not just do it all as a solo player.

- *Integrity*.

  It used to go without saying, but integrity needs to be front and center. Your CAO must be honest, morally and ethically well grounded, and hold those around him or her to the highest of ethical standards. It's worth doing a little digging to ferret out past problems with expense accounts or fudging numbers to meet goals.

Where to Look for a Chief Advancement Officer

Good people in advancement are hard to find, and when you do find one, his or her salary expectations may surprise you. The field is getting more competitive, and people with experience can name their price. Don't just hang out an ad in the daily paper and expect to attract the best in the field. Here are some ideas for recruiting a strong CAO:

- Advertise nationally in *The Chronicle of Philanthropy*, the leading nonprofit weekly.

- Advertise locally online with your local fundraising professional group. In many communities this is the AFP, the Association of Fundraising Professionals.

- Talk to professionals in the field and get them to spread the word to their colleagues.

- Ask your fellow board members to send the job description to the advancement professionals they know from their other board relationships.

- Hire an executive search firm or a consultant to find your CAO (this is expensive, but may be worth it if you are looking for someone with national experience).

- Hire someone away from another organization that has a mission similar to yours.

- Don't forget to look internally—your best candidate may be waiting in the wings.

TIPS AND TECHNIQUES

Five Ways to Evaluate Candidates for CAO

❶ Identify and pursue references beyond the professional references offered by the candidates to learn more about their abilities and ethical standards.

❷ Ask candidates to go with you to have lunch with a prospect or current donor to your organization and observe the quality of their interaction, especially their ability to listen.

❸ Ask candidates to describe in detail one example of the process of identifying, cultivating, and closing one major gift they were responsible for. Look for qualities such as creativity, humor, ability to connect with the donor, passion for the mission, and integrity in the donor relationship.

❹ Observe candidates' skills in a group setting. Can they move around a room, talk with a variety of people, enter into and leave conversations easily, think on their feet? Do they present a good image for the organization?

❺ Do the candidates treat everyone with respect from the secretary to the chair of the board? Ask the administrative assistants how they rate the top candidates—they are pretty savvy about spotting the difference between the hot-air balloons and the real deals.

Building the Advancement Team

There are many kinds of specialized advancement staff members who take part in large fundraising campaigns. Here is a brief description of standard advancement positions and their duties. Your organization may not need every one of these positions filled, but this will provide you with an overview of the duties and potential areas of interaction between each staff function and your work as a board member.

In most organizations, the development committee reviews staffing, organizational charts, and budgets for the development operation. If you are a member of that committee, you may be asked for budget approval to hire some or any combination of these staff professionals. You may want to offer to help with the interview and selection process. An engaged and knowledgeable board member can be a very useful adjunct to any search committee.

Annual fund director—Leads the fundraising to meet annual fund goals, which is usually defined as funds for current operations. Often runs the direct mail and phone room operations. Can establish and support a cadre of volunteers to make personal fundraising calls. Emphasizes larger numbers of prospects giving smaller dollars. Needs to be very organized and systems oriented.

What it means to you as a board member—If you make annual fund calls, you will be staffed by this person. When you give to the annual fund, your gift will be stewarded by this office. As a fiduciary, you should be very interested in whether the annual fund meets its goals or not.

Leadership annual fund program director—Leads the growth and management of programs that ask for $1,000 to $25,000 annual gifts through personal calls. Requires training, organizing, motivating, and recruiting volunteers. Can be organized on a reunion or class basis at schools and universities.

What it means to you as a board member—Board members are often at the head of the pack in leadership annual fund solicitation. You can be the head of the committee, on the committee, or just give at this level, but you will probably have some interaction with this staff person. This is an area where much of the dollar growth can occur in your annual fund.

Direct mail supervisor—Prepares and plans for all solicitations sent by mail. Nowadays, this task is often farmed out to experts who specialize in buying lists, printing materials, and tracking results. Can be expensive per dollar raised but also is a good way to expand an organization's donor base. Requires experience and systems knowledge, or hire a good direct mail consultant.

What it means to you as a board member—Keep an eye out for costs and effectiveness of this program. Ask questions and be familiar with the materials sent out. Don't opt out of receiving these materials, even if you don't intend to give this way. This keeps you in touch with what outside constituents and lower level donors are seeing from your organization.

Development communications expert—Writes and produces the materials needed to make the fundraising operation effective. Can include print and electronic materials ranging from newsletters to annual reports to brochures. Can be farmed out to specialists, but often best results come from in-house staff who know the organization well.

What it means to you as a board member—You will use the materials provided by this person in your fundraising work. If you think there is room for improvement, give your feedback in a helpful manner. Offer to serve as a focus group member if testing is to be done on new materials. Be proactive about showing the staff good materials you get from other nonprofits. Stay engaged in a positive way with how the organization presents itself and how it makes the case for giving, because communication is an important component that underlies the success of everyone's efforts to raise more money.

Gift recording/gift accounting function—Requires data-entry skills; sometimes this function is assigned to the financial staff rather than development. There are a number of legal requirements for gift accounting and gift use that must be satisfied. Hire someone who knows the ropes or let your CFO supervise this function.

What it means to you as a board member—Board members tend, rightly enough, to get frustrated with mistakes in gift and pledge recording. Good record keeping in general is important for the board to play its proper fiduciary role. Inform the staff about any mistakes that you see or learn about. The development committee of the board is responsible for policy oversight and seeing that the legal requirements of donors are met. You might advocate for an audit, a new computer system, more training, or more staff if gift recording becomes a problem area.

Proposal writer—The art of writing a good proposal never goes out of style. There are outside contractors who do this function well once they learn about your organization, but a good proposal writer on staff may be literally worth his or her weight in gold.

What it means to you as a board member—If you have been part of a solicitation, ask to review the proposal that goes to the prospect. Offer to sign a cover letter. Make sure that you see the written follow-up to any prospect you have solicited, especially if it's over your name. A consultant can provide a strong template for proposals and letters if you think the organization needs help in this area.

Prospect researcher—Prospect researchers pull together all the available information about individual prospects, including a summary of the giving history of that prospect to your organization and to other nonprofits. This information will help you develop a sound basis for developing a gift strategy, including how much to ask for. There are electronic prospect screening services that provide personal and wealth data on your prospects for a fee, but these do not take the place of a human prospect researcher, who is often skilled at pulling together disparate pieces of information about your prospects.

> *What it means to you as a board member*—*Information is power. Having information on both the personal and wealth background of your prospect is important to your success on a call, so your prospect researcher can help you look good. Make sure that your organization handles all prospect research confidentially and ethically. (Ask to see your own profile if you want to cause a stir.)*

Development information systems (database administrator, data-entry workers)—As in all other fields of endeavor, computers and data-based information systems have become very important to the success of the fundraising endeavor.

> *What it means to you as a board member*—*As a volunteer, what you need to know is what information you can get out of the system, its level of accuracy, and getting the information formatted for easy use. You can also advocate for better systems and enhanced staff in this area if you aren't receiving what you need.*

Corporate fundraiser—Handles corporate giving and prospects, corporate sponsorships, corporate alliances; may overlap with marketing efforts. Can work on either a local, regional, or national basis depending on the sophistication of the nonprofit. This position is often combined with foundation fundraising duties in smaller and medium sized nonprofits so that corporate and foundation fundraising is handled by one person.

> *What it means to you as a board member*—*You will interact with this person if you have good corporate contacts or if you pursue funds from corporate prospects. Ask for help from this person, for instance, if you are seeking a sponsorship for a new program or event.*

Foundation fundraiser—Handles foundation prospects, usually both family and national foundations. Has access to subscription-based foundation databases in order to search for foundation giving interests, geographic areas of giving, names of trustees, and other relevant information..

> *What it means to you as a board member*—*This person can check to see if your prospects have access to any foundation money. They can also support your calls on foundation trustees with information about size of gifts, purpose of gifts, family members' names, and other related information. Foundation fundraisers often write proposals, stay in touch with foundation program officers, and identify likely prospects. They can accompany you on calls to foundation trustees.*

Major gifts officer—the fundraiser who handles all major gift prospects. Major gifts are defined as gifts from individuals at the level of $25,000, $100,000, or higher, depending on the sophistication of the organization. These are the field officers who identify prospects, manage their cultivation, and make sure that donors are solicited by the best team in a timely manner. Often major gift officers have regional assignments or are assigned to fundraising for a specific program or school.

> *What it means to you as a board member*—*The major gift officer may be the main person you interact with as you are making your calls on prospects. You may have a major gifts staff member assigned to you who will work with you to identify prospects, create strategy, oversee cultivation efforts, arrange for the solicitation meeting, and keep a record of your efforts. This staff member may also accompany you on calls and help to close the gift.*

Event planner—Plans and directs all event work, from large fundraising galas to intimate cultivation dinners for major gift donors.

> *What it means to you as a board member*—*You will most likely interact with this person when you buy event tickets, sell tables to galas, or attend or host events for prospects. The quality and sophistication of the events you attend or host can be a factor in your success as a fundraiser, so this can be an important staff position to help you in your efforts.*

Planned giving director—Directs, manages, and solicits planned gifts. Often the largest gifts to an organization involve a long-term planned gift such as a bequest or trust. These positions are often filled by attorneys or financial planners who understand tax law and estate planning.

What it means to you as a board member—*If you make calls on major gift prospects and they ask questions about planned gifts, you will want to make use of this staff member's expertise. The planned giving director can help you in setting strategy for your prospect calls if you think planned giving is an option, accompany you on a call with a prospect, or provide follow-up materials on estate planning, trusts, and other planned giving alternatives.*

Donor stewardship manager—Stewardship is the ongoing relationship created with a donor after the gift is made. From thank-you letters to annual reports, good stewardship can affect a donor's decision to give again. Full-time donor stewardship managers often work with endowed fund donors to track endowment gifts, produce and track pledge reminders, and coordinate communication with donors.

What it means to you as a board member—*You may be asked to help with this effort by signing thank-you letters, making calls to thank donors, and attending recognition events. Good stewardship usually leads to repeat gifts from happy donors, so the quality of this effort can affect your ability to go back to a donor for additional gifts.*

Special gifts fundraising—In larger organizations, as well as in many fundraising campaigns, prospects are divided by potential gift level and assigned to staff members responsible for gifts at that dollar level. Special gifts could mean gifts above $250,000, gifts above $1 million, or even mega-gifts above $5 million, depending on the sophistication of the organization, the size and wealth of the prospect pool, and the size of the campaign.

What it means to you as a board member —*Not every board member is suited to raising gifts of $1 million or more. If you are (or if you want to be) associated with prospects and asks at this level, this is the staff person who will support your efforts. Usually asking for gifts at this level is a highly choreographed process, and* *you will want to be involved with setting the strategy for each contact with the prospect, from opening the door to closing the gift.*

Standards for Staffing and Cost per Dollar Raised

Not every fundraising operation needs dozens of staff members to cover every function described above. Many mid-sized nonprofits, such as independent schools, small museums, and social service organizations, get by with a group of four to five development professionals in the advancement office.

Exhibit 4.3 outlines the advancement staff needed for a nonprofit that is midsized, defined here as raising $2 million to $3 million per year. This type of

---

EXHIBIT 4.3

Recommended Staffing Configuration for a Mid-sized Organization Raising $2 million to $3 million per Year

Development Director—manages the office, works directly with board members on all their development assignments, raises money from larger donors, and supervises all programs.

Annual Fund Director—manages lower-level volunteer group, manages direct mail and phone room, responsible for reaching the annual fund goal, and interacts with board for leadership annual fund gifts only.

Major Gifts Officer—works with board members and other volunteers on all prospects for gifts of $25,000+, shares responsibility for board's work on major prospects with development director, travels and meets with potential donors to determine their level of interest in the cause, works on cultivation events, and can solicit alone or as a team member.

Prospect Researcher/Proposal Writer—provides support for all personal calls, does not have personal contact with the board, but supplies research, letters, and proposals for board members' work with prospects through the development director and the major gifts officer.

Administrative Assistant—provides data entry, gift accounting, and thank-you letters; may have significant contact with board members (or their assistants) for appointments, meetings, calendars, signatures, etc.

---

configuration allows for some specialization (e.g., they have a prospect researcher who also writes proposals), but everyone in this office will still need to pitch in and help out for major events and activities.

RULES OF THE ROAD

Fundraising costs should be in a range between $0.03 and $0.20 per dollar raised. Check with industry reports and peers to set a benchmark for this ratio that fits your organization. The American Association of Museums (AAM), for instance, publishes an analysis of fundraising costs for museums derived from a survey of member organizations.

Costs per dollar raised have become the industry standard for judging how big the budget should be for an advancement operation. Fundraising costs should range between three cents and twenty cents per dollar raised for most nonprofits. Unusual situations may cause some variability in costs (such as fundraising for new organizations, disaster fundraising, or recovery from a scandal).

There is a lot of variation in fundraising costs from organization to organization. Costs depend on a variety of factors, including the total dollars raised (raising higher gift levels is more efficient and costs less), the type of nonprofit, the type of fundraising being conducted, and the region of the country where your organization operates. Advancement staff salaries, for instance, can vary widely by region, by level of experience, and by the type of organization doing the hiring.

Big Gifts Are Much Less Expensive to Raise Than Little Gifts

This may sound counterintuitive, but the time, energy, and effort that goes into getting one million-dollar gift is often less than the effort it takes to raise one $10,000 gift. And then it takes 100 of those $10,000 donors to add up to one million-dollar gift! So fundraising efficiency is greatest where the gifts are largest.

Efficiency may not be the only factor to consider in the budget for the development office, however. Some types of fundraising (such as raising small gifts for the annual fund) may cost more per dollar raised than larger gifts, but they are absolutely essential to meet the operational requirements of the nonprofit. Most organizations seek to have a broad base of smaller donors to provide operating funds and go to their major gift donors for special needs, like capital and endowment gifts.

Direct mail, for instance, is much more expensive than having volunteers making calls, and it can cost even more than the total dollars it raises. But direct mail can reach thousands of people whom volunteers don't know and would never be able to reach, and it adds people to the donor pool who may continue to give for years. If your goal is to build up your donor base for the long term, direct mail may be worth its higher price to your organization.

Every organization needs to define its goals and the type of money it needs to raise in order to determine how large a staff and budget it requires to get the job done.

Fundraising Consultants

The time may come when your organization needs to hire a fundraising consultant. The board is often involved in this decision, either through a committee, or through having individual board representatives meeting with consulting candidates. It can be an important decision, and it is one that deserves your involvement.

Just as in the for-profit world, consultants come in all flavors and sizes. There are huge national firms, small independent contractors, and everything in between. Which firm you hire is a factor of what your organization needs, how much money you want to spend, and whether you are mounting a local, regional, or national fundraising effort. Some organizations spare no expense on consultants; others count every penny spent.

On the legal side, make sure your nonprofit understands and follows the IRS requirements for "independent contractors" and that your consultant is not an employee. See IRS guidance on this issue at http://www.irs.gov/businesses/small/article/0,,id=99921,00.html.

Many states have adopted charitable solicitation laws designed to protect donors and charities from fraud. Fundraisers may be required to register with the state before they can work with your organization. Check with the relevant state authorities to determine if your consultant is registered. Not all states require registration of fundraising consultants.

IN THE REAL WORLD

The Mystery Performance

The consultant promised great fundraising returns and sent large monthly bills to support a high amount of travel and activity with prospects. After a few months, the development committee chair asked for a report on funds raised. He was told that all the visits were for cultivation purposes, and that progress was being made. This went on for several more months. Finally the exasperated committee chair demanded a meeting with the consultant.

"What's going on?" he demanded to know. The consultant presented him with a vague story about seeing dozens of prospects, but no concrete visit reports, no strategy for solicitation, no asks, no money, and no follow-up activity. Basically, there was nothing to show for thousands of dollars' worth of work. The consultant was fired, and the board had to start all over again with their fundraising plan.

It's hard to believe, but some consultants don't want to share with you what steps they are taking with your prospects. If you encounter a mystery performer like this one, ask for specifics: Who are they seeing, where and when, what was discussed, and how much was the prospect solicited for? Look for transparency and accountability in your work with consultants— you have the right to expect it.

Do You Need a Fundraising Consultant?

Fundraising consultants have become an integral part of the fundraising process, from advising on annual fund and direct mail campaigns to providing capital campaign expertise. You will want to help your organization carefully weigh the pros and cons of bringing in an external consultant to work on your fundraising efforts. You will need to take into account the level of expertise available on your staff, particularly that of your chief advancement officer.

While consultants do cost money, they can also save you money. It can be expensive and time-consuming to learn how to run a capital campaign, for instance, while you are in one. The cost to your organization of mistakes and missed opportunities may be more than if you had hired outside expertise to begin with.

Some tasks, such as conducting campaign feasibility studies, are given to an outside consultant because the objectivity and confidential nature of the interviews requires an external provider. Other tasks, such as cultivation of high-level donors, may be a better fit for someone inside the organization, such as the executive director or a board member. See Exhibit 4.4 for a list of the pros and cons of hiring a consultant.

EXHIBIT 4.4

Pros and Cons of Hiring a Fundraising Consultant

Reasons to Hire a Consultant

Offers objectivity and credibility.

> A consultant can analyze the organization's fundraising needs and programs without preconceived biases, leading to greater credibility.

Provides experience and expertise.

> A consultant brings experience with what works and what doesn't work from other organizations so that you don't have to have the expertise in-house.

Increases productivity and can speed up results.

> A consultant can focus on specific tasks and get them done quickly because of prior experience; he or she can provide knowledge and shortcuts that can help you achieve results faster.

(continued)

EXHIBIT 4.4

Pros and Cons of Hiring a Fundraising Consultant (Continued)

Increased expense.

Hiring a consultant usually costs more than having in-house staff or volunteers do the same work; however, you have to consider whether anyone in-house can do the work, and how well they can do it.

Some firms apply a "cookie cutter" approach.

Some consulting firms use a standard methodology with all clients, and their approach may not fit your organization's needs.

Requires a learning curve.

A consultant has to quickly learn your organization's strengths and weaknesses, and how to appeal to your donors. He or she may not know your community, your mission, or your board. Familiarity with the organization and its culture is important to fashioning a fundraising strategy that works.

How to Hire a Consultant

Decide in advance who will be involved in hiring the consulting firm. The best combination is a team that might include several board members who are experienced in fundraising, the CEO or executive director, and the CAO or development director. If you are engaged in the process you will want to know more about how to find and hire the right consultant for your organization.

Your team will need to decide first what the organization needs from a consultant. Do you want someone who will conduct a campaign feasibility study? Do you need a full-service consultant who will stay with your organization throughout an entire multiyear campaign? Do you want someone in your area who can work with your staff side by side, or someone who flies in for one day a month? The better you can define your needs in advance, the more success you will have in identifying a consultant who will meet your needs.

Finding good outside counsel can be a challenge. Make sure that you present your fundraising needs and your organization completely and honestly to potential consulting partners, for you will get the best results from someone who understands your organization, warts and all. You want someone who will communicate with you directly and honestly, but who is sensitive to your needs.

Consultants can be paid by several means: by the hour, by the project, or put on a monthly or annual retainer. Do not pay a consultant a percentage of the dollars raised, as this is considered unethical. Ask consulting candidates how they expect to be paid, as the payment methods can affect their relationship with your organization and with your donors.

RULES OF THE ROAD

The AFP (Association of Fundraising Professionals) considers it unethical to pay consultants or fundraising staff members a straight percentage of a gift made to the nonprofit. AFP publishes a *Code of Ethical Principles and Standards* which all members are required to sign and adhere to. The standards relevant to compensation and contracts appear below (original numbering has been changed):

Compensation and Contracts

1. Members shall not accept compensation or enter into a contract that is based on a percentage of contributions; nor shall members accept finder's fees or contingent fees. Business members must refrain from receiving compensation from third parties derived from products or services for a client without disclosing that third-party compensation to the client (for example, volume rebates from vendors to business members).

2. Members may accept performance-based compensation, such as bonuses, provided such bonuses are in accord with prevailing practices within the members' own organizations and are not based on a percentage of contributions.

3. Members shall neither offer nor accept payments or special considerations for the purpose of influencing the selection of products or services.

4. Members shall not pay finder's fees, commissions or percentage compensation based on contributions, and shall take care to discourage their organizations from making such payments.

(continued)

RULES OF THE ROAD (CONTINUED)

❺ Any member receiving funds on behalf of a donor or client must meet the legal requirements for the disbursement of those funds. Any interest or income earned on the funds should be fully disclosed.

From AFP Code of Ethical Principles and Standards, amended 2007, at http://www.afpnet.org/files/ContentDocuments/CodeofEthics.pdf.
A pdf of a longer version of the AFP Code, including guidelines and examples of ethical practice, is available to download at: http://www.afpnet.org/files/Content-Documents/CodeOfEthicsLong.pdf.

Percentage-based compensation is viewed as unethical because it deprives the organization of the full benefit of the charitable gift, which should be used to further the mission and purposes of the nonprofit, not used to reward fundraisers. In addition, charitable gifts can take many years to come to fruition and may not be directly linked to the actions of any single fundraiser at the time the gift is made, just as activities the fundraiser undertakes at this time may results in gifts made years down the road.

Whatever payment terms your team negotiates with the consulting firm selected, make sure the terms are clear, in writing, and understood by all concerned.

TIPS AND TECHNIQUES

How to Hire a Fundraising Consultant

- Develop a team to lead the process. The team should include board members, executive staff, and advancement staff.
- Ask your peers on other boards for names of firms they have used.
- Interview two or three firms to compare costs, services, and experience.
- Make sure you know who will be assigned to your account and meet with him or her in person before agreeing to take on a large firm.
- Choose a firm experienced in nonprofits similar in size and type to yours.

- Ask for a written contract that spells out the services to be provided, the costs, and the terms for payment.

- Ask for regular reports on progress and activities undertaken by the consultant so that you can measure the value of the consultant's work as the project moves forward.

OVERCOMING COMMON BARRIERS TO SUCCESS

WE CAN'T AFFORD TO HIRE A BIG DEVELOPMENT STAFF

Many organizations are experiencing increasingly tight budget constraints where large staff and program expenditures are simply not affordable. One way to deal with this limitation is to hire one individual, or a very small core group of staff, to manage the process, and then have them hire consultants, part-timers, contract help, or other external specialists on an as-needed basis. (See the nearby *Tips and Techniques* for development areas that lend themselves to this kind of contract work.) By avoiding hiring full-time staff, your organization will keep overhead and expensive staff benefits to a minimum.

A warning: There are good reasons to invest in advancement staff. In general, the more contact an individual has with your prospects, the more you want him or her to be a member of your staff, rather than a consultant. This is due to the importance and value of the long-term relationships developed between the development professionals and your most important donors. You want that relationship to be strongest with those who will be with you the longest—whether that is professional staff, board members, or volunteers.

ETHICAL WAYS TO REWARD STAFF FOR GOOD RESULTS

Percentage-based pay in fundraising is considered unethical and may not be supportive of the long-term goals of the nonprofit. Your advancement staff is not comparable to the sales staff in a business enterprise; your team, after all, is part of a *not-for-profit* enterprise.

There have been cases where gifts have been manipulated to match the reward structure of fundraisers. The practice of paying a percentage of the gift to the solicitor (whether it is a consultant or an in-house staff member) can encourage the solicitor to pressure the donor to close the gift, from which he or she will derive immediate financial benefit, instead of working in the best interests of donors and nonprofits over the long term.

In order to build a strong team environment, you will want to find other ways to motivate and reward strong staff performance. Here are some ideas for motivating and rewarding successful fundraisers. The first two are based on examples of ethical practice found in the AFP Code of Ethical Principles and Standards (long form, p. 31):

- Establish a bonus using criteria including financial indicators, such as budget savings, cost effectiveness, meeting or exceeding dollar goals, and increasing the average gift.

- Set a bonus including non-financial criteria, including increases in the number of volunteers, the number of renewals, and the number of prospects seen or cultivated.

- Consider nonmonetary benefits and rewards, such as expanded vacation time, special parking privileges (this is a big one at universities), access to a private office, or hire an assistant to help make your top performer even more efficient.

TIPS AND TECHNIQUES

Consider Hiring Part-Time or Contract Help in These Areas

- Selecting and installing a new development information system.
- Prospect researchers.
- Event planners.
- Direct mail experts.
- Phone solicitation managers.
- E-mail, electronic, and social network development experts.
- Publications work (annual reports, brochures, and case statements).
- Web site development.
- Planned giving program management and materials.

Summary

It takes a team to raise money. Advancement staff may cost a lot, but they also have a lot of expertise to offer. Investing in strong staff members who create relationships with your best donors and stay for years is a long-term investment in your organization.

Learn how to hire a strong chief advancement officer and know what kind of staff support he or she will need. The roles and responsibilities of board versus staff will vary depending on the size of your staff, the complexity of the organization, and the goals that have to be reached.

Invest in a good fundraising consultant if your organization needs more expertise. Take the time to find one who matches your needs and understands your culture. Building the advancement team takes time and money, but in the end, having a high-performing team on the staff side will provide better support for your own work on the board. Their job is to make you look good. Remember that it takes money to raise money, and build the best team you can afford.

CHAPTER 5

The Annual Fund
Raising Money for Operations

The use of money is all the advantage there is in having it.

—Benjamin Franklin

After reading this chapter, you will be able to:

- Raise more money for operations.
- Create a leadership society for annual gifts of $1,000+.
- Ask for an annual gift of $1,000+.

Raising Money for Operations

Funds raised for operations are often called annual funds, because the programs that are used to raise them emphasize giving every year. Most nonprofits develop ongoing programs to ask donors to make regular small gifts, month by month or year after year, in support of operations. These gifts are also called unrestricted funds, because they can be spent where the need is greatest—their use is not restricted by the donor.

The annual fund goal is built into the nonprofit's annual budget as a revenue item. Most organizations raise these funds in the year that they are spent, meaning that not reaching the annual fund goal could incur the possibility of an operating deficit. Holding several months of reserve cash is a good way to offset this potential liability. So is raising the money for next year's annual fund during this year's fundraising activity period (working a year ahead), but we have yet to encounter a nonprofit executive who can afford this relative luxury.

Some annual fund programs are well established and extremely structured, with cadres of volunteers, prospect call assignments, phonathons, giving clubs, and donor benefits. Other organizations rely heavily on direct mail to support their ongoing operations. Some organizations rely on a top tier of $1,000+ leadership annual fund donors to provide the bulk of their funds raised for operations. Expanding this top-tier fundraising effort provides a potential growth area for many annual fund programs.

Newer electronic methods of outreach, from texting gifts in on the phone to social networking and e-mail messaging, are usually focused on raising funds for operations. Special events and galas can also contribute to operational fundraising. We will explore these options in this chapter and discuss how you as a board member can contribute to improving your annual fund results.

Annual Fund: Setting the Goal

There are three basic ways to set the annual fund goal. Your organization may use one exclusively or mix all three. Here is a brief description of each method; then see the sample annual fund goal outlined in Exhibit 5.1.

1. *The incremental increase method.*

Take last year's goal and either hold it at the same level or add a small incremental increase. Moving up the goal by 3 to 5 percent is probably aggressive in these days of flat lined giving. Look at the trend line for the past five years to help determine if setting next year's goal higher than last year's total raised is a realistic option. If the goal is moved up substantially (more than 8 or 10 percent), then either new programs or new staff should be added to meet the challenge.

EXHIBIT 5.1

Sample Annual Fund Goal

Here is the annual fund budget for an organization that has set its goal 4% over the actual amount raised the previous year. They expect direct mail and gala results to decrease, while at the same time they are implementing a leadership annual fund program to raise more $1,000+ gifts.

Annual Fund Program	Last Year Actual Raised	Goal for Next Year
Direct mail	$ 50,000	$ 45,000
Phonathon	$ 25,000	$ 25,000
Online giving	$ 13,000	$ 20,000
Leadership gifts ($1,000+)	$ 4,000	$ 10,000
Annual gala	$ 28,000	$ 25,000
Totals	**$120,000**	**$125,000** (increase of 4%)

2. *The gap method.*

Take the total of all the sources of revenue in the operating budget and subtract that from the total of all the expenditures. The difference is called the *gap*, or the amount needed to balance the budget on an annual basis. This gap becomes the annual fund goal. As a method of financial planning, this method drives the need but has no relationship to how much can be raised. In other words, the board and staff will still have to figure out how to meet the gap through targeted fundraising.

3. *The programmatic method.*

Consider the sum total of all the programs that will be utilized to raise money for annual operations. Set a budgeted goal for each program. Identify areas of the program mix where a dollar increase (or decrease) is expected based on estimates of program activity.

YOUR ROLE AS A BOARD MEMBER

As a fiduciary, you should be aware of what the annual fund goal is and how it is set. If you serve on the development committee, you should be given the opportunity to approve all fundraising goals. If you serve on the finance committee, you should be aware of all the components that make up the revenue side of the operating budget, including the annual fund goal.

Don't approve annual fund goals that are set unrealistically high (high in the current environment means more than 5 percent above the previous year's annual fund total), since this can throw off the entire operating budget and risk incurring deficits for the organization. Ask for regular reports on annual fund results, monitor progress, and make sure that stopgap measures are put in place if fundraising results look weak (like freezing expenditures).

The Importance of Board Giving

As a board member, you should make a gift to the annual fund. Every board member should give to the annual fund every year. Don't make excuses or take excuses. Give as much as you are able. Many organizations ask board members to give at the leadership level of the annual fund; find out what this level is and try to reach it.

RULES OF THE ROAD

One hundred percent board participation in the annual fund should be the goal for every board.

Board members who don't have substantial financial means can make a pledge and stretch their payments over months, make electronic payments, or just write a check for $25. The goal of 100 percent participation should be repeated often by the board leadership, made a part of the board orientation, and explained to all new members at the time they are recruited to the board.

It is more difficult to move a board into full giving mode if they have not ever been asked for funds or told that giving is part of their responsibility as board members. While the lack of a history and tradition of board giving may produce some holdouts, make an effort anyway. Explain why the board needs to give. Make a good case for 100 percent participation. Get the board leadership to make their gifts first. And don't forget to tell new board members what the giving expectations are while they are being recruited to join the board.

Annual Fund: The Moving Parts

There are only so many ways to ask for money. Many annual fund professionals use them all. Measuring and tracking the effectiveness of each method is important to help focus future budget and staffing decisions. Here is a brief synopsis of the basic ways that annual funds raise money to meet their goals.

Direct Mail

Many organizations find that direct mail is an effective way to raise small gifts from people over a diverse geographic area. There are consultants who are very knowledgeable about all aspects of direct mail, and if your organization is trying out this technique for the first time, you may want to call in an expert.

Direct mail is most effective if the mailing list is targeted in some way to people who are likely donors. This may include current donors to your organization, last year's donors (LYBUNTS—an acronym for last year but not this year), or previous years' donors (SYBUNTS—an acronym for some year but not this year). Direct mail can also be used to bring in new donors, although purchasing lists of potential donors can be an expensive proposition.

The cost of getting a new donor through direct mail may actually be more than the dollars raised. While this high cost may seem prohibitive (why would anyone spend more than they make to bring in a new donor?), adding a new donor to the giving base can provide future cash flow if the donor makes repeated gifts, year after year. Repeated gifts from the same donor allow the organization to amortize the original cost of acquiring the donor over a longer period of time.

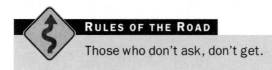

RULES OF THE ROAD

Those who don't ask, don't get.

You will probably be familiar with different kinds of direct mail from your own experience. It varies widely in terms of quality and personalization, which are factors of cost. Annual fund solicitations by direct mail usually are comprised of a letter, a brochure, a pledge card, and a return envelope. Volumes have been written on the exact combination of factors that generates the best returns. (Stamp the return envelope? Personalize the letter? Use a celebrity to sign the letter? There are advocates of every possible technique, along with some you probably haven't even thought about.) Your organization's best bet, in addition to hiring an expert, is to test different packages and see which combinations pull the highest returns.

Direct mail is often combined with other methods of fundraising, such as phone calls, e-mails, invitations to events, and peer-to-peer solicitation. In fact, all of these factors influence the donor, and it is often difficult to determine just how effective each segment of the fundraising program actually is in delivering the gift. It may be that the incremental effect of receiving a variety of solicitations is more productive than weighing the benefits of one type of contact. Testing and measuring returns continue to be popular, however, and have become a mainstay of the business.

As a fundraising technique, direct mail results have been declining in recent years for many nonprofits. There are many possible causes for this trend. It may be due to the rise of new kinds of electronic fundraising, since most young people rarely use "snail mail" anymore, and online giving is growing fast. It may be that donors are wary about giving by mail, are tired of being solicited by mail, or just receive too much mail and throw most of it out. If your organization is experiencing a decline in direct mail results, it's time to consider other forms of asking.

Phone Solicitation

Twenty-five years ago phone banks were at the cutting edge of fundraising. Like direct mail, these calls were often managed and scripted by trained professionals with expertise in marketing to a targeted sector. But like direct mail, solicitation by phone is becoming less productive, at least for cold calls by paid callers.

Things have changed. No-call lists, caller ID, and ubiquitous answering machines have resulted in lower returns for phone call banks. Many people now use cell phones instead of landlines and thus their numbers are harder to match to their names. Answering the phone at dinner now, you are more likely to hear from a personal debt consolidator than from a nonprofit.

There are some exceptions. Schools and universities still find that students and parents can connect over the phone with annual fund prospects. Leadership-level annual fund solicitors (those making $1,000+ asks) are effective using peer-to-peer phone calls, since the prospect either doesn't recognize the phone number of the solicitor or knows that it is an acquaintance. Religious and cultural organizations may also find that phone call banks are productive ways to reach past donors who need a reminder to make their annual gift, and trained solicitors can help to raise the gift level over the phone.

YOUR ROLE AS A BOARD MEMBER

Volunteers at the board level are often recruited to make annual giving asks by phone on behalf of an organization. Your staff may conduct a training session to help you make calls, or you can practice with a role-playing exercise. The structure for a sample call is listed in Exhibit 5.2.

EXHIBIT 5.2

Sample Outline for an Annual Fund Phone Call

1. Introduce yourself: Identify who you are and why you are calling.
2. Connect with the donor: Explain briefly how you got their name and how you know them (if you do).

(continued)

EXHIBIT 5.2

Sample Outline for an Annual Fund Phone Call (Continued)

3. Make the case: Provide information about why the organization needs their money and what it will do with the money (specific examples are good).

4. Support the case: Provide some recent highlights showing the organization's effectiveness.

5. Make the ask: Ask for a specific dollar amount, starting one or two steps above their last gift level.

6. Listen to the donor: Let them respond and ask questions.

7. Respond to their concerns: Try to answer their questions, or offer to get answers and get back to them.

8. Close the gift: Circle back around to the ask. Try to reach an agreement about what specific amount they are willing to give.

9. Agree on method of delivery: Be explicit about how they will send in the money, whether you need to mail them a pledge card, take a credit card number, or refer them to the giving page online.

10. Thank the donor: Thank them for being supporters and re-emphasize how important their gift is to the organization.

11. Keep a record: Write down what they agreed to and any questions or issues that arose. It is surprising how easy it is to forget the details of each call after making several calls to different donors, so keep your records straight!

IN THE REAL WORLD

Clever Ways to Expand Annual Giving

The fundraisers for a symphony orchestra tried out a "choose your own benefits" program to improve their annual fund results. A mailing was sent to all past and current donors, as well as ticket holders, explaining the new plan. The donor could select his or her own benefits from a menu of items that was linked to giving levels. For instance, a $125 donor could select a CD, a reception with a visiting artist, or an upgrade in seating at the next concert. The $500 donor could select from a free companion ticket to a concert, a higher-value CD set, or a special benefit concert.

While the organization had always offered various benefits tied to giving levels, the new twist here was to let donors select which benefit they wanted. The program not only brought in new donors, but it encouraged current donors to increase their giving levels in order to select the benefit they preferred.

Giving Electronically: Online, Through E-Mail, or Texting a Gift by Phone

This is the most promising area of growth for annual fund gifts, especially among younger donors and for smaller gifts. If your organization is seeking a larger number of gifts at a small dollar level, this is a great way to go. Online giving programs are increasingly effective as comfort levels grow with giving electronically among donors of all ages.

Improving social networking can also bring new names and new followers to nonprofits. Social networking can be very productive at turning out more attendance at events, raising the profile of the organization, and providing positive PR. There is less evidence, however, that social networking actually results in more giving.

Start with Online Giving

Make sure that your organization has made online giving easy and straightforward. Look at your competitors' sites to compare ease of giving; using PayPal may be less attractive to donors than being able to enter a credit card, for instance. The site's giving or contributions button should be on the home page and easy to access. Don't make donors have to click into your site too many times to make a gift, or they may click away from your site.

Both e-mail contact and solicitation by e-mail is quickly rising in importance, especially since it is easier to manage and much less expensive than direct mail or phone solicitation. The key here is to use e-mail as a communication tool, not just a solicitation tool.

National and regional political campaigns can provide a good example for e-mail communication and solicitation patterns. They have learned to use e-mail to keep users informed, to stay up-to-date with issues, and to become involved in campaign activities through regular communication, and not to ask for money in every e-mail.

TIPS AND TECHNIQUES

E-Mail Solicitation

One model used by political campaigns that has proven effective is to e-mail the recipient four times with a nonmonetary communication for every ask made online. The communications come every week or so, with only one solicitation per month.

The four nonsolicitation communiqués are not just messages to "read this." Each e-mail is built around asking the recipient to take an action. This promotes interaction online and increases the recipient's involvement with the cause. For instance, the recipient is asked to watch a video, e-mail information to a friend, click on a site, enter a contest, buy a T-shirt, or take part in an online survey. Then after three or four communiqués, there is an e-mail requesting a gift—usually a small one of $5 to $20. Small gifts add up!

Phone texting gifts of $5, $10, and $20 has also become a popular way to raise a large number of small gifts and to respond to charitable needs. The Red Cross, for one example, uses this method after a disaster because it is quick, easy, and requires little staff time.

 IN THE REAL WORLD

Online giving is increasing substantially, according to two fundraising software companies that have analyzed their clients' online giving data.

Blackbaud reports that online gifts *increased more than 34 percent* in one year to $495 million total for the 1,812 nonprofits they track.

Convio, which tracks 1,400 nonprofits that use their online system, reported an *increase of 40 percent* to $1.3 billion total giving online in 2010.

From Nicole Wallace,"Online Giving a Bright Spot in 2010," *The Chronicle of Philanthropy*, March 15, 2011.

In order to employ e-mail as an effective means of communication, your organization must begin capturing donors' e-mail addresses. You can capture the e-mail addresses of visitors to your web site, users of your services, or current donors through requests for updates and surveys. Some groups put together contests and raffles just to collect e-mail addresses.

YOUR ROLE AS A BOARD MEMBER

Some nonprofits have been hesitant to experiment with using electronic tools in fundraising for a number of reasons. Perhaps they don't have the expertise on staff, or they don't think they can appeal to younger audiences, or they don't feel they have the time to experiment with new ways of communicating and giving. There are also doubts about whether online giving fits the needs of older donors or wealthier donors.

Most of these fears are misplaced. See the reports from Blackbaud and Convio in the nearby In the Real World for the statistics on the incredible growth in online giving. You can help by providing support, advice, encouragement, and examples of effective electronic communication. The best places to start are for the organization to make it easy for a donor to give online, and to create an integrated communication/solicitation plan with donors using e-mail.

TIPS AND TECHNIQUES

Ways to Engage in Online Fundraising and Social Networking

- Help the organization determine how to collect more e-mail addresses.
- Provide technical support through equipment, servers, or software.
- Forward samples of good electronic communications that you receive from other nonprofits to your staff as examples.
- Help your organization develop a plan for social networking.
- Offer to write blogs, Twitter feeds, or send event info to followers.
- Review your organization's web site and online giving process and provide useful critiques.
- Don't assume that "our donors don't do online giving." All donors of all ages are moving to online giving, and you don't want your organization left behind.

Making the Case for the Annual Fund

It's not easy to raise money for general operations. Many donors prefer to restrict their gifts to specific programs, capital campaigns, or something they can actually get their arms around.

The best way to make your case is to talk about the positive benefits that a gift will produce. The closer you can tie a specific gift to the actual benefits it will produce in the organization, the better. See Exhibit 5.3 for an example of making the case by linking dollars given to benefits provided for an animal welfare group.

RULES OF THE ROAD

In making the case, give specific examples of how the money will be used by your organization. Find ways to measure the outcomes of your organization's work and communicate those outcomes to the donor.

You may also wish to focus on the recent accomplishments of the organization when making the case. The implication, stated or otherwise, is that with

EXHIBIT 5.3

Making the Case

Here is an example from an animal welfare group that makes the case for annual fund gifts by linking gift levels with an outcome for each level of support:

$15 can provide micro-chipping for a shelter animal.

$25 allows a feral cat to be spayed or neutered.

$50 enables a dog to receive an annual examination.

$100 spays or neuters a shelter pet.

$250 can supply five elevated beds for our adoptable animals.

$500 offers heartworm treatment for a shelter dog.

$2,500 can provide spay/neuter services for 50 animals.

$5,000 can enable us to provide daily care for 10 animals until adoption.

$10,000 can provide medical care for one month to our animals.

additional resources, the nonprofit can continue to achieve these same kinds of accomplishments.

In our increasingly competitive world, measurement of outcomes has become a key concept that donors look for. Find ways to prove that your organization is already achieving excellent outcomes with the money it has. Then make the argument that with this outstanding record of accountability, the donor's gift will be put to good use.

Giving Levels, Giving Clubs, and Benefits

Annual fund drives can benefit from establishing tiered giving levels and societies that are associated with various dollar amounts. In these programs, giving at a certain level often confers specified nonmonetary benefits on the donors who support them.

Giving levels and giving societies provide a social benefit, since donors know exactly where their gift stands in the hierarchy of giving for that organization. Giving societies also provide a means of donor recognition, since many organizations publish the names of annual donors by giving level or invite donors to events based on their giving level. See Exhibit 5.4 for IRS rules on giving benefits to donors.

EXHIBIT 5.4

IRS Rules for Charitable Donations

The IRS requires a statement on all gift receipts to the effect that "no goods or services have been provided in consideration of this gift." If benefits are incurred that have a monetary value, then the full market value (not the cost to the organization) of these benefits must be declared to the donor, who is then advised to deduct that value from the tax-deductible portion of his or her declared charitable contribution.

Many nonprofits now give the donor the option of accepting or denying the benefits offered with the gift, a decision that will help the donor to determine the extent to which the full gift is deductible by law.

Giving levels are often listed in order by dollar level of the gift, and the donor is provided with a check-off box on the pledge card or return envelope that lists each giving tier. Dollar amounts for each giving level can be linked to a specific use of the funds to help strengthen the case for giving (as in the example in Exhibit 5.3).

Benefits can range from getting your name on a published list to coffee mugs to invitations to special events. Nonprofits should be cautious and not overdo benefit offers for gift items, such as mugs, CDs, posters, clothing, accessories, desk items, and such. First of all, these items cost money and expand overhead fundraising costs. Secondly, many donors hate to receive these items, because they know that their gifts are paying for them. And finally, if the item has real market value, that value has to be declared to the donor and can affect the tax deductibility of the entire gift.

That said, there are some benefits that do seem to work well with most donors. See the nearby *Tips and Techniques* for ideas that many nonprofits use for smaller donors.

TIPS AND TECHNIQUES

Sample Benefits for Annual Fund Gifts

- **Name recognition**: Annual fund donors can be listed by giving level on walls, plaques, online on the organization's web site, and in newsletters and annual reports. This recognition is attractive to many donors and is a tried-and-true method of encouraging donors to consider making a larger gift. (You should provide your donors with the option of remaining anonymous if they so desire.)

- **Small gifts**: Small gifts below the $5 level are still okayed by the IRS without affecting the donor's tax deduction. Use fun stuff like refrigerator magnets, pens, small Frisbees, or other giveaways that carry the logo of your organization. Swag is fun to get and many donors will use or display the items with your logo.

- **Special invitations to events**: Exclusivity is attractive to many donors. Consider holding a reception or thank-you event for all donors above a certain dollar level. Annual donor events with a cutoff for giving (e.g.,

$500 or $1,000) are a good way to keep people giving at leadership levels and provide a reason for asking donors to increase their giving.

● **Special access or special rates**: Museums, symphonies, parks, zoos, and other nonprofits that offer public access or events can use special access to help drive their membership levels, which often are used to support ongoing operations and are similar to annual fund gifts. "Behind-the-scenes" tours have become attractive for memberships above a certain level, for instance.

Making a Splash behind the Scenes

The Audubon Aquarium of the Americas in New Orleans is a first-class family attraction. But in an incident that took place almost a decade ago, things got a little more exciting than officials had planned. According to a CBS News report on the incident:

Ten people found themselves swimming with the sharks after a catwalk over an aquarium tank collapsed unexpectedly and dumped them into the water.

Aquarium staff quickly helped the visitors out of the water after the incident. . . . The ruckus apparently scared the sharks, which are about 8 feet to 10 feet long, away from the frightened swimmers. The sharks are well fed and are accustomed to people being in their 400,000 gallon tank, because divers are frequently in there.

Officials at the Aquarium of the Americas were investigating what caused the accident at the Gulf of Mexico exhibit, which includes about 24 nurse sharks and sand tiger sharks. The aquarium web site warns visitors: "You'll be glad you're on the outside looking in."

The catwalk is normally reserved for staff but was opened for a behind-the-scenes tour for aquarium members. When it buckled, the group was thrown into the 20-foot-deep, 400,000-gallon tank.

Source: http://www.cbsnews.com/stories/2002/08/08/national/main517954. shtml (emphasis added)

Galas and Fundraising Events

Fundraising galas can be fun, glamorous, and highly productive in terms of raising money for the nonprofit. They can also be horrible, expensive, and total disasters. Some organizations make very little money on fundraising events and galas, but there are a few groups that raise over $1 million from one event.

In addition to the issue of whether or not your organization will make a net profit, most galas take a tremendous amount of time and effort on the part of staff, volunteers, and board members to mount successfully. This is time and energy that could be spent on more productive fundraising efforts. If you decide to add a major fundraising event to your nonprofit's calendar, beware of the wide variation of results and enter into this territory with your eyes wide open!

Most charity events are used to support annual operating budget needs, which is why they are grouped here under the annual fund. Some events that raise money for a special cause, such as a person who is ill or the victims of a disaster, are probably better viewed as restricted fundraising projects.

In many organizations there is a little tug of war that develops with donors between directing gifts to the annual fund and selling tickets and tables to the gala. This comes under the heading of "creating your own competition." If there are too many competing fundraising options, they tend to undercut each other, and the entire program suffers.

Try to keep your fundraising programs discrete and distinct from one another. Don't keep asking the same donors for money five different ways. Donors complain about being asked for money from too many different directions for the same cause, and it can hurt their loyalty to your organization over the long term.

Leadership Annual Fund Programs

One proven way to grow your annual fund dollars is to create a leadership annual fund program. These programs often start at the $1,000 or $1,500 giving levels and move up through several levels including $2,500, $5,000, and $10,000. Larger organizations with established, more sophisticated fundraising

TIPS AND TECHNIQUES

Don't Settle for Dull Bake Sales

Refresh your events by finding new ways to attract new audiences. Here are some ideas for improving your event planning:

- Use social networking to attract a younger crowd to give your event more zing.
- Change venues to someplace less formal or hold the event outside under a tent.
- Add a patron party before the event or a dessert party after.
- Tie the add-on parties (patron party, dessert party) to new levels in the ticket pricing structure to maximize revenue.
- Update the evening's program to kick your event up a notch; use a celebrity, show a video, or feature people who have benefited from using your services.
- Add live bands and dancing.
- Add fun drink options or find a liquor sponsor who will provide drinks.
- Use raffles and auctions to provide additional revenue.
- Give out awards to community leaders; try adding an award for a young person who is volunteering for your cause.
- Be creative, mix it up, and make things fun!

YOUR ROLE AS A BOARD MEMBER

First, ban those endless charity dinners where the MC drones on and on about each of 22 honorees. Make your events fun to attend for all. From a fiduciary viewpoint, make sure that overhead and benefits don't eat up all the funds raised. See that your organization is following IRS guidelines for receipts, tax deductibility, and providing the cost of benefits to donors.

From a marketing point of view, you can bring new ideas to your organization for how to attract new event attendees, sponsors, table purchasers, and donors. Bring in interesting samples of invitations and benefit parties that you receive. Find new ways to tie in celebrities or honor community leaders at your events. Encourage the organization to review its event giving levels and benefits structure—they might be in need of an overhaul. Help your organization to integrate new and innovative ways to use social networking, e-mail, and phone texting into their event strategies. (See Exhibit 5.5.)

programs should include $25,000, $50,000, and even $100,000 giving levels in the annual fund.

These $1,000+ annual giving societies are often given "elite" names such as the Associates, the Founders, the Pillars, or the Headmaster's Circle. Some organizations break out special names for each giving level above

---

EXHIBIT 5.5

How You Can Support Annual Fundraising Events

- Offer to review invitation and mailing lists and add names.

- Help find a new and exciting venue.

- Provide new ideas for music, decorations, themes, food, and programs.

- Assist with PR and publicity related to the event.

- Help the organization learn to use social networking tools to attract younger audiences to their events.

- Sign letters and make calls to help sell higher-level patrons party tickets or tables.

- Buy tickets yourself.

- Sell tickets or tables to friends, neighbors, and colleagues.

- Find or donate auction items.

- Help create a new award that will attract a new constituency to your event.

- Pull in a celebrity if you have the contact.

- Provide catering, printing, or other special services to offset costs.

- Solicit corporate sponsorships for events or activities.

$1,000, while others group together all donors under one name for the whole society.

What makes a leadership annual fund program work?

The attraction to most donors is a powerful coupling of philanthropic appeal with the achievement of a desirable social stature. Of course, providing enhanced support for the cause motivates most high-level gifts, but there is more to it than just philanthropy. Talk to leadership annual fund donors at a university, a museum, or a school, and you will find they are very aware of the benefits they receive for their level of giving.

The benefits for leadership society members should include exclusivity and the opportunity to rub shoulders with those who give at the same level. Perhaps there is a special event or reception where the donors want to be included. Who asks who for the gift becomes an important component. Seeing their name listed at the leadership level of giving in the annual report is attractive to many donors.

Adding and promoting a leadership annual fund program can give your annual fund a huge boost. Consider Exhibit 5.6, which illustrates the results of a museum's annual fundraising efforts before and after adding a high-level donor society. Note that some lower levels of giving actually experienced a decline (gifts are down at the $500 level, for instance), while the higher gift levels increased strongly. This reflects the organization's effort to ask its $500 donors to increase their giving to one of the new leadership levels.

RULES OF THE ROAD

Raise more money for operations by starting a leadership society for annual giving donors at the $1,000+ level. Focus on higher-level annual gifts and moving donors up the ladder of giving.

In a more mature organization, with a board that is used to making gifts, the board may agree that every board member should be required to make a leadership level annual gift. This requirement is usually stated at the point of board

EXHIBIT 5.6

Annual Fund Results Before and After Adding a Leadership Giving Society

Before Adding a Leadership Giving Society:
Annual fund results when the highest annual fund giving level = $1,000

Gift Levels	Total Number of Donors	Total $$$
$1 to $99	403	$ 20,150
$100 to $249	329	$ 41,125
$250 to $499	232	$ 69,600
$500 to $999	45	$ 27,000
$1,000	12	$ 12,000
Totals	**1,021 donors**	**$169,875**

After Adding a Leadership Giving Society:
Annual fund results after three years of promoting new leadership giving society; highest annual fund giving level = $20,000

Gift Levels	Total Number of Donors	Total $$$
$1 to $99	450	$ 22,500
$100 to $249	367	$ 45,875
$250 to $499	225	$ 67,500
$500 to $999	32	$ 19,200
$1,000	25	$ 25,000
$2,500	8	$ 20,000
$10,000	10	$100,000
$20,000	2	$ 40,000
Totals	**1,119 donors**	**$340,075**

Note that after three years of work on the leadership giving society, the non-profit has only improved its total number of donors by 9%, but it has doubled the dollars raised!

This example shows that your annual giving program can grow through pursuing a small number of gifts at substantially higher dollar levels rather than by simply bringing in more donors.

YOUR ROLE AS A BOARD MEMBER

The **Tips and Techniques** box nearby contains a step-by-step guide to help you get your organization started with a leadership giving program that will bring in these important higher-level annual gifts.

As a board member, you can encourage your organization to take this step toward larger annual fund gifts. Team up with the advancement staff, the executive director, and the development committee to build the program and implement it with your donors. If you have the means, you can make a gift at this level. And if you have the commitment, you can call on your fellow board members and other prospects to ask for gifts at this level.

TIPS AND TECHNIQUES

Step-by-Step Guide: Starting a Leadership Annual Fund Giving Society

❶ Establish the structure for the giving society.

  a. Select a name and logo for the society.

  b. Set achievable goals for Year I for both members and dollars raised.

  c. Set giving levels—begin with $1,000, $2,500, $5,000, and $10,000; later you can add $20,000, $50,000, and more if appropriate.

❷ Establish the counting rules (these are meant to serve as examples; each organization can count their gifts as they determine what is best for their needs).

  a. Count only gifts received in the same fiscal year.

  b. Count matching gifts toward the individual's total.

  c. Count cumulative gifts made within the same fiscal year.

  d. The purpose of the gifts should be for annual operating support.

  e. Decide whether to include gala tickets and other special funds in the total. (You are advised against this in order to avoid donor confusion and to keep giving programs discrete.)

❸ **Decide what types of benefits will be offered** (these can vary by giving level).

   a. Provide a gift with membership identification (e.g., lapel pins, baseball caps).

   b. List donors' names on an annual donor wall by giving level.

   c. Invite donors to a special annual event for all members of the new society.

   d. Offer discounts on tickets, memberships, special tours, or gift shop items.

   e. Initiate a thank-you call from a board member.

   f. Recognize board leadership donors by name at board meetings.

❹ **Identify prospects** (help to create a list).

   a. Begin with current board and past board members.

   b. Current donors of $250, $500, and $1,000 should be asked to move up.

   c. All past annual donors of $500+ should be asked to give again.

   d. Review names of all $500+ donors to tribute funds, restricted funds, and galas; select those who have the capacity to make an additional gift.

   e. New prospects—identify new names for outreach into the community.

❺ **Set an annual calendar** (the dates here are just examples).

   a. September 1—First mailing, includes a personal letter, brochure, and pledge card as well as an invitation to the kickoff event.

   b. September 15—Kickoff event to introduce the new society.

   c. October, November—Personal follow-up calls and visits from volunteers and board members.

   d. Late November—Second mailing, emphasizes year-end opportunities for giving.

   e. January, February—Follow-up calls from board and volunteers continue.

   f. Spring—Step up mailings to current $250 and $500 donors.

   g. End of the fiscal year—Thank-you event for all donors and volunteers.

❻ **Recruit and train board members to make calls on prospects.**

   a. Develop the volunteer committee—write a job description.

   b. Recruit and train committee members.

c. Ask volunteers to do these four things:

Identify the names of five prospects.

Agree to make calls to ask for money.

Make their own gift at the $1,000+ level.

Help to plan and attend the events.

➐ Prepare materials (assign a staff member or volunteer to create these).

a. Materials needed: Stationery, brochure, pledge card, reply envelope.

b. Develop a new logo for the giving society. (Optional, but gives it an identity.)

c. Prepare an introductory letter or email to send to prospective donors before the volunteer's call is made.

d. Secure the signature of a leader well known in the organization for the letters (use the board chair, volunteer chair, CEO, or a celebrity).

e. Determine how to integrate $1,000+ prospects into direct mail (or delete them from direct mail so that their contact is all personal).

➑ Next steps.

a. Assess and report on progress at the board level.

b. Ask all board members to attend events to show support.

c. Ask all board members to make a gift at the new leadership level.

d. Invite board members who make the gift to join the program as volunteers.

recruitment so that it shouldn't be a surprise. (Note: It may be best to move in this direction gradually if your board has no requirement for giving at this time.)

How to Ask for a Leadership Annual Fund Gift

Personal asks play a key role in the solicitation of leadership annual fund gifts. These gifts are not likely to come in without some kind of personal contact, either over the phone or in a face-to-face meeting. Exhibit 5.7 provides a script on how to ask for gifts of $1,000+ over the phone. Calls for $5,000, $10,000, and higher are more effective if made in person, face to face. You can learn the skills needed for face-to-face personal calls in Chapter 7.

Your organization can assign prospect names to you or you can bring names of prospects to your staff. Prospect assignments should probably be limited to three to five names for personal calls, but if you are willing to do more, then by all means, take more names.

Some board volunteers like to call on people they already know, figuring that they can be more effective with someone who recognizes their name. Other volunteers like to call people they don't know because they find it less awkward to ask strangers for money. You should try both kinds of calls to see which feels better for you.

Don't forget that you are asking for money on behalf of a cause you care about. The gift is not for you, nor is it for your family's benefit, but it is all about your community's benefit. If someone says no, don't take it personally, since you are not asking for a personal gift. Getting a "yes" means that you have conveyed well how important this gift is for advancing your organization's mission.

The best way to start is to make your own gift! You will be much more effective as a $1,000+ fundraiser if you can say that you are asking the prospect to do what you have already done.

 TIPS AND TECHNIQUES

Preparing for the $1,000+ Phone Call

Study the basic information about the prospect before making the phone call.

These are the data points about the prospective donor that your advancement staff should be able to provide you:

- Full name, nickname, spouse's name.
- Best phone number and time of day to reach him or her.
- Annual giving history for the past three years.
- Any additional giving to this organization, like a campaign pledge or buying patron tickets to the annual gala.

> • Prospect's relationship to the organization, for example, current board member, past board member, volunteer, user of the organization's services, graduate, or grateful patient.

Make the call from a quiet place. Taking assignments home might be preferable to calling from a noisy phonathon room, depending on your tolerance for group efforts. Ban all barking dogs, crying children, and hungry spouses. You have work to do!

Think about what you are going to say and make notes on your script before you get on the phone. (See Exhibit 5.7 for a sample annual fund phone call script.) It can be hard to think, talk, and listen all at once. Practice with a spouse or friend first, and don't get discouraged if the prospect turns you down. Your skills will improve quickly with experience!

EXHIBIT 5.7

Sample Annual Fund Phone Call Script

This script is for a $1,000 ask for the new leadership annual giving society for an independent school, City Prep. This phone call follows an initial letter that went out over the board president's signature about the new giving society.

1. *Introduction: Explain who you are, what your relationship is with the organization, and how you know this person.*

   "Hi, I'm Susie Smith; I'm on the board at City Prep School. I know that your son is a student there, and I'm a City Prep parent too; our son, Ben, is in eighth grade. Didn't we meet at the soccer game last month?"

2. *Explain why you are calling, reference the letter mailed, and thank the donor for past gifts.*

   "I am calling to talk to you about giving to City Prep. First, let me thank you for your past gifts to the school. We appreciate everything you have done to support our programs.

   "I want to talk to you about our new leadership giving group, the City Prep Scholars Society. We recently sent you a letter from Bobby

   (continued)

EXHIBIT 5.7

Sample Annual Fund Phone Call Script (Continued)

Jones, our board president, about it—did you see it?'' (If they didn't get it, offer to send a copy, but keep on going.)

3. *Introduce the new giving society and review the benefits provided.*

"The City Prep Scholars Society is our new giving program to honor our most important annual donors, those who give $1,000 or more. All donors to this important group will be recognized by listing their names in our annual newsletter and on our web site. We will also hold a special event for all the members next spring at our board president's home.''

4. *Make the case: talk about why the donor should give.*

"It's important that we have additional funds to meet our operational needs this year. As you know, you pay for your child's tuition, but the amount of tuition per student doesn't cover everything we provide. In fact, there is an annual gap of about $150,000 that must be raised to support our outstanding programs and activities.''

5. *Making the case continued: tie the gift to examples of ways the money will be used.*

"Your gift of $1,000 will provide benefits like these:

- "Coaching and equipment for our soccer team to play one home game.
- "Care and maintenance of our lovely grounds for two weeks.
- "New computer equipment for the middle school computer lab.''

6. *Make the case, continued: "do what we are doing.''*

"My husband and I have decided to give $1,000. We hope that you will consider doing the same. It's really important to us to have a school like City Prep available to our family.''

7. *Make the ask and then keep quiet until the donor responds.*

"Do you think that you and Buddy could join us as members of the new Scholars Society with a $1000 gift?''

8. *Listen and respond to any objections.*

"Oh, I'm so sorry that Junior got a D in Environmental Science. I'm sure you can talk to his adviser about that. Ben didn't like that course either.''

9. ***Bring the conversation back to the gift under discussion***.

   "But we do want to make sure that Junior still has access to all the good programs at City Prep, and it takes leadership donors to make that happen. What do you think about joining the Scholars Society?"

10. ***Reach agreement and close the gift***.

    "I hope we can count on you for a gift to the Scholars Society. Can I put you down as a founding member?" (Pause and let them respond.)

11. ***Confirm the amount and how they will make the gift***.

    - "Thank you for your pledge of $1000. This is a great way to support our school."

    - "Did you get the pledge card and envelope with the mailing? Just mail your check to City Prep in that envelope."

    - "I'll send you a pledge card with a return envelope in the mail tomorrow."

    - "Did you know you can make a gift on the City Prep web site? Go to the home page at cityprep.com and click on giving."

    - "I can take your credit card number over the phone if you want to take care of things right now."

12. ***Thank them for their gift, no matter what the response is***.

    "We really appreciate your support. I hope you will consider giving at the $1,000+ level next year, but every gift matters."

13. ***Record the response***.

    Keep good records of who will give and how much. It is easy to get confused after making several calls, so write notes down as you go.

The individual you call on may have questions, comments, or complaints about the organization. Your role is to listen, try to respond, and then bring the conversation back to the matter at hand: Will they consider making a gift to the new leadership society? Take all questions and comments seriously and offer to find answers.

It is important to practice calls before making them. Hearing someone else make calls can be helpful; so can role-playing with other board members in a training session. If you have a business or retail background, think about how you would make a sale to this customer. Draw on the experience you have from your professional life (or other volunteer positions) to help make this call work.

TALES FROM THE BOARDROOM

The members of a small nonprofit board had just committed to starting a new $1,000+ annual giving leadership donor society. A long-time board member in her late 60s was hesitant to ask her friends for a $1,000 gift, even though she had made a gift at that level herself. She came from the old school, where talking about money was considered a little crass.

She persevered, though. First she attended a training session run by a consultant and learned the basics of how to ask. Then she worked on a script she was comfortable with. She wrote down all the reasons she herself had made a $1000 gift and used the list to help her make the case to others.

The development director helped her to choose five prospects—they were all people she knew, and she thought they all had the capacity to make a gift at the $1,000 level. She made her calls by phone from her home, where she was more comfortable.

When the group reconvened to share notes, she had raised five new gifts at the $1,000 level! How did she do it?

It turned out that she had promised her friends that she would take them out to dinner if they made a $1000 gift. She ended up spending a little more than she had counted on with all those dinners, but she got to see her friends, she brought in $5,000 for the organization, and she had a successful experience doing it!

OVERCOMING COMMON BARRIERS TO SUCCESS
IT'S NOT MY JOB

The cause you believe in will not grow or meet its goals without your commitment to ask others. Think about money as a tool to make things happen. Don't focus solely on the money—focus on the cause and what it takes to make the services your organization provides better and stronger.

It is easy to assume that someone else will do the fundraising. People have a natural tendency to avoid doing hard things unless there is some incentive and reward. It is hard to fundraise. If the culture of your nonprofit does not encourage board fundraising, it probably isn't going to happen.

Many organizations do have professional, trained staff members to do fundraising. Staff members have an important role to play: They should be able to provide plans for fundraising, drive the activity, and see to the implementation of key programmatic elements. But staff alone can't make the largest gifts happen: They can't provide the entrée to key prospects, they can't talk peer-to-peer about resources, and they don't have the fiduciary responsibility for seeing that the organization meets its goals.

Some organizations turn all the fundraising responsibility over to the board development committee or to a campaign committee. While such committees do have an important role to play in the overall fundraising picture, they cannot operate effectively in a vacuum without board oversight, board input, board giving, and board members reaching out into the community to open doors. It is easy to burn out good board members if only a few people do all the fundraising.

The leadership has to come from the top. The executive director/CEO, the board chair, the executive committee, and the development committee chair must all agree that fundraising is a key component of every board member's responsibilities to develop a fully effective fundraising program.

You know that wealthy donors are inundated with solicitations. They may find it difficult to assess the value of the work of organizations they don't know much about. You can give them information from a trusted source— your own experience. Your commitment and your personal gift to the nonprofit you lead are the best examples you could provide.

I Can't Ask Someone to Make a Gift that Big

The best person to make an ask is a volunteer or board member who has already given to the organization. Giving is the key, not how much has been given. If you have "stretched" to make a gift that is at the top of your capability, you will have the confidence to ask the prospect to make that "stretch" in his or her own personal giving.

Passion and commitment to the cause are highly contagious. The energy, enthusiasm, and sincerity with which you make your presentation will help to sway those who have much more capacity to give than you do.

TIPS AND TECHNIQUES

If you are worried about asking for $1,000 or more because you can't give at that level, use one of these techniques:

- Team up with a staff member or a friend who has given at that level and make the call together.
- Ask the development office to prepare a list of all the $1,000+ donors, and show it to the prospect to talk about his or her group of "peer" donors.
- Have a board chair or committee chair follow up on your call with a note, e-mail, or phone call encouraging the prospect to give and mentioning his or her support.
- Leverage a big gift by asking the donor to use it as a challenge to bring in additional gifts from others who are at a lower level of giving.
- Focus on the case, including the reasons that you yourself support this cause, the benefits to the donor, and all the good reasons why he or she should give $1,000 or more.

As a well-prepared and passionate board member, you can play an important role in asking for the largest gifts, as long as you have made the best gift you can afford to make in support of the cause yourself.

Summary

Fundraising for operations is the most important kind of money most institutions have to raise, but it can also be the hardest to raise. Your involvement and willingness to help raise annual fund gifts could make a big difference in the programs that your organization can afford to offer.

Annual funds use a wide variety of fundraising techniques, including direct mail, online giving, phone calls, and giving societies. The best way to improve the amount of annual fund dollars raised is to focus on higher-level gifts. You can be influential in starting and participating in a leadership annual fund giving program. Such programs need volunteers like you and your fellow board members to identify prospects, make calls, ask for gifts, and to help provide high-level recognition benefits, such as invitations to exclusive events.

Most people don't give more unless they are asked to do so. Don't expect donors to make a $1,000 gift unless they are asked for a $1,000 gift. These programs really work, so get your plan ready and go! Your organization will be stronger and more flexible with more funds available for annual operations.

CHAPTER 6

Major Gifts and Mega-Gifts

My theme for philanthropy is the same approach I used with technology: to find a need and fill it.

—An Wang

After reading this chapter, you will be able to:

- Identify major gift prospects.
- Cultivate prospects for a major gift.
- Prepare your organization to look for mega-gifts.

An Introduction to Major Gifts

Larger gifts made for a specific purpose, or major gifts, are at the heart of the fundraising effort in most nonprofits. Major gifts are defined here as gifts of $25,000 and more (gifts can be pledged over three to five years) from individuals or family foundations. Some organizations set the major gift level lower, at $5,000 or $10,000, and some set it higher, at $50,000 or $100,000. The level your organization chooses will depend on the number of high-level donors at these levels and how well developed your major gifts program is.

This chapter and the following one are all about individual giving. Individuals gave 73 percent of the $290 billion in total charitable gifts made to nonprofits last year (source: Giving USA 2011). Individuals thus represent your best prospects for major gifts. Large gifts from national foundations and corporations require a more specialized giving process and will be discussed in more detail in Chapter 10.

Major gifts are important for several reasons. First of all, they bring in more money to the organization than annual gifts do. Donors are usually unwilling to make major gifts that are totally unrestricted to pay for general operating expenses because donors of larger amounts of money tend to want to see exactly where their money is going. In fact, most major gifts are restricted by the donor to provide specific support for identified needs such as program, capital, and endowment.

Another reason for the importance of major gifts is that they tend to be given in clusters. Oddly enough, once a few major gifts are being made to an organization, they tend to attract other major gift donors, especially if the donors and gifts made are handled well by the nonprofit receiving them.

The Ripple Effect

This tendency for donors to follow other donors with large gifts could be called the "ripple effect." The ripple effect predicts that a prominent organization that has already attracted a number of large donors will continue to attract new large donations. There is a momentum that develops around major gift fundraising. You could also call this "giving to success," since people continue to give to successful institutions even though there may be greater needs at other institutions providing similar services. In fundraising, rich institutions tend to get richer.

Why does this happen? Perhaps the majority of donors are hesitant to break new ground and tend to follow a path set by earlier donors. Perhaps the prestige and recognition of giving to a more visible organization trumps the needs of another less visible nonprofit that is still doing good work. There seem to be "hot trends" that develop in giving circles that favor certain nonprofits over others. It's also possible that some institutions just do a better job at fundraising and keeping their donors happy.

When satisfied, major gift donors often give again to the same organization, thus providing the potential for ongoing financial support. Because of this potential for long-term gift giving, a donor who has already made a major gift is someone who must be treated very carefully by the organization, a process referred to as "stewardship." Stewarding a major gift donor can often involve personal meetings, recognition, ongoing communication, and other methods of keeping the donor engaged in the work of the organization.

The Process Behind Major Gifts

Successful major gift solicitors view giving as a process. The process has four distinct stages: prospect identification, cultivation, solicitation, and stewardship. (See Exhibit 6.1 for an illustration of the linear giving process.) Each of these stages will be covered in more detail in this chapter and those following.

A personal relationship must develop between one or more individuals representing your organization and the donor before a major gift can be secured. It is very rare for a major gift to come immediately from a cold call on a wealthy donor (although this has been known to happen, it's probably more a factor of luck than skill).

Most major gifts take months or years to ripen. Closing a major gift in 12 to 18 months from the first meeting with a prospective donor is considered an average time period. Many anecdotal reports from professional fundraisers attest to the fact that as economic times have become more difficult, the amount of

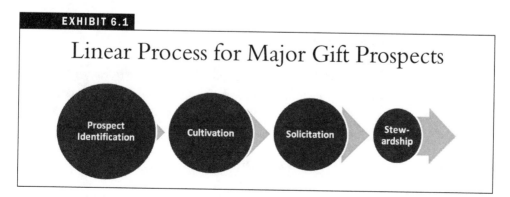

EXHIBIT 6.1

Linear Process for Major Gift Prospects

Prospect Identification → Cultivation → Solicitation → Stewardship time needed to close a major gift has lengthened. It can take several years to close a large or complex gift.

Time is needed to bring the donor closer to the people, mission, and goals of the organization before asking for money. The cultivation process must show respect for the needs and desires of the donor, as well as the needs of the organization. The donor must become engaged in the work of the organization before being asked to make a major financial investment in its needs. After the ask is made, there may be an additional period of discussion or negotiation about the size of the gift, the purpose, and what assets the donor will use to make the gift.

Most major gift programs start with a larger number of prospects and move them from left to right through each stage in Exhibit 6.1. Naturally, some prospects decide not to continue building a relationship with the organization and fall out at some point during the process. This fallout results in the organization dealing with a smaller number of prospects at each point in the process. The ratio of major gift prospects to gifts actually made is often estimated at 3:1 or 4:1.

Some fundraisers prefer to talk about a giving circle. In this model, rather than constructing a linear process from identification through stewardship like the one in Exhibit 6.1, the donor comes back around after the stewardship phase to make another gift to the organization.

There are some other tweaks to the giving model. It is possible to integrate a lifetime giving model into the major gifts continuum by thinking about bringing a prospect from small annual gifts (as a younger donor) through major gifts (middle age) to a planned gift (e.g., a gift through the donor's estate), thus involving the donor in a lifetime of giving to the nonprofit.

 IN THE REAL WORLD

"Museum of Modern Art Leads Nonprofits in Billionaire Board Members: Twelve billionaires sit on the board of New York's Museum of Modern Art, the most for any nonprofit institution in a recent survey by *Forbes* magazine."

As reported in the *Chronicle Board Report*, January/February 2011, p. 8.

YOUR ROLE AS A BOARD MEMBER

Board members are integral to the major gift process. A board member may actually be the most important component of the decision on the donor's part to make a major gift. Relationships do count. Knowing about and respecting your commitment to your nonprofit can be highly influential in the donor's decision about where to give and how much to give.

So where do you come in? You can play an important role at every stage of the process. In the very beginning, you can help by identifying people whom you know or you can open the door to those who have the capacity to make a major gift. At the prospecting stage, you can review lists, identify names, open doors, make phone calls, send letters, and talk to colleagues. Not everyone with money is a prospect—you can help to identify those who have a real interest in the mission and goals of the organization.

Your role continues with the cultivation process, which brings the prospect closer to the work of the organization through engagement with its people and programs. Board members can host events, provide tours, accompany donors on site visits, and take the prospect out to lunch with the executive director/CEO. If it is done well, cultivation helps not only to bring in a major gift, but also to increase the size of the gift, because the donor becomes more committed to seeing the organization succeed through his or her involvement.

You can also be influential in the solicitation process. Asking for money is something almost anyone can learn to do well if they want to do it. You can still be a member of a solicitation team even if you have some reluctance to ask. Making the case, talking about your own giving, and showing your enthusiasm for the organization are all appropriate roles for board members on a solicitation call.

And finally, stewardship is not just a staff function, but also an area where your involvement can be very helpful. Having a board member thank a donor for his or her gift often is highly appreciated. You can write letters, make thank-you calls, attend dedication events, and find other ways to honor donors. The result of good stewardship is that the giving cycle works—satisfied donors are more likely to give again.

Who Are Our Prospects?

Working with major gift donors begins with prospect identification. Prospects are the core of any fundraising effort. In the broadest possible terms, a prospect is anyone who might make a gift to your organization, which could include millions of people. In order to focus the board and staff efforts *on the most likely prospects to make a major gift,* however, it is useful to do a little research and set priorities.

IN THE REAL WORLD

Wealthy People Could Give More Away

A recent survey shows that the wealthiest Americans give away less than 10 percent of their income, and that their rate of giving is dropping. The 2010 Bank of America Merrill Lynch Study of High Net Worth Philanthropy from the Center on Philanthropy at Indiana University reported on the giving patterns of 800 families reporting an average household wealth of $10.7 million (excluding primary residences). These high-net-worth families reported giving away 9 percent of their annual income to charitable causes in 2009, down from 11 percent in 2007.

Source: AFP e-wire, November 23, 2010.

YOUR ROLE AS A BOARD MEMBER

If you were starting a business, you would want to have some market research on potential customers so that you had a better idea of who your customers were and how to reach them. The same process exists in the nonprofit world through the use of prospect research.

You may be fortunate enough to have a prospect researcher on staff who can provide everything discussed in this section. Your organization can also consider hiring a part-time researcher, a consultant, or a prospect research firm. Understanding your options starts with knowing more about the research process.

Sources for Information on Prospects

There are now many online information sources, some with a fee attached, that are available to a prospect researcher to help identify personal and wealth factors. These resources can be used to find new names or to learn more about names that are already in your organization's database. The information available goes far beyond a casual "googling" of your prospect names.

Some nonprofits, especially large ones, have full-time, trained research staff members on board who help identify prospects and develop profiles on potential donors. If your organization has one of these talented people, you are lucky! Make sure that the names of prospects you supply are sent to the researcher for additional workup.

There are also research consulting firms and electronic prospect screening firms that can help your organization to zero in on those most likely to give. It may be worthwhile for your organization to make an investment up front in prospect research to get the best possible information about potential donors, their interests, and their capability to make a major gift. This investment in research is especially appropriate before a major fundraising campaign.

There are some board members who object to the concept of researching people who might be donors to the organization. Development research is similar to (and often less intrusive than) the market research most for-profit companies do automatically on prospective clients. Done in an ethical manner, and with the information kept confidentially, research on prospects is one of the most useful tools that your organization could employ in the fundraising process.

Prospect research is a tool that allows you as a volunteer and your nonprofit to focus your limited resources on those prospects who are most likely to have the means and the interest to make a major gift. Without research, board volunteers and staff can flounder around and spend a lot of time and money pursuing inappropriate prospects. See Exhibit 6.2 for some of the resources commonly used in prospect research.

These resources require user fees or memberships, so your nonprofit will need to decide whether to invest in prospect research. If you do make this

---

EXHIBIT 6.2

Where Prospect Researchers Find Information

Most of these resources require membership or fees:

Dun & Bradstreet®—provides private company information.

Thomson Reuters Database—provides public company information.

Fidelity Data Services—provides real estate and property information.

FEC data—the Federal Election Commission lists all donors to federal elections.

NOZA™—bills itself as the "world's largest searchable database of charitable donations available for use by nonprofit organizations," identifies who gives to what organizations.

Marquis Who's Who®—provides biographical information on prominent people.

The Foundation Center—provides Foundation Directory Online, an online searchable directory of foundations, including giving interests, trustees, and assets.

LexisNexis® for Development Professionals—provides Web-based information resources from public records, news media, and company information.

---

investment, be sure that there is a staff person in the advancement office identified and trained to help the organization maximize the benefit derived from these resources.

Electronic Prospect Screening

The availability of information about people, their interests, and their assets has grown exponentially with the Internet. Several firms have developed the capability to screen large numbers of prospect names quickly to help prioritize them according to likelihood of giving and potential giving level. These groups are for-profit businesses, and they charge per name or for groups of names researched.

Most of the information these firms provide is publicly available from sources like those listed above, but these firms also collect additional proprietary information to build their own private data resources. It is probably best to have advancement staff on board who have the ability to develop and use this kind of service before you invest in it. While you might consider that using electronic prospect screening would take the place of research staff, actually the opposite is true—the information should be analyzed, checked, and prioritized by a staff member before being acted on by a board member.

The advantage of electronic prospect screening is that you can use it to identify major gift prospects who are "hidden" in your database (names of people who have made a gift to your organization but whom you don't know much about). Then the results can be used to prioritize the prospects that have been identified for attention from staff and board members.

Electronic screening only fills out part of the picture. It can tell you who owns what property, who gives to what organizations, and whether a corporate officer owns company stock. This type of research has its limitations. A prospect researcher should be able to fill in the blanks on the interests, assets, and connection to your organization for the top priority prospects identified in the screening process.

TIPS AND TECHNIQUES

Electronic Prospect Screening Firms

The companies offering services in this area have consolidated in recent years. These two companies are well-respected in the field:

Wealth Engine at http://www.wealthengine.com/

Blackbaud's Target Analytics at http://www.blackbaud.com/

Major Gift Prospects: What to Look For

Nonprofits often need to find new ways to reach new prospects. As a board member, you can help with this process by keeping your eyes open for prospective donors who might be able to help out your organization. For purposes of the discussion in this chapter, we will define major gift prospects as those with the capacity to give a minimum of $25,000, or $5,000 per year over five years.

Prospecting in development is an analytical process focused on certain identifiable qualities, which are discussed in the following section.

Giving Capacity

The ability to give should be the main factor in prospect identification. Most Americans give from 2 to 5 percent of their income away to charity. Even the wealthiest individuals are unlikely to give away more than 9 or 10 percent of their income. So if you are looking for a donor who will give away $5,000+ per year ($25,000 over five years), you need to find someone with an annual income of at least $100,000.

The individual's total assets are also important to the equation. Most donors won't mortgage their home to give your organization a gift, but they may sell some stock that has appreciated or make a donation from a retirement fund. In most cases, however, the annual income is the key factor unless you are talking to the donor about a planned gift.

Philanthropic Intent

It may sound like a truism, but the best major gift prospects are those who already make charitable gifts (even if they aren't giving to your organization). It is sad, but some people of wealth just don't think of themselves as giving their money away. It is possible to make a donor out of someone who hasn't been a philanthropist previously, and it can be very rewarding on a personal level, but it takes more time and effort to raise a major gift from a first-time giver than it does to work with a donor who is already committed to philanthropy. So start with those who are already generous, and continue to educate the rest.

Interest and Commitment to Your Cause

Some experienced board members give this factor the heaviest weight in prospect identification. Interest has to be coupled with assets, because a wonderful, loving, compassionate member of your community who just lost his job is probably not a strong major gift prospect. It takes interest and commitment to the area your organization provides services in to make a major gift, and this commitment takes time to develop. The cultivation of a major gift prospect should always show respect for the donor and build his or her interest and commitment to the cause through enhancing relationships, volunteer activity, introduction to those who use the nonprofit's services, and similar activities.

Connection to the Organization

The best result of prospect identification is the discovery of a connection between a wealthy prospect and the organization. Connection is usually identified as a common interest, a family member's tie to your organization, prior giving, or something personal that ties the prospect more closely to your cause. There are many types of connections, and this is where board members are at their most useful. Your knowledge of or acquaintance with a prospect could be the key to finding his or her connection with your organization.

IN THE REAL WORLD

Reasons for Giving

"When asked about their charitable behavior, high-net-worth households reported that their top motivations for giving were:

- Being moved by how their gift can make a difference (72%).
- Feeling financially secure (71%).
- Giving to an organization that will use their donation efficiently (71%).
- Supporting the same causes or organizations annually (66%)."

Quoted from AFP wire report on the 2010 Bank of America Merrill Lynch Study of High Net Worth Philanthropy, conducted by Bank of America and Merrill Lynch in partnership with the Center of Philanthropy at Indiana University. The study focused on 800 high-net-worth households. Respondents' household incomes were greater than $200,000; net assets were at least $1 million; and the average household wealth was $10.7M million excluding the value of their residences. Over 98 percent donated to charitable causes.

YOUR ROLE AS A BOARD MEMBER

Start by making a list of possible major gift prospects whom you already know. Personal connections come in all shapes and sizes. Think about people who might be interested in the services your organization provides and who have the financial capacity to make a major gift.

Give the names of people you think of to your contact on the advancement staff, to the executive director, or, if you have no staff, designate a board member to coordinate prospect lists and assignments. Ask that additional research be compiled on your prospects if your organization has a research staff member.

Reviewing Lists with the Board

The advancement staff should collate lists of potential prospects and review them on a regular basis with board members. This is a useful exercise at a board retreat, a campaign committee meeting, or a development committee meeting. It is preferable to review lists with the entire board, however, rather than with just one committee, in order to increase the chance that connections will be identified. A designated board member can produce and compile prospect lists if the organization has no advancement staff.

Lists should be clean, easy to read, and not too lengthy. If your organization wants to have the board review hundreds of prospects, divide them into smaller lists and review them over the course of several meetings.

These are the questions to ask during a list review process with your board:

- Do you know this person?
- Do you know the person well enough to open the door to him or her for our organization?
- Could you ask this person for a gift (after appropriate cultivation)?
- What do you think might be the giving capacity of this individual?
- Do you know about this person's interest in our cause?
- Do you know of a possible connection with this organization?

Where do the names of the prospects on these lists come from? See the ***Tips and Techniques*** nearby for some common sources of major gift prospect names.

Places to Look for Names of Major Gift Prospects

- Current donors at all levels.

    Ask your staff to run the names of all current and past donors through an electronic prospect screening program to identify those with higher-level giving capacity.

- Past and current donors of $1,000 per year or more.

    Past and current donors are the most likely to know your organization and want to support your organization. They will also take the least amount of effort to cultivate. Start with the names of donors of $1,000+ in your own database.

- Donors of major gifts to other groups that have a mission similar to yours.

    Look for donor walls, donor lists, and donor announcements from other nonprofits that do work in a similar field to see who is giving at higher levels. Not every donor will be interested in your organization, but good cultivation could engage them in the work of your nonprofit.

- Members of foundation boards that give in your region.

    You will need to find out if your mission matches their interest, but this is a good place to start, because you know the capacity exists to make a gift.

- Names featured in the business section of your local paper, or those active in real estate transactions in your region.

    See who is selling their company, making a new investment, selling or building a big house.

- Top professionals in your community.

    Doctors, lawyers, accountants, real estate developers, and others who have a steady income from their professional activities.

- Owners of successful private or family-owned businesses in your region.

    Again, you will need to find out if your mission fits their interests, but many locally owned business owners like to invest in their community.

- Corporate officers and board members of national companies that operate in your region.

    Look at corporate web sites for a summary of their giving interests. You may also want to look up the names of the community giving directors (or corporate foundation officers), since they often direct corporate giving decisions.

Don't forget the lessons of *The Millionaire Next Door,* the well-known book by Thomas Stanley and William Danko, published in 1996. It taught that many people who have wealth don't show it off. It is very difficult to identify the wealth of a baby boomer who just inherited $5 million from his World War II–generation parents or the elderly widow with all the stock certificates hidden away. That is why it pays to treat everyone well!

Cultivation

Cultivation can be thought of as a process that brings the potential donor closer to the nonprofit through education, building relationships, and engagement. Once major gift prospects have been identified, the organization must develop a plan for their cultivation. Individualized plans are best, especially for prospective donors who don't know your organization well. You can participate in or lead the cultivation plans for donors with whom you have a connection.

The goal of cultivation is to show respect for the donor and to give him or her time to understand the mission and vision of the nonprofit in a personal way. A gift solicitation is more likely to succeed if the donor is familiar with and educated about the services the organization provides. The ideal cultivation process results in the donor asking, "What can I do for you to further the goals of the organization?" instead of your asking the donor for his or her gift.

Three Stages of Cultivation

As indicated in Exhibit 6.3, cultivation steps can be thought of in three stages, moving from less personal encounters to highly individualized ones.

The cultivation process often moves the donor from participation in larger group events to smaller, more personal encounters (like a site visit or a volunteer activity) that help the donor to become more engaged with the nonprofit and its services.

Cultivation also should provide the donor with the opportunity to build relationships with people associated with the nonprofit. Having access to the

EXHIBIT 6.3

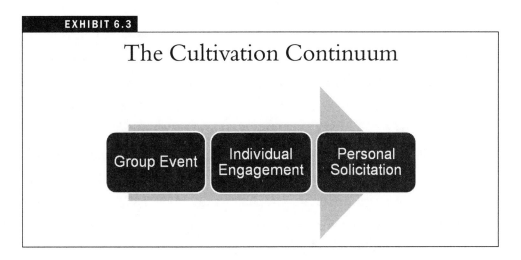

The Cultivation Continuum

Group Event → Individual Engagement → Personal Solicitation

nonprofit's leadership, including board members, helps to build a stronger relationship between the organization and the donor. Relationships can also be developed between the donor and the executive director/CEO, advancement staff members, program directors, and other professionals associated with the nonprofit and its work.

Cultivation plans should be developed to meet the interests and needs of a specific donor. Participation in volunteer activities, for instance, can provide a highly rewarding experience for a potential donor, immersing him or her in the service culture of the organization and creating a bond that supports future giving.

The cultivation process culminates in a personal solicitation meeting with a volunteer, staff, or board member (often a team) who asks the donor to give to the organization. There is often more discussion, essentially continued cultivation, that takes place after the ask is made to help close the gift.

Cultivation is often the step that is skipped when organizations move too fast to raise money to meet their needs. Major donors are more likely to make a meaningful gift if they develop a true understanding of the organization's needs, values, and services. This process takes time.

Cultivation toward a major gift is at least a 12- to 18-month process, and it can often take years to motivate a donor to make a six- or seven-figure gift. Real passion leads to real gifts, and it takes time to develop passion about an organization. Because of the time it takes to move high-level prospects all the way through the cultivation process and to close a gift, major gift work must be viewed as a long-term investment on the part of the organization.

Without adequate cultivation, the solicitation is at risk for several reasons. If the ask for a major gift is made too soon in the relationship, the donor may make a smaller gift than she is capable of making. A solicitation made too early can result in a refusal or an excuse for putting off a decision on the part of the donor. An ask made too fast can also anger the donor if she feels that she is being taken for granted, or being valued solely for her money, and not respected for her non-financial contributions.

Respect for the individual, coupled with ongoing high-level contact, is integral to the relationship between a nonprofit and its major supporters. Have respect for the donor and give her time and access to build a real relationship with the organization and its principals. Find out where her interests lie and develop her connection to your organization in a manner that meets her interests. Treat the donor as you would want to be treated: with courtesy, integrity, and individual attention.

But don't forget to ask for a gift! Asking for money too soon can depress the value of a major gift. Never getting to the ask is even worse, because you and your organization have invested considerable resources in working with each potential donor, and those resources should not be squandered.

TALES FROM THE BOARDROOM

A wealthy long-time donor was in his 80s when he was asked to make a final, lifetime gift to endow the athletics department at his old prep school.

"Why not see the good your gift will bring while you are still with us to enjoy it?" urged the board member soliciting him. "Our boys need your support now."

"Well, you know that I already have you in my will," replied the donor. "And I'm afraid that you won't pay a bit of attention to me once I make that gift, so let's keep things the way they are."

YOUR ROLE AS A BOARD MEMBER

One of the most important roles that you can play is to bring a potential donor into the cultivation process. Your personal knowledge, enthusiasm, and support for the organization can influence others. A potential donor who has taken the time to be educated and involved with your nonprofit at your invitation will make a better gift than one who is rushed into a solicitation with little preparation.

If you know or have been asked to work with a potential major donor, take the time to get him or her engaged in the work of the nonprofit. Bring them in to meet the executive leadership. Encourage them to accompany you on a site tour. Invite them to join you at an event or to participate in volunteer activities. Share your own interest and excitement about the work of the organization with others in your community who have the capacity to support the needs at high levels.

TIPS AND TECHNIQUES

Examples of cultivation steps with a major gift prospect:

- Invite the prospect as your guest to an event that showcases the organization, such as the annual fundraising gala.

- Host a small group of potential donors for dinner in your home with the executive director. Present a short program about the organization but don't ask for money; just use the time to educate the prospects.

- Invite the prospect to participate in a tour of the site and meet him or her there.

- Introduce the prospect to individuals who have benefited from the services provided by the nonprofit.

- Make a personal call on the prospective donor just to provide information about the organization—don't ask.

- Ask the donor prospect to join you as a volunteer in a program at the nonprofit.

- Ask the prospective donor to help the organization in his or her area of expertise.

Transformational Gifts: Giving at the Top

Really big gifts have become more common in the past decade. As wealth increased, the number of millionaires and billionaires went up, and the incentives to give (whether personal or financial) become more attractive to higher-level donors. With the exception of the most recent year (2010), the gifts at the top of the philanthropic pyramid are becoming larger and more donors are giving them.

The new mega-gift donors are not like the philanthropists of an earlier era. A generation of dot.com entrepreneurs, many of them younger than the major donors of earlier decades, has set a new tone of engagement and involvement in the charitable organizations they support. Increased financial accountability, sophistication in financial investments, transparency of governance, and a commitment to measurable outcomes have all come into play with the advent of donors of transformational gifts.

IN THE REAL WORLD

Big Giving Goes Down

"The year 2010 brought a lot of talk of philanthropy by the super-rich—but not much giving. Despite more than 50 billionaires announcing last year that they would ultimately devote at least half of their wealth to charity, few made big gifts in 2010.

Just 17 people on *The Chronicle*'s annual list of the 50 most generous donors also appeared on *Forbes* magazine's list of the 400 wealthiest Americans.

Over all, the donors on *The Chronicle*'s list—which actually numbered 54 this year, thanks to some ties in the rankings—committed a combined total of $3.3 billion, the smallest sum since *The Chronicle* began to track the biggest donors in 2000. The list measures the cumulative total each individual gives to charitable causes, not simply the biggest donations of the year. Just nine people on the list committed more than $100 million in 2010, compared with 16 in 2007 and 18 in 2006. The median gift was $39.6 million, down from $41.4 million in 2009, $69.3 million in 2008, and $74.4 million in 2007."

Quoted from Maria Di Mento and Caroline Preston, "After a Frugal Year, 2011 May See a Jump in Top Donors' Giving," *The Chronicle of Philanthropy*, February 6, 2011.

How Big Is Big?

The largest gifts come from individuals as well as from the huge national foundations like Gates or Annenberg. While any of us would consider $5 million or $10 million to be a big gift, the biggest ones are now well into the hundreds of millions of dollars. For purposes of discussion in this book, we will consider a megagift to be a gift of $5 million or more.

Billionaire donors, as well as some prominent organizations like national museums and universities, now view a $1 million gift as an "entry-level" gift into the big time for players in the upper echelon of philanthropy. Gifts or bequests of $20 to $50 million are now relatively common, and more are announced monthly.

One way to look at the rise of these huge gifts is that nonprofits are doing a better job of cultivating and motivating donors. The entire spectrum of philanthropy—from identification of prospects to pricing of naming recognition—has become much more professionalized and more sophisticated. Nonprofits are improving their marketing, their solicitation techniques, and giving more attention to the relationships that lead to the biggest gifts.

IN THE REAL WORLD

Getting a Gift of $10 Million+ Could Take 33 Years

"Getting donors to the point where they will make such a big contribution often takes decades," said Ronald J. Schiller.

Mr. Schiller, who gained national attention in March when he was caught in a video sting while working at NPR, referred to an analysis of donors to the University of Chicago, which was done when he led a $2.3 billion capital campaign there. *An average of 33.5 years elapsed between the time donors who gave $10 million or more made their first gift and their biggest one.*"

Quoted from Holly Hall, "How to Win Very Big Gifts," *The Chronicle of Philanthropy*, June 14, 2011 (emphasis added).

Don't panic—the time frame of 33 years for a mega-gift referred to in the *In the Real World* story is a special example of the lifetime relationship built between a university and its graduates. Naturally the first gifts from young graduates are going to be small when they are just starting out. And most donors don't reach the capacity to make a gift of this size until later in their careers. Concentrate your efforts on building the kind of relationship that will deliver a gift of this size, however long it takes.

Donor intent is a big factor in the growth of mega-gifts, too. Donors are seeing opportunities for making change, making an impact, and making the world a better place. The Gates initiative to encourage the super-wealthy to devote half of their assets to charitable causes has attracted attention worldwide, bringing mega-gifts to the forefront of charitable giving.

There are also numerous movements that have been started in philanthropic circles to build support for solving global issues through private philanthropy.

Two examples where mega-gifts have been made to solve global problems: Solving the AIDS problem in Africa has attracted large grants and a whole new way of building infrastructure to provide Third World health care solutions, led by the Bill and Melinda Gates Foundation. Fixing the problems of big-city public schools has become a national priority, with foundations like Annenberg, Broad, and the CEO of Facebook, Mark Zuckerberg, contributing resources to create new educational models.

Funds targeting cancer and other specific diseases have enrolled the support of celebrity names in order to attract bigger gifts, from Lance Armstrong to Christopher Reeves. Hurricanes, tsunamis, and earthquakes have elicited a tremendous outpouring of support, both big and little, to alleviate suffering.

Donors have seen that larger gifts make more of an impact, because more can be done with more resources.

The private sector, from foundations to corporations to wealthy individuals, has made a huge commitment to solving the problems of the world, often going above and beyond the efforts of local, state, and national governments. The basic motivations for private philanthropy—to alleviate hardship, to make the world a better place to live in, to have impact, to give back to others, and to create change—have moved nonprofit work in new and creative directions funded by the major infusion of financial resources through mega-gifts.

YOUR ROLE AS A BOARD MEMBER

How Can You Help Your Organization Find a Really Big Gift?

The place to start is to find a donor with the resources to make a very large gift. See Exhibit 6.4 for some ideas of where to look. No organization receives a gift of $10 million from a donor with $5 million in assets. Look for a donor who is ready to give from assets, not just from income. Even very wealthy people give away less than 10 percent of their income to charity on an annual basis; this means that to give away $5 million from income, the donor must earn at least $50 million. Most mega-gifts from individuals are made from assets earned over a period of years, not from annual income.

Having good prospect research available on your current donors and prospects should help you learn what kind of assets might be available for mega-gift giving. Ask your organization to use an electronic research tool to search for wealth in your current donor base. Watch the business news and keep track of sales of family-owned businesses and entrepreneurial activities among your supporters. Learn about planned giving tools and educate yourself on how to approach donors using them, since the largest gifts are often made using planned giving vehicles.

Other mega-gifts come from foundations or corporations that have a particular interest in the focus or service provided by your nonprofit. Become familiar with the foundations that give in your field of interest and keep abreast of large gifts made to other organizations that do work in the same field as yours.

Networking is a wonderful tool for finding hints about potential mega-donors. You can talk to peers, attend national conferences held about your organization's cause, and stay involved in nonprofit circles to keep up with information on large donations, giving patterns, and the interest areas of well-known donors.

You or your fellow board members may already have a connection with a potentially big donor. Ask about the names of prominent philanthropists that your fellow board members might know from other boards or businesses that they are involved with. Review personal and business links, such as national suppliers to local corporations and national investors in local business enterprises. Talk to bankers, stockbrokers, and investment advisers who work in your region.

Your goal is to learn who has made great wealth, who has invested great wealth, and who among your fellow board members knows people of great wealth whom they can open the door to for your organization.

EXHIBIT 6.4

Where to Find Potential Donors of Transformational Gifts

- Identify who among your supporters sits on corporate boards and how much stock they own in the company

- Watch for indications that someone in your region is selling their company, especially a family business

- Learn who owns or develops large pieces of real estate in your area

- Identify the names of individuals of great wealth who give to your cause, no matter how much or how little they have given to your organization in the past

- Keep track of large corporate and foundation gifts to other nonprofits that do similar work to yours

- Stay abreast of corporate buy-outs and mergers, and look into the national companies that come into your market

- Look for connections to national corporations and individuals of wealth among your vendors, including banks, insurance companies, investment firms, and other professional service providers

- Read *The Wall St. Journal* to stay on top of business news

- Study the Forbes billionaire's lists to see if your organization has any connection to people listed among the wealthiest

- Read *The Chronicle of Philanthropy* to learn about large donors and new gifts in your field. The Chronicle devotes one issue a year and many additional articles to profiling high level donors, foundations, and their charitable interests.

Planning for Super-Sized Gifts

Mega-gifts require both creativity and rigorous planning by the institution's leadership to be both attractive to the donor and at the same time to be successfully integrated into the needs and mission of the nonprofit. Some nonprofits talking to donors about large potential gifts have found that the intended purpose of the gift could take them off-mission, or would force them into doing something they don't want to do. Others have found that new donors shy away from giving to them after a mega-gift has been announced, thinking that they don't need any more money. All of the possible consequences require thoughtful analysis at the highest levels of the nonprofit, from the board to the executive director/CEO.

TIPS AND TECHNIQUES

Transformational Gifts

David Dunlop, who spent his career working for Cornell University, described how he gradually came to understand that fundraising boils down to three types of pitches: solicitations to win modest gifts (ideally every year); appeals for capital campaigns and other projects that require big donations for specific purposes; and building relationships that lead to large "transformational" gifts.

"Transformational gifts are different from the others because they are motivated by a donor's personal hopes, dreams, and individual timetable, not the institution's," Mr. Dunlop said.

Quoted from Holly Hall, "How to Win Very Big Gifts," *The Chronicle of Philanthropy*, June 14, 2011.

When considering transformational gifts, careful financial and strategic planning is required to make sure that the gift will do what the donor wants it to do. Questions to ask when considering a mega-gift:

- Does the organization have the knowledge, expertise, and human resources to deliver on what is promised?

- Does this gift fit into the organization's mission and objectives?

- What will it cost? Does this gift cover all the costs, and if not, where will the rest of the money come from?

- Will it provide leverage? Is there a way to use this gift to encourage other donors to give to this purpose?

Transformational gifts also take time. While there are a few well-publicized cases where a donor approached for the first time by a nonprofit is completely swept away by their passionate presentation and commits to a gift of millions on the spot, these occasions are not the norm.

Most donors of large gifts know the organization they are giving to, many have served on the board, and all are familiar with the good work that the nonprofit does in their field of service. Sometimes mega-gifts take decades, as the donor develops from a young annual supporter to a middle-aged major gift contributor to a mega-gift donor at the end of his lifetime. Patience is a virtue in development, where lifetime relationships produce lifetime gifts.

Talking About Really Big Gifts

Once your organization identifies a possible mega-gift donor, your work has just started. Now you need to develop a connection with the donor, build a relationship, and decide what to ask for. Consider these issues when transformational gifts are under discussion:

- What will really get the donor excited?

- What about the gift will make things different for the organization and the people who use its services?

- What impact will the gift have on the problem or issues being addressed?

- How will the gift be announced and recognized?

- What kind of involvement will the donor have in the implementation and use of his or her gift?

IN THE REAL WORLD

The Dot-com Billionaire

The engineering school of a major university proudly claimed one of the wealthiest of the Silicon Valley entrepreneurs as their alum. When he was in school, the entrepreneur had been a classic computer geek, sitting in the front row of every class and earning straight A's. He had been famous among his professors for being unwilling to speak up, not even to ask a question in front of others. When offered the honor of giving the graduation speech as valedictorian he had refused, citing his unwillingness to speak in front of a crowd. The dean kindly agreed to appoint another speaker, thus sparing the young man untold embarrassment.

Now, 12 years later, the university president flew out to California with a board member to ask the young billionaire for a large gift to the engineering school's big capital campaign.

"What would you think about giving us our first gift of $20 million?" the eager board member asked.

The young man, still in his early 30s, glanced at them and then looked away. He was wearing the classic dot-com uniform—a rumpled T-shirt, jeans, and tennis shoes. "Would I have to give a speech?" he finally asked. The president assured him the gift would be speech-free, and the deal was struck for $20 million.

Asking for huge gifts can be daunting. Just to begin with, it's probably going to be hard to find someone from your board who has made a gift of the same size, so using a peer who has made the same level of commitment to make the ask is not likely.

Sometimes board members are afraid to broach a large gift with a donor because, if they get turned down, it means a great disappointment for the institution. Not surprisingly, blame can begin to fester and fingers are pointed when large numbers are at stake. The nervous board volunteer might want to invite a "heavyweight" solicitor, such as the board chair or the executive director, to accompany him or her on such a call. As in any major solicitation, however, the strongest approach comes from the member of the team who has the best relationship with the donor.

Remember that most donors who have enough assets to give away $5 million or $10 million are very smart and know about running a business. They will ask hard questions and will expect hard answers. Be prepared to discuss the big picture, because this is a big picture gift. Talk about the organization's future, its strategic initiatives, its priorities, its finances, its governance, its programs, and its potential.

Asking for Too Much

Asking for big gifts—gifts of $5 million and up—will not always be successful, but just the act of making an ask for a gift this large can position the organization for success in closing larger gifts. Asking for gifts of $5 million, $10 million, and even $50 million indicates that the nonprofit has big ideas.

Big vision is almost always an asset in fundraising, since many successful and wealthy business people and entrepreneurs pride themselves on exhibiting this same quality. Of course, the institution needs to have the planning and capacity to back up the vision, but for some organizations, the situation becomes a self-fulfilling prophecy: Seeking $25 million becomes a way of "getting on the map" with the largest donors, those who have the capacity to give $25 million. And if asking for $25 million results in a $5 million gift, who is going to be disappointed?

"Asking for too much" from a high-capacity donor is therefore almost an oxymoron. Donors are seldom insulted at the assumption that they can make a large gift. Asking at the mega-level raises the sights for all those involved. It can even raise the gift levels of the team members who are involved in the solicitation (this includes board members and volunteers who are simply informed about the pending meeting with a high-capacity donor).

TIPS AND TECHNIQUES

Increasing the Size of the Gift

Sometimes, even when a big ask fails, the organization can still benefit. A donor who is asked for a gift of $10 million, for example, might respond that that is much too high; but after hearing the case, he is swayed into giving

$1 million instead. Later he admits that he was really planning to give only $500,000, so the institution doubled their gift size by making an ask on the high side of what was deemed possible. "Asking for too much" thus can be used as a technique to raise gifts that are larger than the institution had expected from that donor, or even higher than the donor had expected to make himself.

The Downside to Mega-Gifts: Is There One?

Yes, surprisingly enough, there can be a downside. You might think that getting lots of money for your organization is always good, but it depends. Look carefully at what the gift is for, how much else needs to be raised to meet the donor's goals, and how the establishment of the gift will affect the organization's mission, services, and goals. You will also want to delve deeply into the demands and the motivation of the donor.

In one recent case, for example, the board of a nonprofit was told that a donor would make a transformational gift if the entire board quit. That gift didn't happen, needless to say! Very large gifts often come with strings attached, like changing the name of the organization to honor the donor. This is fine as long as you and your fellow board members are privy to and agree with the terms.

There is a danger that if a huge transformational gift is realized, other (smaller) donors will feel that their funds are not necessary for the success of the institution. Hospitals and universities that have received gifts of $100 million and more have learned ways to successfully counter this problem. One option is to create and market attractive giving options at the $1 million to $5 million level, below the mega-gift, that will still attract key donors and build a strong base of support. Obviously it is not wise for the organization to depend solely on one donor, no matter how wealthy and generous he or she is!

There are other ways to continue building the major donor base, even after receiving a large gift. Identifying a portion of the large gift as a challenge gift, for instance, might help leverage new gifts or bring in bigger gifts from previous donors. And some transformational gifts are planned gifts that really won't have a big impact right away on the institution, so an effort must be made to explain the long-term nature of the gift's impact to other donors when the big gift is announced.

Other stipulations can also be troublesome. Watch out, for instance, when donors require that gifts be used to support a specific moral or political slant. Unless your donor is clearly of the same persuasion as the overall organization, this is bound to cause trouble. And donors who get too involved in hiring and making appointments can be problematic. Most universities don't let donors select endowed chair holders or scholarship recipients, for example.

Remember that you and your fellow board members are there to lead the organization. Ceding too much control of the organization's direction and leadership to one donor, no matter how much he or she gives, is a poor decision. It turns off other board members, deters additional gifts, and can even hi-jack the mission of the entire nonprofit.

OVERCOMING COMMON BARRIERS TO SUCCESS
HOW TO KNOW WHEN A PROSPECT IS READY TO BE ASKED

Timing of the major gift solicitation is one of the trickiest components of the major gift process. You don't want to rush the process, since you do want to respect the donor and give her time to engage with the organization. Board and staff members who are experienced in major gifts suggest that it can take from 12 to 18 months or longer for a donor to be ready to make a major gift.

When is a prospect ready to be asked? Here are a few hints to look for:

- The prospect has developed relationships with several people associated with your organization (this could be at the staff or board level).
- The prospect has begun to show active interest or volunteer in a specific aspect of your organization or cause.
- The prospect has made an initial gift, an annual gift, or something that could be considered an "entry level" gift, and you know they could give more.
- The prospect shows the intention of wanting to get more involved in a formal way, for example, asking about board membership or joining an advisory council.

- The prospect begins to talk to you about other prospects that he or she can open the door to for your cause.

SIMPLIFYING CULTIVATION STEPS

Creating an individualized plan for cultivating each prospect sounds like a good idea until you have hundreds of prospects to work with. Here is a simple 4-step plan that shows respect for the donor and gives him or her time to develop a relationship with the organization and its leaders. This plan can be used with almost any organization.

❶ Invite the prospective donor to an intimate, small group event, such as a dinner or reception, held at a board member's home. Use the evening to introduce the prospect to the organization and its leadership. Don't ask for a gift, but do talk about the needs of the organization.

❷ Bring the donor to your nonprofit's site for a personal tour. Meet her there or offer to pick her up and bring her there. Use the time to introduce her to the executive director and make sure she connects with clients or users of your organization's services.

❸ Set up a small luncheon with just the executive director, the prospect, and you. Ask her what interests her about the organization and draw her out on what her giving interests are. Use the luncheon to answer her questions and find out what you should be asking her for.

❹ Identify your solicitation team (it could be you, along with the executive director or advancement staff member) and set up the call. Make the ask and see what her response is. Realize that it may take multiple meetings and discussions with the donor to close the gift.

Summary

Think about major gift giving as a process. Start by identifying prospects who have the capability to make a major gift, and look for a possible interest or connection with your organization. Use prospect research to gain a better understanding of the prospect's giving potential and interests. Review lists of potential major donors with your peers on the board and offer to open the door to prospects whom you know.

The next part of the process is cultivation, and it should be individualized for each donor. Before being asked for a major gift, the potential donor must become engaged with the organization. This can be accomplished through building relationships, getting to know the work of the group, and perhaps making a site visit. Don't ask until the donor is ready, because their level of knowledge and passion about the organization will directly affect the size and nature of their gift. Respect the donor's interests and timetable in getting to know the nonprofit.

Landing transformational gifts—gifts that change the way an organization approaches its work—takes special planning and a special approach. Realize that meeting the donor's interests is paramount, and find ways to excite the donor about the potential for your organization. Even if the number and size of really big gifts is slowing down, it will only take one to make a huge impact on your cause!

CHAPTER 7

How to Ask for and Close a Gift

Always desire to learn something useful.

—Sophocles

After reading this chapter, you will be able to:

- Prepare for the call.
- Make a successful solicitation call.
- Overcome objections and close a gift.

Preparing for a Successful Call

The time needed for cultivation before making a successful solicitation is unique for each donor and requires a judgment call by the person closest to the prospect. As noted in Chapter 6, the cultivation process may take months or even years. Proceed with respect for the time needed to develop the donor's interest and engagement in the organization. Once the donor is deemed ready for a solicitation there are several steps to take to prepare for the solicitation call.

Determine the Best Team for Each Solicitation

The most important element of a successful solicitation call is who is selected to meet with the donor. Usually a team approach is preferable, as it makes the ask go a little more smoothly, and different team members can present different parts of the solicitation. The team should be from two to three people, and often includes one or two volunteers, including board members, the executive director/CEO, and perhaps a member of the advancement staff or someone else at the nonprofit who knows the donor well. Taking too many people on the call can crowd the donor and make him or her feel ganged up on.

The basic development rule is that the person who knows the donor the best goes on the call. It is also appropriate to have a volunteer or board member along who has made a gift near the level that the donor will be asked. For example, a board member who knows the donor well, but who is not himself a high-level donor, might add a team member who has given $250,000 if the donor is to be asked for a six-figure gift.

Consider the different ways that each member of the team might contribute to the ask. The executive director/CEO, for instance, might be better able to address a donor's concerns about the financial details of an upcoming project. A board member might be the best person to present the case and share her passion for the organization. The development staff member who knows the donor well can contribute by making the actual ask if the board member is uncomfortable with that role.

Assign Roles to the Team

Each participant should be assigned a role in the meeting. Hold a practice session if necessary, or prepare talking points, so that the actual call goes smoothly. It is up to the staff member supporting the call to make sure everyone understands his or her role, to provide an ask level and purpose for the gift, to prepare information about the donor's previous giving, and to provide talking points or a script if needed.

A well-prepared team is more likely to succeed than a group that fumbles and hems and haws its way through a meeting. Many wealthy donors are quite familiar with the solicitation process and expect a high level of professionalism from nonprofits that approach them. Don't disappoint them.

Set the Appointment

Ask the board member who is closest to the prospect to set the appointment. In some cases, when working with business people or busy civic leaders, the appointment can be set by contacting the donor's assistant. Say that you are coming to discuss the nonprofit, or that you are coming to talk about the donor's support for your nonprofit, but try not to explicitly say the amount you will ask for over the phone.

This isn't to hide the fact that you will ask—it's to avoid your having to make the ask over the phone, when it is much easier to deflect your ask or put you off. Getting to a face-to-face meeting is important, so try to work around any efforts to defer your call to others, to send in a letter ahead of time, or to make the ask over the phone. These are less productive contacts.

Always meet in a place that is convenient for the prospective donor. In general, it is better for you to go to him, rather than the other way around. This puts him in the leadership role, which will help him respond positively to your visit. If the prospect lives out of town, a visit by a delegation from your nonprofit to his city shows that you are making his involvement a priority for your organization.

The actual meeting space could be the donor's office, your office, a conference room, or a boardroom. Coffee shops and restaurants are popular meeting places, but they don't offer the privacy and quiet space that a good call requires. Use public spaces and meals for cultivation meetings, as opposed to solicitation meetings, where possible.

If you intend to use any electronic materials (PowerPoint, videos, and live web sites), make sure that the proper equipment is available and ready to go. Bringing your own laptop is usually better than depending on staff and equipment you are not familiar with. It can be really embarrassing to hit the go button on the big show and have nothing happen.

Decide What You Are Going to Ask For

This is the most sensitive part of the preparation for a call. A call will be effective if the ask is made by the best person for the right amount and the right project at the right time. How do you know in advance what amount and what project to ask for?

Start with the prospect's giving capability. Giving capability can be determined from the prospect research provided to you, by your own experience and knowledge of the donor's past gifts, or by your board colleagues' rating of the donor's capacity.

Then look at what you know about the donor's interests. Some donors always give to capital projects; others prefer endowment funds. Find out what services and programs your organization offers that are of interest to this donor. One of the goals of the cultivation process is to get to know your donor well enough so that you can select an appropriate giving area to meet his or her interests.

Finally, try to match the donor's giving capacity and interests with a specific area on your organization's Table of Needs. Some solicitors like to give donors an option of two or three gift ideas. We prefer settling on one option to present to the donor, but be prepared to move to other areas as a backup plan.

Just as each nonprofit has different needs, each one also has a different history and culture for giving. Plan your ask within the parameters of the organization you are representing. For some small community organizations, $25,000 may be a large gift, and that call deserves extensive planning and preparation. Another organization might give this level of attention to a $1 million ask. Making a personal solicitation call will require you to follow the same steps, whether you are asking for $25,000 or $1 million.

TALES FROM THE BOARDROOM

The eager young board member made one of her first calls on the biggest donor in town. She was part of a larger team that included the executive director and the board chair. Everyone met in the donor's boardroom, but she missed the introduction to several people in the room she didn't know.

After the presentation there was an informal discussion period. She approached one of the men in the donor's group who hadn't said much. "What did you think of our project?" she asked.

"I don't really know much about it," the man responded. "I'm just the limo driver."

The Five Elements of the Successful Ask

There are five identifiable elements in every personal solicitation call. These elements include the opening moves, making the case, making the ask, listening and negotiating, and the close, which often determines when and how the deal will be clinched. The entire call should take between 30 minutes and one hour. A shorter call time usually means that steps were skipped, while longer calls often mean the team is wearing out its welcome.

Exhibit 7.1 outlines the key parts of every solicitation call. The recommended times are meant as a guideline. Timing for each element of the call may vary, depending on who is on your team, how much the donor already knows about your organization, and the nature of the questions and discussions that take place after the ask is made.

What follows is a step-by-step guide to each element of the solicitation call. You and your fellow board members may want to try some role-playing or experimentation with each portion of the call, or you can work with a consultant or a training video to see how experienced solicitors handle various challenges that arise.

Note: Board training materials, along with several sample scripts modified for role-playing, are available in the Appendix. These materials, including a PowerPoint presentation on "The 5 Elements of the Successful Ask," can also

EXHIBIT 7.1

Five Elements of the Successful Solicitation Call

	Elements of the Call	Recommended Time
1.	Opening	5 minutes
2.	Making the Case	10 to 20 minutes
3.	Making the Ask	5 minutes
4.	Active Listening and Response	10 to 20 minutes
5.	Closing the Ask	5 minutes
	Total Call Time: 30 minutes to one hour	

be downloaded from www.wiley.com/go/boardfundraising so that you or your advancement staff can personalize them for your organization.

The Solicitation Process

Remember that each donor is unique and will have his or her own reasons for giving. Taking time to learn the techniques of how to ask is not meant to imply that all donors respond in the same way. The process outlined here is simply to help you develop a feel for the pace, the content, and the flow that most solicitation calls take. Respect each donor's needs and stay flexible so that you can adjust to the donor's personal style.

Opening: 5 Minutes

Use the opening portion of the call to make the potential donor feel comfortable with the solicitation team. One team member should take charge of the meeting and lead the conversation. This role is a good one for a board member or colleague of the donor. Introduce each team member and explain his or her role within the organization clearly. The team should strive to set a familiar tone, to put everyone at ease, and to get the group ready for the business portion of the meeting. Establish up front how long the prospective donor has set aside for the meeting and leave plenty of time to cover the key points.

Making the Case: 10 to 20 Minutes

Making the case is the heart of the call. This is the part of the meeting where you will want to display passion, show the need, and explain how the money will be used. The team member assigned to make the case must be well informed about the organization in order to make this portion of the call effective. Real passion can be very persuasive. The person who makes the case can be a board member, the executive director, or an advancement staff member, as long as their commitment is knowledgeable and real.

The person who makes the case must explain clearly what the need is, why the need is there, and what the donor can do to meet the need by making this gift.

> **RULES OF THE ROAD**
>
> "We need the money" is NOT making the case. Making the case means explaining why the money is needed, what it will be used for, and why it is important for this donor to make this gift at this time.

If supportive materials are going to be used, this is the portion of the meeting in which to display them. Materials might include a video, a PowerPoint presentation, a brochure, or renderings of a building in a capital campaign. Videos and/or PowerPoints should be brief and to the point (8 minutes is considered the maximum length during a presentation, and less is preferable). Make sure all the technology works in advance of the presentation.

Many successful solicitors like to tell a story about a recipient of the nonprofit's services to help illustrate the need for the gift. Experienced fundraisers tend to prefer to rely on their own words rather than using extensive prepared materials, such as brochures and videos. Your best bet is to use the materials that you are comfortable with and to find a way to express your personal commitment to the cause at hand.

If the potential donor has been properly cultivated, she should already be familiar with the organization, its mission, its vision, and its goals. Making the case at this point should focus on the specifics: where the need is, how her gift will meet that need, and what opportunities her investment at this time will create for the organization.

Make sure you are not just talking **at** the donor during this exposition. Ask her questions, keep her interest engaged, and listen and respond to her comments. No one likes being lectured to—make sure that you aren't talking down to her or simply delivering a canned speech. At the end of the case presentation, pause and ask the prospect if she has questions about anything that has been said.

Making the Ask: 5 Minutes

The actual solicitation should include a specific dollar amount, a purpose, and a mention of the specific recognition that could be awarded to the donor for the gift under discussion. These elements should be incorporated into one phrase or a short summary statement that encompasses the entire solicitation in a clear, focused manner. See the nearby *Tips and Techniques* for examples of solicitations that include these elements.

Above all, don't apologize for asking for money! Be bold, have confidence in what you are doing, and your confidence will help to convince the donor that this is a project well worth his support.

TIPS AND TECHNIQUES

How to Ask for a Major Gift

Always include a specific dollar amount, the purpose of the gift, and any recognition that accompanies a gift of this size. Here are some examples:

- We would like to ask you to make a gift of $2 million for the new classroom building. A gift of this size would be recognized by naming the building for your family, if you wish to do so.

- Would you consider giving $25,000 to underwrite our new program for the first year? You will be identified as the founding sponsor in our printed materials, on our web site, and at the opening reception.

- Please help us by contributing $100,000 to the endowment for an equipment purchase fund. Your name will be listed as a Founder-level donor in our annual report, and you will be thanked at the annual gala. We also will mount a permanent plaque in the lobby to recognize your family's generous support.

RULES OF THE ROAD

After the ask is made, the solicitation team should remain QUIET and wait for the donor to respond.

The self-imposed silence that should follow the actual ask can seem painfully long and awkward as the seconds tick by, but don't break it! The donor must be allowed time to think, react, and respond before the team jumps in.

Active Listening and Response: 10 to 20 Minutes

The job of the solicitation team after the ask is made is to listen carefully, respond, and deal with objections as they are rendered. It is called active listening because the team has to move conceptually with the donor, following his line of thought and reacting to his concerns.

It is unlikely that the donor will agree immediately to the amount and purpose as posed in the solicitation. It is more common to have the donor respond with questions, ask for clarification, make a counteroffer, or air grievances. The donor's responses need to be evaluated seriously and given due attention from the team.

Be prepared for a range of questions from the simple to the complex:

- Sophisticated: What percentage of my gift goes to actual programs?
- Recognition based: Where would our name be placed on the building?
- Informational: What did you say the goal was?
- Financial planning: Can I pledge it over five years?
- Personal: Can you give me some materials for my wife about this?

The fact that the donor asks questions is a good sign, because asking questions shows interest and engagement with the institution. All questions must be answered openly and honestly. If you don't know the answer, don't make it up! Offer to find out the answer and get back to the donor as soon as possible.

Closing the Gift: 5 Minutes

Closing a gift is an art, not a science. While experienced solicitors tend to fare better with closing a gift, there are techniques that can be learned by anyone.

The key to closing the gift is for the donor and the solicitation team to agree on a next step and the time frame for that next step before leaving the meeting. The next step should be developed as a response to the reactions or concerns that the donor expressed during the active listening and response period.

The close should be personalized to the needs of the prospective donor and the situation at hand.

The team member closing the meeting can identify a specific follow-up activity, such as agreeing to draw up a pledge letter. The team may have to promise additional research or a meeting to answer complex questions, such as those involving institutional investments and returns. The prospective donor must leave the meeting feeling that his or her concerns have been heard and that they will be addressed in an adequate manner.

It is useful at the end of the meeting for the closer to make a brief statement that summarizes what has been agreed to. Repeat the donor's main concerns, explain how they will be resolved, and set forward a timetable for the resolution.

See the nearby *Tips and Techniques* for some examples of closing statements. The closing agreement assures that all parties have come to a similar understanding in the meeting, even if no final decision on the gift has been reached.

TIPS AND TECHNIQUES

Examples of Closing Agreements

- Thank you for making a pledge of $25,000 over five years. We'll draw up a pledge letter and send it to you by the end of the week.

- I understand your concerns about that problem with the operating fund that was in the newspaper last week. We will look into it and get you the real facts about what happened. Can I call you to follow up next week?

- We would be happy to talk with your wife about the gift. When do you think would be a good time to meet with both of you?

- We would like to invite you to visit our facilities to see the program for yourself. Do you think you could come for a site visit next week?

- We'd like to prepare a proposal for you that outlines some of the ideas we discussed. I'll have it to you by next week. May I call you to follow up?

- We would really like to wrap the campaign up before the end of our fiscal year in June. Do you think we could meet with you again at the end of May?

Once you make an agreement to follow up with the donor, make sure that you or someone from the organization takes the promised steps. Staying in touch with the prospective donor should be assigned as a task to a team member. Touching base to ask about the progress of the gift is a role you can perform well as a peer, but don't overdo it; no one likes to be harassed about making a charitable contribution. Talk to the donor once a month or so until the gift is actually closed.

YOUR ROLE AS A BOARD MEMBER

You can play any role you are comfortable with in the solicitation process; however, you must make your own gift first. You may be particularly effective at presenting the case, for instance, if you are knowledgeable and excited about the project being presented. On the other hand, a board member who has already made her own gift can be especially good at making the ask, because she can point to her own support of the nonprofit and ask the donor to do what she has already done.

The most important thing you offer on a call is your role as an articulate, educated, committed advocate of the organization. Your willingness to make your own investment of time and money in the nonprofit provides a powerful model for the donor. Done well, a successful solicitor will make such a powerful case that the donor will be left asking, "What can I do to help?"

TALES FROM THE BOARDROOM

Two hospital board members made a solicitation call on a very wealthy old gentleman who did not have a history of major philanthropy to their organization. They asked him for $5 million to name their new building. He appeared to be interested and asked a lot of questions, but finally they left his office with no assurance that he would make the gift.

Time went by and they didn't hear anything from him. They took turns calling him once a month, using the calls to update him on the hospital and staying in touch in a friendly manner. They didn't badger him, but they did talk about the project they had asked him to fund. He never said yes, but he never said no either, so they kept in touch.

After two whole years he sent them a letter outlining a charitable lead trust he had created, which would give the hospital $5 million over 10 years. It turned out that he had been working on the gift all along as part of his estate planning.

Moral of the story: Persistence pays off. Respect the timetable and needs of the donor when asking for gifts.

Common Issues in Negotiating and Closing Gifts

The following examples comprise five of the most common issues faced when negotiating and closing gifts.

The Donor Wants to Consult with His Wife, His Children, or His Foundation Trustees Before He Can Respond

Donors often want to have time to consult with others, and this is a very common request. Taking your case to the family or to the trustees gives you the potential to develop new friends and new supporters for your mission. View it as an extension of your cultivation efforts and as a positive development.

In this case, agree to the consultation, and ask if you can make another presentation to the additional parties. Try to establish a date for the next meeting if possible, or agree on a time frame for setting it up.

It is possible that you could have dealt with this issue up front by including the spouse or the trustees in the call to begin with. Knowing your prospect is the key to the decision of who should be present during the call. Some families are very open about giving, but others are not so eager to share the decision making. Be flexible, be sensitive to family issues, and make sure that a team member follows up with the donor after the promised interval.

The Donor Is Interested in Naming the New Building, but He Can Only Give $1 Million, Rather Than the $2 Million Asked For

If this happens in your organization, don't agree too quickly to a drop in the price of one of the major naming options. You may not be playing fair with your other donors, and giving away a big naming opportunity for less could hurt the organization's ability to raise the full amount of money that is needed.

Certain donors seem to enjoy the art of negotiating and enjoy pushing for a "special deal" from the organization. If your organization is ready to drop the price, go ahead, but know that special deals never stay secret. Dropping the price of a major naming opportunity may affect the prices your organization can ask from all the remaining donors.

Of course you can accept the gift at the lower level if this gift is your best alternative. You may want to hold on the offer and see if any other donor appears to be interested for the higher price. But other appropriate responses might include the following:

- Ask the donor to pledge the money over a longer period of time (suggest 10 years instead of 5 years; this affects campaign counting and may affect your cash flow, but it's better than not getting the gift at all).

- Introduce the idea of funding the gift through a charitable lead trust (see Chapter 10).

- Ask him if he will put up $1 million, and tell him that you will continue to look for a second donor with $1 million, and that the two donors will have to share the name of the facility.

- Ask him to make the $1 million gift and convince him to take charge of the effort to raise the additional $1 million from his friends and colleagues.

- Gently refuse this offer and offer him another naming opportunity for $1 million.

The Donor Is Involved in Some Estate Planning Right Now and Isn't Ready to Make a Decision

This situation provides an opening to move the gift discussion toward planned giving options. Offer to send him some information, ask him whether you or your organization's planned giving officer can talk with his financial adviser, or offer a specific planned gift tool (a charitable lead trust, for instance) that might meet his goals for the gift currently under discussion.

Additional hints that indicate the time is right for a planned giving discussion include statements about imminent retirement, explanations about the need to take care of a spouse or child, or a pending change of financial status, such as the sale of a family company.

The use of planned gifts in major gift giving is discussed in more detail in Chapter 10. At least one member of every solicitation team should be familiar with the major vehicles in planned gifts. The point is not to negotiate every detail of the gift at this meeting, but to know enough to bring up the concept of making a planned gift, discuss the appropriate vehicle, and open the door to further discussions with the donor or his financial advisors.

The Donor Responds That the Gift Level Is Too High

Don't immediately offer to drop the gift level. Consider some or all of the following options:

- *Try to find out more about what is motivating the donor.*

  Find out what she is really interested in seeing the organization accomplish and explain why this gift level will meet her goals as well as those of the organization.

- *Ask the donor what she has in mind.*

  Listen to her ideas and consider how she can best help to move the organization forward with the gift she has in mind. Suggest that she meet with the executive director or a program director to flesh out some of her ideas.

- *Explore other payment options.*

  Maybe this donor requires a longer pledge period than you had in mind. Consider offering a 5 or 10-year payout if your organization can afford to handle the cash flow issues.

- *Explore other timing options.*

  The donor may want more time to consider the gift. The donor may be making some financial decisions that will affect her giving that she isn't prepared to talk to you about. Try to determine if giving her more time would be helpful to closing the gift. Perhaps your estimate of her readiness was a bit aggressive and more cultivation is needed.

- *Explore other giving resources.*

  Ask the donor if he or she would consider making a portion of the proposed gift with the remainder coming from family members. Suggest that it might be possible to include the family foundation, the business, the children, or other resources in the gift. Sometimes pulling together a multigenerational family gift is a great response to this problem.

- *Judgment call —decide if you should try to close the gift in this meeting.*

  It may be better to leave the ask open and return for another conversation if there is still room for negotiation, rather than closing the gift at a reduced level.

- *Then consider dropping the gift level.*

  Of course there are occasions when the best response is to suggest a gift at a lower level—this, too, is a judgment call. Bring along a list of naming options at various levels so that you are prepared to make a lower offer. Don't drop the dollar level too suddenly, however. Going from asking for $1 million to $10,000 without an intermediate step is too big a drop. Try to land somewhere in the middle.

The Donor Repeats an Old Complaint About the Organization and How He Has Been Treated in the Past

At times the donor will air a grievance he holds with the organization during the solicitation call. Some people are harder to ask for money than others.

A donor can make the nonprofit spend a lot of time jumping through hoops trying to answer a grievance or explaining some perceived injustice.

When faced with a negative comment about the organization, respond to complaints by giving the donor a sympathetic hearing and providing due process in the follow-up. Then come back to the ask by reinforcing the need to finalize the discussion about the gift.

Your job is to focus on the gift. Take the donor's concerns seriously, try to address them, respond with an answer to the best of your ability, and then ask for the gift again. A good fundraiser views a complaint as an invitation to fix something, not as a door closed in the face. You may have to agree to return once the problem is resolved. Negative engagement is still engagement, challenging though it may be!

TIPS AND TECHNIQUES

Framing the Ask

Learn to use techniques that give the donor a context for his or her gift. Select one of these options and ask the staff to help prepare the materials you will need:

- The solicitor displays a gift chart for the entire project, showing the donor the gift levels that have already been met, and explains how important it is to meet the higher levels to make the project work.

- The solicitor shares a list of the names of current donors who have made gifts directly above and below the level the donor is being asked for. Make sure the other donors agree to have their names and gift amounts shared before you do this!

- The solicitor displays a list of only the naming opportunities and recognition available at gift levels near to the dollar level the donor is being asked for, so he or she won't select something much lower on the chart.

- The solicitor mentions his or her own gift: "I've already made my own gift of $25,000 for a classroom in the new building, and I'd like to ask you to do the same."

Multiyear Pledges

It's a good strategy not to bring up multiyear pledges as part of the initial ask. The pledge period can be presented as a point of discussion during the listen and response part of the call.

Why? Let the donor decide what his own financial requirements for the gift are. If he can write a check for the entire gift, let him do so; it will only benefit your organization. Offer the pledge option as a response if the donor indicates that the gift being asked for is too large for him to handle all at once.

TIPS AND TECHNIQUES

How to Present the Pledge Period

Hold off on presenting a pledge option until after the ask is made and the donor responds.

If the donor says, "I want to support your work, but $25,000 is a little high for me right now," you respond, "Well, a gift of $25,000 could be pledged over five years, which means you would be giving $5,000 a year for five years."

Before you offer a pledge schedule, make sure that the organization can afford to take the pledge over a number of years. If the program or building being funded requires the cash in hand this year, five-year pledges aren't going to be of much help.

When to Make a Double Ask

Fundraisers refer to the "double ask" when they are asking a donor to make a small annual gift at the same time and in the same meeting that they are asking for a larger major gift. This may sound inappropriate; after all, why would you ask a donor for $1,000 and in the same meeting ask for $50,000?

Experienced solicitors will tell you that it is easier to bundle up requests for all the gifts that a donor will be asked to make to one organization in one call, rather than spreading them out over multiple calls with multiple solicitors.

Think about your organization's fundraising efforts: Multiple calls are often made for different purposes, including the annual fund, tickets to a gala, capital campaigns, the endowment, and even planned gifts. All these calls can irritate or annoy even the most loyal supporter. So from a certain point of view, you are doing the donor a favor if you make one call and ask him or her for more than one purpose.

The best technique for making the double ask is to make the various gifts, needs, and timetables very clear to the donor. This can be done in writing, if that helps the donor understand the issues. For instance, clarify if the annual gift is to be made for one year or is part of a multiyear pledge, and the same for a major gift. Recognition will probably be different for each gift. The purpose will probably be different for each gift. Spell it all out, on paper if necessary, so that everyone involved understands what is being asked.

TIPS AND TECHNIQUES

Example of a Double Ask

Mrs. Jones, we would like you to consider making a capital gift of $50,000 in support of our new building. This gift can be made over 5 years and would be recognized with the naming of a new classroom for your family.

We would also like to ask you to continue your leadership commitment to the Annual Fund, which is so important for meeting the growing demand for our services. Please consider pledging your current annual gift of $5000 per year for the next 5 years.

Your total gift would then be $75,000 for the campaign, or $15,000 per year. $10,000 would go for the classroom gift and $5,000 for the annual fund. A gift of this size would provide an incredible leadership gift for our campaign and would inspire others on our Board to make a similar commitment.

OVERCOMING COMMON BARRIERS TO SUCCESS

FEAR OF REJECTION

It is time to put aside any fear you may have of making a solicitation call. First of all, the donor usually is prepared for the call. It is rare for a prospective major donor to accept the appointment unless he or she already intends to make a gift. Often the core decision in the call is how much the donor will give, not whether she will give.

Even in those meetings that fail to secure a gift, the person being called on is most likely friendly to the organization. Most donors are gracious and understand the role of the volunteer solicitor; in fact, most donors have done this work themselves for other organizations. They will give you a warm reception at best and a polite hearing at worst.

Secondly, asking for money for a purpose and organization you care about is not crass or demeaning. You have no reason to be embarrassed or shy about sharing your enthusiasm for the organization with someone new. You have made your own gift, after all; you aren't asking this person to do anything you haven't already done.

And finally, the people you will be calling on should be capable of making a major gift, or you wouldn't be there in the first place. In some cases your call may determine which organization will receive a gift from a pool of charitable giving dollars that the donor has already set aside. Don't you want your organization to win out? Let your commitment to the organization trump any reluctance you may have to ask.

Experience helps to mitigate anxiety. Ask a more seasoned colleague on your board to show you the ropes. Go along on a call with someone who has more experience and watch how that person handles the ask and questions from the donor. Fundraising is not a rare art form; it is a series of techniques that can be learned by anyone willing to practice and try. You may actually learn to enjoy it! It can be very exhilarating to bring a new donor into the fold and watch your organization benefit.

ADD URGENCY TO YOUR CASE

Prominent donors are often besieged by many well-respected but needy organizations that offer important services in the community. Each need is hard to weigh against the next; how is the donor going to decide which area to fund?

Making your case more urgent can help your nonprofit rise to the top of the donor's giving priorities. Here are some ideas for **focusing on the immediacy of your organization's needs**:

- Measure the increased need for your nonprofit's services now as compared to past years. Show the donor how his or her gift will meet that increased need.

- Create a video presentation or a brochure that highlights the experiences of people who have used your services. Personalize the need for services through pictures and stories to evoke emotion.

- Find a way to measure what would happen if your services weren't able to be provided. Create a worst-case scenario for the donor to show the importance of his or her gift to the continuation of these services.

- Identify one or more recipients of your services who can speak eloquently about how their life has been changed because of your organization. Introduce them to prospective donors at a reception, meeting, site visit, or even bring them on the solicitation call.

There are also a number of **fundraising techniques** that can add urgency to the request for a gift. Discuss the impact of these techniques with the advancement staff before you employ them, since they may involve internal deadlines or finding additional donors.

- Challenges.

  Challenge gifts made with a deadline can help build momentum in a campaign. If your organization risks losing a large gift unless a challenge is met, this can motivate the donor to give now rather than later.

- Year-end gifts.

  Annual funds commonly cite the end of the fiscal year as a reason for urgency in giving, and the donor who cares about the fiscal solvency of your organization may respond to this rationale for giving. Many donors also respond to year-end giving prompts because making the gift will provide them with a tax deduction. Giving is usually far stronger in October, November, and December than at other times of the calendar year, so take advantage of this propensity and ask for more gifts in the fall.

- Leveraging additional gifts.

  Most donors love to know that your organization can leverage their gifts by going to other donors and using their gift as a base from which to raise new money. Emphasize the leadership nature of this donor's gift and how much you think this gift will help you raise from others.

Being the "first in" with a big gift can be a rewarding position for the lead donor as others follow his or her example.

- Honor rolls and donor lists.

Set a cutoff date for printing the donor honor roll. Call or write all donors who are still on the fence and tell them that the deadline is near. Consider preparing a "draft" honor roll **without** their name on it and e-mail it to them to urge them to take action.

- Dedications and fundraising events.

If your organization is planning a big fundraising event, a building dedication, or another public ceremony, call the donors and let them know that they need to make their gift in advance of the event in order to receive recognition. Recognition might mean having their name in the program, sitting on the stage, being introduced, or even saying a few words, depending on the situation and the size of the proposed gift.

- Campaign deadlines.

Capital campaigns always have deadlines. Perhaps the building needs another $500,000 raised before your organization can break ground. Perhaps there are only two classrooms left to name at $25,000. Good solicitors use the campaign time line as a method of creating urgency for the project at hand.

IN THE REAL WORLD

Beginner's Luck

A new board member became very involved with the capital campaign at a major medical school. For her first major solicitation call, she agreed to be part of the team to solicit a prominent donor who had supported other projects in their city but had never given to the medical school. As the appointment grew closer, she became increasingly nervous. What if the call failed? Would the donor even listen to their case?

She brought along a friend of the donor's as a team member on the call. This friend had supported the medical school with a major gift himself. She also brought lots of materials: a video on the project, floor plans, a brochure, and a list of all the naming options and prices in the new building.

The donor was very gracious and the meeting went smoothly until the ask. They had agreed to ask for $1 million to name the entrance hall of the new

(continued)

IN THE REAL WORLD (CONTINUED)

building. She went through all the materials, made the ask for $1 million, and then stayed quiet, just as she had been trained.

It seemed as if whole minutes of silence ticked away. She began to count silently and had gotten all the way to 15 when the donor stirred in his chair.

"I like the project," he said, much to her relief. "But I don't think I want to do the entrance hall. How much does it cost to name the whole building?"

And that's exactly what happened—he made the naming gift for the whole building.

Summary

Asking for a major gift can provoke anxiety. Find ways to demystify the process, and you and your fellow board members will be much more willing to take on this important role. Experience, training, role-playing, and learning specific techniques can help to mitigate any lingering fears.

Prepare your team, practice, and follow the five basic elements of the solicitation call. Be prepared to answer questions, negotiate, and come back with more information. Experiment with different ways to add urgency to your case to help to close the gift within a timetable that meets both your organization's needs and the needs of your donor. Respect the donor and the process, and you will be successful in this important enterprise.

CHAPTER 8

Getting Ready for a Fundraising Campaign

Fit no stereotypes. Don't chase the latest management fads. The situation dictates which approach best accomplishes the team's mission.

—Colin Powell

After reading this chapter, you will be able to:

- Select the right type of campaign for your organization.
- Decide whether to do a feasibility study.
- Set realistic goals.
- Use the basic tools of campaign structure: phases, timetables, and gift tables.

An Introduction to Fundraising Campaigns

Fundraising campaigns are a unique and complex endeavor that requires significant board leadership and involvement in order to succeed. They also can be a rewarding enterprise to be involved in because a good campaign will unite disparate factions of an organization behind one common goal. Let's start with the basics to learn more about this sophisticated enterprise.

While every campaign is unique in its timetable, objectives, and goals, your organization must determine what type of campaign will serve your needs best. In order to make the best choice, you should know the five basic campaign types:

- Capital campaigns
- Endowment campaigns
- Annual campaigns
- Comprehensive campaigns
- Mini-campaigns

These models can be mixed or combined, as long as the components are clearly understood by those involved in giving and asking for the money. Each type is introduced in the following section.

Types of Campaigns

The following are definitions of different types of campaigns.

Capital Campaign

A capital campaign is a set of fundraising and related outreach activities that raises funds for one-time capital expenses; usually, to build a new building or to renovate a facility. Capital campaigns may raise funds for a portion of a facility, more than one building, or for an entire complex.

A capital campaign may also include funding for expenses related to the facility, such as furnishings, equipment, program, staffing, exhibits, technology, and maintenance. Recently there has been a trend to include an endowment component in capital campaigns to cover long-term building maintenance and repairs.

Endowment Campaign

An endowment campaign is a set of fundraising and related activities used to raise funds for the organization's endowment, that is, a gift in which the principal is invested for the long term, and only the interest or income from the principal can be spent. The use of the interest or income is often determined by the donor at the time of the gift.

An endowment campaign may stand alone; it can be combined with a capital campaign; or it may be one component of a larger comprehensive campaign.

Annual Campaign

An annual campaign is a set of fundraising and related outreach activities used to raise funds for annual operating expenses; usually, the annual campaign, as its name denotes, is recurring every year.

An annual campaign may be combined with a capital campaign, especially if the nonprofit wants to count all funds raised during a specific time period toward the campaign. Sometimes campaign solicitors will make a "double ask," comprised of asking for two gifts for one campaign; for example, you might ask the donor to make a (smaller) annual gift for operations, which will either be pledged over a period of several years or repeated each year, and a (larger) one-time gift for a specific campaign purpose, which can be pledged over a period of several years.

Comprehensive Campaign

A comprehensive campaign is a set of fundraising and related outreach activities used to raise all types of funds during a defined time period. The comprehensive campaign includes goals broken out for the annual fund, endowment, program, and capital gifts.

Mini-campaigns

A mini-campaign is a set of fundraising and related outreach activities used to raise funds for a set of small focused projects. These smaller projects are marketed together like a capital campaign for one organization.

A campaign can be structured to take a sequential, or phased, approach that includes more than one model. An example would be to begin a campaign with a capital phase, and then to end the campaign with a phase for raising endowment.

YOUR ROLE AS A BOARD MEMBER

If you are involved in making a decision about which campaign is right for your organization, start with a determination of what kind of funds your organization needs, whether it is endowment, operating, or capital. Then decide whether to include the annual fund in the campaign. In some organizations, it may make more sense to keep the annual fund separate so donors don't get confused. In others, adding the annual fund into the campaign is a boost because it helps to give every donor at every gift level a place in the campaign.

You may want to select a hybrid variety, like a comprehensive campaign, that includes everything, which helps to maximize the total dollars raised. Take the time to study the campaigns of several nonprofits in your area and talk with peers who have conducted campaigns to determine which type will work best for you.

TALES FROM THE BOARDROOM

The wealthy industrialist made a gift of $5 million to his old engineering school. His old buddy from his graduating class, who was on the board, called to ask him whom he wanted to invite to the big dedication ceremony.

"Are there any of our old professors still alive?" asked the donor. "I want them to see that the boy they all gave C's to turned out pretty good."

Preparing the Campaign Plan

Make sure that your organization draws up a campaign plan, whether it is done by internal staff members or an external consultant. This plan will provide the blueprint for the board's activities during the campaign and keep everyone focused.

Capital campaigns for nonprofit organizations are among the most complex of civic group endeavors encountered in today's highly networked communities. Like winning a hard-fought election or playing a competitive team sport, the capital campaign requires careful preparation, extensive teamwork, and skilled execution in order to succeed. A good campaign plan keeps everyone on task and highlights the path toward the campaign's ultimate success.

Developing a campaign plan can meet a number of objectives:

- Build enthusiasm and support for your organization's future needs.

- Harness the energy of those who work and volunteer for your organization.

- Focus everyone's efforts in the same direction.

- Share the organization's mission and vision with new audiences.

- Enhance relationships with donors and prospects.

- Provide the organization's leadership with a blueprint for success.

Exhibit 8.1 outlines the major components of a campaign plan. With this plan in hand, you and your fellow board members will know how long the

---

EXHIBIT 8.1

Basic Components of a Capital Campaign Plan

1. Review of the external environment for a campaign
2. Assessment of internal readiness of the organization for a campaign
3. Feasibility study (or the executive summary) if one has been conducted
4. Preliminary campaign goal and table of needs
5. Campaign timetable and phases
6. The case for the campaign: major themes
7. Campaign leadership and volunteer structure
8. Prospect identification strategies
9. Prospect cultivation strategies
10. Leadership gift fundraising strategies
11. Campaign staffing and budget
12. Campaign gift table
13. List of potential campaign chairs and members of the campaign committee
14. Campaign prospect list

---

campaign will last, the level at which the goals will be set, the major components of the case, and the campaign volunteer structure. The whole plan should be shared with the entire board, with the exception of the last two items, the prospect list and the list of potential chairs and campaign committee members, which are usually held confidentially.

Campaign consultants have become an integral part of the campaign planning process and are often hired to prepare a campaign plan. In order to decide if your organization needs a consultant, you will need to take into account the level of expertise available on your staff, particularly that of your chief advancement officer.

It can be an expensive mistake for a nonprofit to learn how to run a capital campaign while it is conducting one. The cost to an organization from missed opportunities may be high. But finding the right consultant is also a challenge; see Chapter 4 for tips on finding and hiring the right consultant for your organization.

Campaign Feasibility Studies

The campaign feasibility study is a marketing technique designed to help your organization learn more about the reception your campaign might receive from various external audiences. The feasibility study tests the capacity and interest of a segment of prospects in order to estimate whether the campaign can meet its projected financial goals. Feasibility studies are usually conducted by an outside consultant to ensure objectivity and anonymity for the donors interviewed.

The best study results are usually derived from personal, face-to-face interviews with a carefully selected cohort of supporters and leaders of the organization. External consultants are hired to conduct these studies because they have the time and expertise, and provide a fresh perspective. A consultant can often elicit comments from a study participant that the participant might not make to a staff member. A study can be useful in creating the campaign plan, and often campaign consultants will provide a feasibility study as one component of the campaign planning process.

EXHIBIT 8.2

The Campaign Feasibility Study: More Than Just Setting a Goal

Feasibility studies are used for some or all of these reasons:

- To cultivate top prospects by asking for their advice and involvement.

- To determine how committed donors are to the organization.

- To test the feasibility of the campaign goal.

- To learn where your organization ranks in donors' giving priorities.

- To see how donors react to the proposed case and themes.

- To test the appeal of your campaign with new potential donors.

- To learn how donors perceive the organization and its goals.

There is more than one reason for conducting a campaign feasibility study. (See Exhibit 8.2.) While the most common reason is to determine whether the preliminary goal can be reached, conducting a feasibility study is also a good way to cultivate prospective leadership donors, because the purpose of the study is to ask for their advice and input.

It is important to understand the limitations of the techniques employed in such studies, since they rely on personal interaction between the donor and the interviewer. The answers they provide may not be completely reliable, especially when a prospective donor is asked how much he or she will give to a certain organization.

Donors have become increasingly reluctant to reveal their future giving plans in these studies. In today's uncertain economic environment, they may not even know their future giving plans. Therefore, it is prudent to view the results from a feasibility study as one data point among several other considerations in setting the goal.

In a feasibility study, the consultant usually asks the interviewees directly if a proposed goal of X dollars is attainable. This goal can be expressed as a definite number or as a range. The answers will help to "test the waters" for a specific goal number and may be useful as one indicator of the organization's ability to reach a proposed goal.

Through the feasibility study, the organization can get an estimate of how deep the support is for campaign objectives, whether the goal can be reached, and how much cultivation the prospects will need before committing to a gift. The consultant who undertakes the study may recommend the proposed goal, a number within the range of goals tested, or additional steps to take before settling on a final goal.

YOUR ROLE AS A BOARD MEMBER

Making a decision about undertaking a fundraising campaign has huge implications for the organization and your work as a member of the board. You should have access to all the available information in time to make an informed decision.

It is possible that you will be selected to be interviewed for the feasibility study. The consultant, the executive director/CEO, and the appropriate staff members usually make these choices. Often the interviewees will include the board leadership, potential campaign committee members, donors who have the capacity to make a large gift, and those board members who are highly respected in the community. If you are selected, your role is to be thoughtful and honest. Your comments will help to guide the organization and the campaign planning process.

The feasibility study results should be submitted for review and discussion by the entire board. An executive summary, or a list of feasibility study findings, can be used rather than reproducing the entire study. The consultant who conducted the study should present the findings in person, so that questions can be answered fully.

In most organizations, the board takes an up or down vote on whether or not to enter into a campaign with a certain goal or range of goals specified. This vote should follow the presentation and discussion of the feasibility study. If you have doubts, issues that need to be clarified, or suggestions, be sure to discuss them at this point. Once the campaign is underway it can be difficult to stop or change plans.

The Feasibility Study that Underestimated the Goal

An independent school about to enter a capital campaign conducted a feasibility study. The study showed that they could raise about $8 million from their various constituencies, alumni, parents, and community members. The board and headmaster decided to take a more aggressive stance and set the goal at $12 million over four years. They chose to do a comprehensive campaign, including annual fund and endowment, but focused on a new classroom building.

The campaign took longer than the board expected, but after five years they had raised $18 million, a huge success for the school. Why was the final amount raised so much higher than the recommended goal determined by the feasibility study?

In looking back at the feasibility study, two things became apparent. First, there were several large donors who had not been members of the school's family when the campaign started. These new donors either enrolled young children or transferred children from other schools during the campaign period. Thus new prospects appeared—something that happens in most campaigns.

Secondly, several of the school's traditional donor families had given modest dollar amounts when responding about their potential gifts during the feasibility study, telling the consultant they would make a gift of $100,000, when they had the capacity to do much more. While the low number was accurate at the time, later in the campaign their interest developed in greater depth. Both as a result of substantial cultivation, and with the attractiveness of the new building's naming opportunities, three of these families gave over $1 million.

Thus some donors gave substantially above the level they had previously identified in the feasibility study. This also is not unusual; donor circumstances change, and donors may ultimately give more or less than they declare during a preliminary study. This is why feasibility studies should be viewed as only one data point in setting the campaign goal. Their assumptions can change as the giving environment changes, as the campaign develops, and as the donors themselves evolve in their relationship with the organization.

Setting Realistic Goals

Ideally, the goal should be realistic within the time frame of the campaign, but also stretch the organization's fundraising capability. If the goal is too high, the organization will struggle to reach it and possibly fail, which could hurt the nonprofit, disappoint donors, and blunt future support. If the goal is too low, the organization could miss an opportunity to realize gifts that might help them for years to come.

Setting the goal for a campaign can be a complex process, depending on the organization's needs and level of sophistication. Your organization's staff and executive director/CEO should analyze your organization's needs, its past giving patterns, and its future giving potential to determine a goal that can be reached. Peer campaign fundraising levels, feasibility study results, and early commitments can also be useful benchmarks.

RULES OF THE ROAD

There are two main considerations in setting campaign goals:

1 How much the organization needs.

2 How much the organization can raise.

In the best scenario, how much your organization needs and how much it can raise will be close to each other. But how does anyone know how much their organization can raise? And what if these numbers are far apart?

The techniques described here can help your organization deal with these concerns. In most organizations these analyses would be developed by members of the advancement staff or the consultant and presented to the board. If your nonprofit lacks staff or the means to hire a consultant, you and your fellow board members can develop some estimates in these areas for yourselves.

IN THE REAL WORLD

Getting Everyone on Board

A $10 million capital campaign to renovate a new education facility was approved by a 15 to 12 vote of a nonprofit's board. The "losing" side, those who thought the project was too big and too expensive for the organization to take on, spread their negative comments across the community. Major donors were scared off by the bad-mouthing of the proposed project and the fundraising foundered.

In the final analysis, the naysayers won their point—the campaign was too expensive for the group to bite off. But the failure was due more to the lack of cohesiveness on the board and the mixed messages given out in the community than to any real fundraising problem.

Moral of the story: Getting enthusiastic buy-in from the board for a campaign is absolutely essential for fundraising success.

Your organization should try to arrive at the goal using more than one method identified below, or develop goals based on several of these methods and see where the numbers converge. The important point is to select realistic goals and to build confidence that these goals can be met.

TALES FROM THE BOARDROOM

The nonprofit had deep roots in the jazz community, and the executive director looked the part; he dressed very casually, with his shirt hanging out over shorts, and he always wore Birkenstock sandals. The night before the big call on a corporation for a program sponsorship, the board member leading the team called him up. "Do you think you could wear shoes tomorrow?" he begged.

Six Methods to Use for Goal Setting

Your campaign staff or campaign consultant can utilize all of these methods and see how the answers converge, or select several methods that fit your institutional model best.

Determine Needs

Many organizations conduct a strategic planning exercise including developing a table of needs to determine their costs before starting a campaign (see discussion in Chapter 3). Prioritize all the needs of your organization and estimate the costs for each need.

For a bricks and mortar campaign, hire an architect and get an estimate of the construction costs. In many nonprofits, this planning process is led by the board or a committee that includes board members. Be sure to consider the full costs—including enhancements in program, endowment, maintenance, depreciation expense, operations, staffing, and construction—that will be required to run a new program or facility.

Some nonprofits stop here and decide to base their campaign goal solely on what the organization needs. But this is only looking at the demand side, not the supply side—how much can your organization raise? It is unrealistic thinking to believe that if you build it, the donors will come, especially in these times of economic uncertainty.

Analyze Past Giving

Undertake an analysis of the organization's past giving patterns. Even with the enhanced activity of a campaign, these patterns will probably not change radically. To be realistic, project future giving levels during each campaign year in reasonable increments over what the organization has raised, as an average, each year for the past five years.

For instance, if your organization averages $100,000 per year total for all purposes, then you may be able to raise 50 percent more per year ($150,000), or twice as much ($200,000), but probably not five times more ($500,000) during a campaign. A campaign goal that requires you to raise more than two or three times the amount of past giving is probably going to be unrealistic, unless there are unusual circumstances, such as a large lead gift. And it would be best if you already knew who was going to give such a large gift.

Evaluate and Rate Your Campaign Prospects

Ask the staff to identify and rate the giving potential of the major campaign prospects on their list, including board members, along with current and previous major donors. For new prospects, add only those whom they realistically think can be reached during the campaign period. Rate each of them for the maximum gift they could give if they were properly cultivated and solicited.

Have the staff or campaign consultant develop a campaign gift table (see the discussion on gift tables in the last section of this chapter). Then fill in each gift level with the names of prospects that have been identified and rated for that level, and see if there are enough prospects to fill out each level.

As a board member, you can help rate top prospects for this exercise. If there are large gaps in the number of prospects identified versus the number of prospects needed, especially at the top levels of the gift table, the organization will need to either adjust the goal downward or invest in new ways to identify more top prospects for the campaign.

Conduct a Feasibility Study

Feasibility studies do provide one assessment of how potential donors will respond to the campaign goals and initiatives. Beware of placing too much faith in their recommendations, however, because respondents are not always willing to share or even ready to identify their own giving level to the campaign.

While feasibility studies are not always completely accurate at predicting campaign results, they do represent a useful data point in the goal-setting process. If your organization hires a consultant to conduct a feasibility study, the study will assist you to cultivate prospective donors and determine where your organization stands in their philanthropic priorities.

Look to Your Peers (but Not Too Much)

Determine how much your peer institutions have raised in their most recent capital campaigns and look at the goals of campaigns that have just been announced. Set your goal in a range near that of these peers. If you are too far above these peers, the broader donor community will be wary of your ability to reach the goal and your campaign will appear unrealistic. If you are too far below your peers, your organization may fall behind its peers in terms of both public perception and the actual services it is able to offer.

Beware of goals set at a higher level simply to trump the goal recently announced by a peer. Competition between institutions is rampant in the nonprofit world; consider, for instance, the current rush to billion-dollar campaigns that is being used to vault universities to a higher place in the national rankings.

Set a Stretch Goal

Many experienced fundraisers set a "stretch goal" as a way to stimulate larger gifts and energize the donor base. To define your organization's stretch goal, estimate the amount of dollars you think the organization can raise, and then add about 10 percent. This extra amount will force staff, board members, and donors to push a little beyond their comfort level in asking for and making gifts. Meeting the stretch goal will help the organization grow its total fundraising potential.

In the final analysis, the members of the board, the campaign leadership, the executive director/CEO, the chief advancement officer, and your campaign consultant should all agree on the campaign goals. It is not conducive to success to have leaders, whether they are board members or part of the executive staff, who don't support the goal. Moving forward with a united front is important to the campaign's ultimate chances for success with the broader community of donors.

If there is disagreement about the campaign goal, or if questions still remain about the feasibility of the goal, your organization can still begin the quiet phase of the campaign without setting a final goal. This can be done by using the early part of the campaign, the quiet phase, to test the goal, as described in the nearby *Tips and Techniques*.

Once the organization decides on a goal or a range of goals that seem feasible, it is time to have the goals approved. This usually requires action by the board or a committee of the board. Having the full board vote on the goal is preferred, because it allows the entire board to take full responsibility for the key decisions around the campaign. Enthusiastic buy-in at the board level is essential for campaign success. Goal setting, like strategic planning, can provide a reason to bring together various stakeholders of the nonprofit to create buy-in for the campaign.

TIPS AND TECHNIQUES

Use the Quiet Phase to Test the Goal

This technique gives the organization maximum flexibility as it explores giving with its leadership donors. It is also useful if the organization has never done a campaign before and needs to test the waters before deciding on a realistic goal.

Set a preliminary target or range for the goal to discuss with early donors. For example, set the campaign goal at a range of $4 to $5 million, estimating that at least 50 percent of the total goal must be raised from these early leadership gifts.

Then if early leadership gifts during the quiet phase are lower than expected, adjust your goal downward by selecting the goal at the lower end of the range, $4 million. If early gifts are strong, announce a goal of $5 million when the campaign goes public.

YOUR ROLE AS A BOARD MEMBER

You may participate in several aspects of the goal-setting process. The board is often very active on the demand side of the goal equation—that is, determining in what directions the organization needs to grow, what areas the campaign will fund, and how much that growth will cost.

As a board member, you should understand and approve the long-range goals of the organization that underlie the needs in a capital campaign. Board committees are often used for hiring architects and developing a set of costs for new buildings. All of these activities support the development of a preliminary goal based on needs.

You should also be aware of the supply side of the goals equation—that is, how much money might be able to be raised. As explained above, the various campaign goal analyses may be produced by staff or a consultant, but you too can play a role:

- Offer to help with rating likely donors.
- Assess the likelihood of using the campaign to bring in gifts from new donors.
- Participate in the feasibility study if you are selected.
- Offer to find out what peer institutions are doing with their campaign goals.
- Ask questions about the methods used to set campaign goals and be aware of the limitations of certain assessment methods, such as feasibility studies, in determining a final goal.

Keep in mind that the final campaign goal must be based not only on a consideration of needs, but also on an assessment of what can realistically be raised.

Campaign Structure: Phases, Timetables, and Gift Tables

Timing is an important element of campaign strategy. Most capital campaigns are multiyear efforts, and many campaigns are divided into phases. Each phase is marked by goals and the solicitation of specific constituencies. The time frame must be long enough to achieve the desired goal, but short enough so that staff, volunteers, and campaign leaders stay focused on the tasks at hand. Campaign burnout is a real phenomenon and must be avoided at all costs.

Selecting the right timetable for the campaign can help to build momentum, an elusive but critical component of all successful fundraising efforts. A campaign achieves momentum when gifts at significant levels begin to roll in, creating a growing sense that the campaign will succeed. When prospects feel that they need to give now or they will be left out, and you sense an increasing swell of support, then you have created momentum for your campaign.

This sense of building toward the inevitable, yet successful, conclusion of the campaign is partly the result of choosing the right timetable for your organization.

The Quiet Phase

The traditional campaign has two phases. The first phase can have one of several names: the nucleus fund, the leadership gift phase, or the quiet phase. It is a highly focused drive to bring in substantial early support for the campaign, usually in the form of leadership or major gifts. During the quiet phase, the campaign volunteers solicit gifts from those donors who are already close to the organization and who can be counted on to "lead the way" or "set the pace" for others who might need more time or more cultivation before they make their commitment.

The board members, the campaign chairs, and the campaign committee members should be solicited during the quiet phase. The quiet phase usually relies on personal solicitations by campaign volunteers or board members for high-level gifts. Who solicits whom is usually a factor of assignments being made to volunteers on the campaign committee.

Soliciting the Board during the Quiet Phase

The quiet phase of the campaign offers an opportunity to engage the entire board in the campaign through their personal giving. Consider the following points when conducting the board solicitations:

- In many campaigns, giving from members of the board accounts for as much as one third to one half of the total goal.

- The campaign chair or the board chair should talk to the entire board about their giving responsibilities at the beginning of the campaign.

- As a rule, like any campaign volunteer, a board member should have made her own gift before soliciting others.

- Both the campaign chair and the board chair should be asked for their gifts first.

- All board members should be solicited during the quiet phase. These board solicitations can be made by other board members, the executive director/CEO, or by members of the campaign committee.

- If you become a member of the campaign committee, your role will be to ask others, as well as to give.

In some organizations, the executive director/CEO solicits the board chair, who in turn solicits the campaign leadership and other members of the board. In other cases, the campaign chair begins the process by soliciting the board chair and campaign committee members. Your strategy will depend on the personalities and experience of the people in these positions. Basically you can select whatever process works within the culture of your organization, for there are no hard and fast rules.

Once they have made their own commitments, the leaders of the campaign and the board then solicit the remaining board members. The goal is to get the maximum possible participation, coupled with a strong financial showing, so that going forward into the campaign the volunteers can point to substantial support from the board and campaign leadership.

Early high-level gifts are particularly important to close during the quiet phase. The size of the gifts during the quiet phase usually sets the range for the size of most of the gifts that the organization will receive during the rest of the campaign.

Some organizations also solicit internal constituencies, such as staff or faculty, at this point to demonstrate internal support for the campaign. The quiet phase can take six months or three years, but it should be short enough to create momentum and long enough to set a strong pace for giving in the remainder of the campaign.

The Quiet Phase Goal

Most campaign consultants suggest setting a relatively high percentage of the total campaign goal as the benchmark for the quiet phase of the campaign. The strategy behind this push is that it allows the nonprofit to have a higher proportion of the campaign dollars in hand when the campaign goes public.

> **RULES OF THE ROAD**
>
> Many campaigns strive to reach 50 to 70 percent of their goal during the quiet phase.

Having a larger percentage of the funds in hand when the quiet phase is completed gives the public phase of the campaign a boost, and it shows the level of commitment from the board and the campaign leadership. All this is calculated to build momentum and give potential donors the assurance that the campaign will succeed.

The Public Phase

The public phase of the campaign has two objectives: raising enough money to reach the final campaign goal, and expanding the campaign to reach new constituencies.

The public phase uses more marketing and PR outreach elements to bring the campaign to a wider audience. In the public phase, fundraisers look for gifts from lower-level donors and reach out to new donor groups, while continuing to cultivate and close higher-level gifts from those prospects who may require additional cultivation before making their commitment.

Many different fundraising tools can come into play in the public phase. Campaigns commonly make use of tools that provide for broader outreach at this stage, including direct mail, telemarketing, newspaper and radio ads, and brick campaigns. The public phase should incorporate aspects of social networking and online fundraising, from the use of e-marketing and interactive web sites to social networking. The object is to use the campaign to draw attention to the benefits that the organization provides in the community, while building a base for future support.

Alternative Timetables

Not all campaigns have just a quiet phase and a public phase. The timetable selected depends on your organization's unique circumstances and needs.

Here are four alternative timetables to consider:

- Phase by timing of construction. Raise money for different components of a building or buildings on a sequential basis. Coordinate the construction schedule with the fundraising schedule.

- Phase by geographic region. Announce the campaign in different parts of the country at different times. Start locally, and then open the campaign in targeted cities on a rolling basis.

- Phase by the type of funding needed. Develop separate phases for capital and endowment needs. Combine all gifts into one overall goal but fundraise for each on a separate timetable.

- Phase by constituency or organizational units. In a complex organization, such as a university, plan to have one unit (such as the medical center) fundraise in the first phase, and then follow with other units.

Using Gift Tables in Campaign Planning

Campaign gift tables are a calculated effort to mathematically determine the number of prospects, donors, and gifts that will be required at various established dollar levels to reach the campaign goal.

Attempting to predict the number and dollar level of gifts that will appear during a campaign is a little like handicapping a political race; you know what the polls say, you can guess who is out ahead, but you really don't know how things will turn out until the votes are all in.

Gift tables are also known as gift pyramids, because, when drawn, they usually show a pyramid shape. The typical model shows a small number of donors making really big gifts at the top, a moderate number of donors making gifts at the middle levels, and a large number of donors making smaller gifts at the bottom levels.

The university athletics director and the big athletic donors on the board cultivated a potential donor all fall, wining and dining him at every football game. Then they asked him to make the lead gift of $2 million for the new practice field on campus. The donor said he wanted to make the gift, but that he needed some time to work it out with his family.

Six months later the gift agreement came in—$2 million for the new early childhood education program. "What happened?" asked the distraught athletic director.

"Well," the donor explained, "It is my wife's money, and that's what she wanted to give it to."

Campaign planners find that this model of graduated gift giving holds true for campaigns of almost every size and type. In recent years, however, those huge campaigns with billion-dollar goals have distorted the gift table by depending on a few mega-gifts (think eight or nine figures), which tilt the campaign heavily toward higher-level donors. This newer model is probably not going to match the majority of campaigns that seek to raise hundreds of thousands or millions of dollars.

Gift tables are usually prepared by staff or consultants, but they can be used as a planning tool in many ways. (See Exhibit 8.3.) Their primary purpose is to help determine how many prospects are needed at different levels of the giving pyramid to reach the required dollar totals. They can be useful in guiding the planning and pricing of various recognition opportunities.

Some board solicitors like to bring gift tables along on calls to help illustrate potential gift levels and the number of gifts needed in meetings with prospective donors. Staff and volunteers can fill in the gift table with the names of donors as the campaign progresses, using it as a tracking tool to determine how many more donors are needed at each gift level.

Sample Gift Tables

The dollar level of the highest gift is the most important factor in creating a gift table for your campaign. The difference between securing a top gift of

EXHIBIT 8.3

Using Gift Tables as a Planning Tool

Use gift tables in these ways:

- To see if there are enough prospects identified at each dollar level to make the campaign work.

- To help define the campaign structure and set realistic goals.

- To price naming opportunities and recognition opportunities.

- To raise sights among board members and campaign leaders.

- To serve as a visual aid on solicitation calls with prospects.

- To track the campaign's progress with prospects at each giving level.

$500,000 and a top gift of $1,000,000 can be dramatic in a campaign with a goal of $3,000,000. (See Exhibits 8.4 and 8.5.)

RULES OF THE ROAD

Gift tables illustrate an important campaign concept: that by raising a relatively small number of gifts at high dollar levels, your campaign can avoid having to raise hundreds of gifts at lower levels.

Note that the number of gifts needed drops quickly for the campaign with the higher lead gift. The campaign in Exhibit 8.4, with the lead gift of $500,000, will require 381 prospects and 127 donors to reach its $3 million goal. The campaign in Exhibit 8.5, with a lead gift of $1,000,000, requires less than half that number, 153 prospects and 51 donors, *to raise the same amount of money.*

The campaign with the higher lead gift of $1,000,000 is more efficient; it will require less work for the staff and volunteers, less money spent on reaching lower-level donors, and less time to reach the goal.

These two sample gift tables use a 3:1 prospect to gift ratio, but some consultants prefer to use a tougher 4:1 ratio. Choose a ratio that you think suits your organization's prospect pool. If many of the names on your list are "cold"

EXHIBIT 8.4

Sample Gift Table for a $3M Campaign; Top Gift at $500,000

Gift Level	Prospects	Donors	Dollars	% of Campaign
$500,000	3	1	$ 500,000	17%
$250,000	6	2	$ 500,000	17%
$100,000	12	4	$ 400,000	13%
$50,000	24	8	$ 400,000	13%
$25,000	48	16	$ 400,000	13%
$10,000	96	32	$ 320,000	11%
$5,000	192	64	$ 320,000	11%
$1,000 and below	numerous+		$ 160,000	5%
Totals	*381+*	*127+*	*$3,000,000*	

EXHIBIT 8.5

Sample Gift Table for a $3M Campaign; Top Gift at $1M

Gift Level	Prospects	Donors	Dollars	% of Campaign
$1,000,000	3	1	$1,000,000	33%
$500,000	3	1	$ 500,000	17%
$250,000	6	2	$ 500,000	17%
$100,000	9	3	$ 300,000	10%
$50,000	18	6	$ 300,000	10%
$25,000	24	8	$ 200,000	6.5%
$10,000	30	10	$ 100,000	3%
$5,000 and below	60	20	$ 100,000	3%
Totals	*153*	*51*	*$3,000,000*	

prospects who will need a lot of cultivation before they make a gift to your organization, choose the higher ratio. Campaigns that convert every prospect into a donor (a 1:1 prospect to gift ratio) probably aren't digging deep enough into their prospect pool and need to increase their outreach to new donors.

YOUR ROLE AS A BOARD MEMBER

You may be asked to help rate prospects for your organization's gift table. Ask to see the gift tables prepared for your campaign and pay close attention to the highest gift levels because of their overall importance. Ask if there are prospects identified for the highest level gifts, and how close the organization is to these prospects. Offer to help introduce the organization to any new prospects you know at these gift levels.

Be sure the plans are realistic—counting on gifts from wealthy donors who have no relationship to the organization is pie-in-the-sky thinking. Help the organization determine the level of the highest gift by identifying real potential prospects for a lead gift. Use the gift tables to plan your own gift and see how you fit into the campaign.

OVERCOMING COMMON BARRIERS TO SUCCESS

WE DON'T HAVE ENOUGH PROSPECTS

Don't panic—this is a common problem. Very few campaigns know all the prospects and donors that they will need to tap at the beginning of the campaign. Part of the work in preparing for a campaign is to search for names of new potential supporters. This work continues during the quiet phase. During the public phase of a campaign one of the goals is to reach new constituencies. The campaign is designed to uncover and attract new support.

Secondly, there are some built-in assumptions that will give your organization some fall-back room. For instance, if your gift chart is built on a prospect-to-gift ratio of 3:1, this means that you only need to close one gift for every three prospect names uncovered. Some nonprofits can improve on this ratio if they have already cultivated a number of key prospects who are close to the organization.

If you need more prospects, go back to some of the ideas presented in Chapter 6 and look for more ways to uncover new prospect names. Your organization may have to invest some resources in prospect identification. Three possible areas to invest in are: Electronic prospect screening, hiring a prospect researcher, and hiring a new major gift staff member to make more calls out in the field.

Even with these considerations, you may want to plan conservatively and make sure that your goals are not set too far out of reach. It may be wise to cut back on the estimates of what your organization needs, or plan for a campaign in several phases. Often the best goal is a compromise between the dollars needed and the estimated total giving capacity of known donors.

How Can We Sight-Raise with our Board?

"Raising sights" means getting the board and potential major gift donors acclimated to the idea of giving larger gifts, and it is one of the psychological underpinnings of a well-planned campaign.

Gift tables are one way to raise sights among board members and other supporters because they are a visual tool that helps donors see the number and size of the largest gifts that will have to be raised to meet the goal.

As a board member, you may have become used to thinking about finding prospects and gifts in a certain range for your organization, let's say between $5,000 and $10,000. Looking at the gift table makes you realize that the campaign will require much larger gifts, including several gifts between $100,000 and $1 million, to make the goal. This raises your consciousness about what kinds of prospects and gifts will be needed, and it also raises your thinking about your own gift, if you have the resources to do more. This process of thinking more seriously about the need for higher-level gifts is referred to as sight-raising.

There are other techniques for sight-raising. Among them:

- Announce the earliest large gifts in a public manner to link the campaign with higher-level dollar amounts in the minds of prospective donors.

- Seek the largest gifts early in the campaign to set the pace for higher-level giving.

- Price the most attractive naming opportunities at the high end of the gift table to attract donors who are capable of making larger gifts.

- Solicit a challenge gift that encourages donors to give at a higher level.

- Talk about and ask for gifts that are larger than the organization has raised in the past.

Summary

Campaigns are complex enterprises and require great dedication from their board members. Select the type of campaign your organization needs by looking at the size, duration, and type of funds you want to raise. Set the goals by estimating how much you can raise as well as how much you need. Feasibility studies may be one way to help estimate whether a goal is reachable.

The structural components of the campaign, including timetables, phases, and gift tables, are meant to help support successful fundraising. Timetables can help build momentum for the campaign and motivate donors, as well as meet the cash flow needs of your organization. Phasing a campaign is useful to break a fundraising project down into bite-size pieces, like constructing a building in phases as the money is raised.

Gift tables can be used to determine whether the organization has enough donors identified at each dollar level to reach the goal. Gift tables also help to raise sights among board members and other potential donors. These strategic elements should be developed by the staff, the consultant, and the campaign committee before the campaign begins and presented to the board for your review.

CHAPTER 9

Fundraising Campaigns
How to Make Your Campaign Succeed

A man always has two reasons for doing anything: a good reason and the real reason.

—J. P. Morgan

After reading this chapter, you will be able to:

- Distinguish between the roles of board members and staff.
- Provide board and volunteer leadership for the campaign.
- Develop the case for your campaign.
- Set appropriate campaign recognition and pricing levels.

Campaign Leadership Roles

Campaigns require leadership in order to meet their goals. Organizational leadership comes from the executive director/CEO, along with the advancement staff, but campaign leadership also must be provided by the board, the campaign chair or chairs, and the campaign committee. All of these groups have to function together smoothly.

Campaigns require a great deal of activity with prospects and donors. While some of the day-to-day support activities should be provided by staff members, your organization will need to recruit, organize, train, and manage a broad array of volunteers to assist in the campaign.

You will need to understand the roles played by the board, the executive director/CEO, and the advancement staff during the campaign. It is important to understand what the CEO and the advancement staff can provide before exploring the roles that can be assumed by board members and other campaign volunteers.

Role of the Executive Director/CEO

Successful campaigns require a heavy commitment of time, energy, and passion from the executive director/CEO. Many campaigns founder because the organization's leader is either not prepared for or not able to commit the required time to the success of the effort. And it is a huge effort! Notwithstanding large numbers of volunteers, staff, and consultants, running a campaign is a tremendous undertaking.

Articulating the Vision

The key role for the executive director/CEO of the nonprofit in a campaign is to set out the vision for the organization. (See Exhibit 9.1.) He or she must be able to share their vision and passion for the cause with prospective donors, and to communicate how the donor's investment in the campaign will move that vision forward.

Many organizations today look for an executive director/CEO who is a proven fundraiser. There is no question that the great majority of nonprofit CEOs now cultivate, solicit, and ask for major gifts for their organizations and are productive doing so. Often, they are the leaders who can best and most effectively communicate their excitement and knowledge about the organization to a prospective donor.

It is not always a best practice, however, for the CEO to ask for or to close gifts all alone. There is also an important role for board members and other volunteers to play with top-level donors. The CEO will often pair up in teams

---

EXHIBIT 9.1

Campaign Roles:
The Executive Director/CEO

- Define the vision for the organization's future.

- Oversee the planning process and build the table of needs.

- Help build the case for why a donor should invest in the organization.

- Engage the board in all aspects of the campaign.

- Staff and budget the campaign to support its success.

- Help to hire the campaign consultant.

- Serve as chief spokesperson for the organization and its needs.

- Participate in the cultivation and solicitation of selected high-level donors.

- Lead campaign events and thank donors.

---

with board members, campaign co-chairs, or the chief advancement officer to meet with leadership donors.

In many organizations, because of the many different demands placed on his or her time, the CEO is focused only on the top-level gifts. Below that level, board members and other campaign volunteers, coupled with an advancement staff professional, can make the asks, close the gifts, and handle follow-up with the donors. Even with a focus on high-end prospects, the CEO should still be the one to articulate the vision for all donors at campaign and cultivation events.

Role of Advancement Staff

Many nonprofit organizations have moved to a staff-driven development function, as opposed to the model of an entirely volunteer-driven development function, in implementing campaign fundraising. This doesn't mean that volunteers and board members are off the hook, it just means that professional staff is guiding the process.

The norm in most campaigns today is for advancement staff working with the campaign consultant to plan, direct, and implement most of the aspects of the capital campaign. The CAO is like the general who oversees the work of the campaign: He or she coordinates all the pieces, such as prospect identification, assignment of calls on prospects, timing of solicitations, cultivation events, prospect management, reporting on progress, and providing stewardship and recognition for donors. In most nonprofits the CAO also staffs and coordinates the fundraising work conducted by the members of the board and the campaign committee.

The CAO should be prepared not only to manage the efforts of others, but also to make calls, ask for money, and to work with a subset of assigned prospects and donors. The CAO's prospect assignment load should be lighter than other full time members of their staff, however, due to their management responsibilities. See Exhibit 9.2 for the key components of the role of the chief advancement officer during a campaign.

Professional staff management has become more common than depending totally on volunteers because campaigns have become larger and more complex. Most board members don't have the expertise, time, or focus needed to make the substantial commitment of time and skill that it takes to keep a large campaign running smoothly.

Perhaps nowhere has the role of advancement staff changed more than in the use of trained development professionals to ask for and close gifts. Nonprofit leaders have found that experience and training do matter in the process of cultivation and solicitation of major gifts, leading to the greater use of professional staff. And the sheer number of prospects who need to be met with has meant that more staff activity is needed.

While there is still a strong preference for using board volunteers and peers in high-level cultivation and solicitation activity, the number of gifts asked for and closed by professional fundraisers is on the rise.

The best method for managing the solicitation process is to integrate the use of professional staff and board members or other campaign volunteers. The

EXHIBIT 9.2

Campaign Roles:
The Chief Advancement Officer

- Help hire a consultant and assist with the feasibility study.

- Develop the campaign plan or oversee its development by the consultant.

- Manage and support all campaign activity by board members, staff, and volunteers.

- Oversee prospect identification, cultivation, and solicitation activities.

- Oversee development of campaign materials and PR activity.

- Accompany volunteers, board members, and the CEO on calls.

- Manage a selected group of assigned prospects, cultivate, ask for money, and close gifts.

- Plan and execute all campaign and cultivation events.

- Oversee management of a database system to track prospects and activity.

- Provide timely and accurate reports on campaign progress and activity.

- Provide appropriate stewardship and recognition for donors.

strategy used most often is to create teams with both staff and board volunteers present for solicitation meetings with the prospect. The board member or volunteer can present the case for the campaign and its needs; then the professional development staffer makes the ask and closes the gift.

The growing emphasis on staff-driven campaigns by no means implies that there is no role for campaign volunteers, the CEO, and board members to play in the campaign. To the contrary, the involvement of these players is more important than ever. However, given the complexity, size, and sheer length of many fundraising campaigns, a professional staff is better equipped and trained to focus on areas like prospect identification and research, event planning, and supporting and tracking prospect activity.

IN THE REAL WORLD

Recruiting the Perfect Campaign Chair

A museum was making plans to mount a five-year capital campaign for a new building. The board chair was eager to get the best volunteer capital campaign chair in the city. After much discussion with the executive director and the staff, the perfect candidate was identified. This candidate had it all—she had campaign fundraising experience, the potential to make a seven-figure gift, and was a respected leader in the community. Although she did support the museum as a high-level annual donor, she was not a member of the museum's board.

The chair took on the role of recruitment. He chose a time when the candidate was just completing another campaign for a different nonprofit. He first invited her to join the board, which she agreed to. Then he asked her to chair the campaign. Not surprisingly, she initially balked: She had just completed a different campaign and wanted time to rest; she wasn't an established member of their board; and she didn't want to carry all the responsibility on her shoulders.

The chairman regrouped. Negotiations took about six months, but the final agreement was a win/win for all sides. The perfect candidate agreed to be one of two co-chairs, responsible for a portion of the campaign. She took on the wealthy individual prospects, and a second co-chair was recruited who was better suited to work with corporate and foundation donors.

The organization also agreed to a two-year term limit for both its campaign co-chairs in order to avoid burnout. By then the candidate had attended several board meetings and was more comfortable assuming a leadership position. She also was closer to making her own leadership gift, which was a necessary step toward her leadership of the campaign. The flexibility shown by all resulted in strong campaign leadership.

Staffing and Tracking of Volunteer Activity

The successful campaign requires the integration of a broad variety of activities and people to be successful. The leaders of the campaign must be able to recruit, train, and motivate an army of supporters, from board members and campaign volunteers to paid staff, and to focus and manage their efforts in a productive manner.

Without effective management, campaigns can deteriorate into chaos, disarray, and nonproductive behavior. Examples of campaigns out of control include volunteers who approach prospects without adequate planning or preparation, and staff who become demoralized and cynical about the organization and its goals.

In today's complex campaigns, where each staff member may be managing hundreds of prospects and numerous volunteers, it is imperative to have a prospect management system that works. In the old days, campaign staff kept index cards in a box under each volunteer's name, with prospect information and activity on each card. In today's world of computerized databases and development information systems, even a small campaign can track prospect assignments and activity on a laptop. This tracking is normally a staff function.

When campaigns lose their ability to staff and track volunteer activity, big problems arise. Campaign consultants can tell horror stories of volunteers run amok, calling on one anothers' prospects, making promises that the organization can't fulfill, asking prospects worth millions for a token gift of $10,000, unintentionally insulting donors, and generally providing such a poor public image for the organization that it can take years to erase the harm done.

Board Leadership in a Campaign

Nonprofit organizations are only as good as their boards. Good boards are even more critical a factor in the success of fundraising campaigns than in the course of other activities the organization pursues because donors look to the board for leadership. The board must be able to provide money, energy, leadership, passion, commitment, and time to make the campaign work.

Board members are often expected to provide a substantial portion of the campaign dollars needed. Consultants estimate that from 30 to 50 percent of the campaign goal should come from the board. There are community boards where this isn't possible, and alternatives can be devised, such as creating a campaign committee with substantial nonboard membership. For those board members lacking experience in fundraising, providing training and professional staff support can help fill in the gaps.

The Role of the Board

The board needs to play a major role in a campaign. The amount of actual fundraising done by board members will vary from organization to organization and from board member to board member. All board members should find ways to help, even if they are not sitting on the campaign committee.

As you will see in Exhibit 9.3, board members can play a variety of roles during the campaign. Board members set the pace for leadership gifts; they influence their peers; they help open doors to prospects; and they serve as spokespersons for the nonprofit. Often, because of their status in the community, the enthusiasm and activity level shown by members of the board is the leading reason that donors cite for making leadership gifts.

EXHIBIT 9.3

Campaign Roles: The Board Member

Before the Campaign begins:

- Board members may be asked to participate in or review the results of a campaign feasibility study, if one is conducted.

- Board members should be given the opportunity to review the goals and funding areas on the organization's table of needs and vote on them before the campaign commences.

Once the Campaign is approved:

- Board members have a fiduciary role to see that the organization secures the resources that it needs to successfully meet its mission.

- Every board member should make a gift to the campaign.

- Board members set the pace for leadership gifts by the level of their own giving.

- Board members can influence their peers in the community through their own gifts and involvement.

- Board members can be outstanding spokespersons for the organization.

- Board members should review lists, identify prospects, open doors to new prospects, and help to develop a plan for the engagement of prospects with the organization.

- Board members should volunteer to serve on the campaign committee or as campaign co-chairs.

- Board members should be active in the cultivation and solicitation of prospects, often as a member of a team.

- Board members should attend campaign events to show support.

- Board members may host small group events such as dinners to help cultivate campaign prospects.

- Board members help build the case by sharing their reasons for giving.

- Board members should thank donors, attend recognition events, and participate in stewardship activities.

Before the Campaign

Many organizations wisely undergo a board self-review process a year or two before attempting a major fundraising campaign (see the *Tips and Techniques* nearby).

There are several ways to build a stronger board before the campaign begins:

- Expand the size of the board to provide for greater outreach.

- Recruit new members to enhance geographic or ethnic diversity.

- Recruit new members who bring expertise in fundraising.

- Recruit new members who have the capacity to make a leadership gift.

- Recruit new members who represent targeted campaign constituencies, for example, corporations, foundations, or specific industries.

It is very important to tell new board members about the organization's expectations for their involvement, including giving, when they are being recruited, even if you haven't publicly announced your campaign. These new members will be more willing to help if they know where your organization is headed, and they won't feel blindsided.

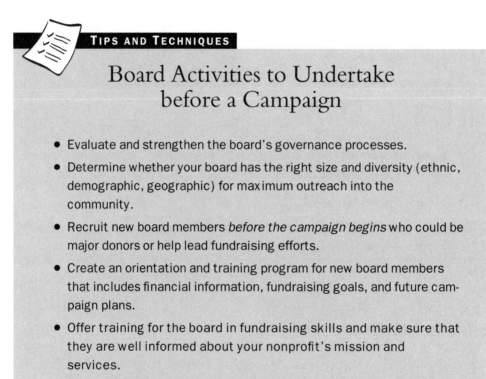

TIPS AND TECHNIQUES

Board Activities to Undertake before a Campaign

- Evaluate and strengthen the board's governance processes.
- Determine whether your board has the right size and diversity (ethnic, demographic, geographic) for maximum outreach into the community.
- Recruit new board members *before the campaign begins* who could be major donors or help lead fundraising efforts.
- Create an orientation and training program for new board members that includes financial information, fundraising goals, and future campaign plans.
- Offer training for the board in fundraising skills and make sure that they are well informed about your nonprofit's mission and services.
- Identify future leaders and create opportunities for them to take on leadership roles.

Campaign Volunteer Structure

It is important to have board members and other campaign volunteers involved in various aspects of the campaign, particularly in outreach to other donors in the community. The more advocates of its mission and needs the organization can produce during the campaign, the better the organization will be served in years to come.

The *campaign committee* is the most common volunteer structure used to support the work of a major fundraising campaign. The campaign committee can be big or small, but 12 to 15 is an effective size. The campaign may have one chair or several co-chairs.

The campaign committee should be separate from the development committee, which should continue to exist for matters of fundraising policy and to oversee ongoing programs like the annual fund and planned giving. The campaign committee should report to the board or to the development committee to ensure that the campaign meets the needs of the organization and follows appropriate policies.

The committee should be comprised of board members and nonboard volunteers. How often the committee meets depends on the work to be done; some meet weekly, some meet monthly, and some meet only in conjunction with board meetings. Because campaigns recruit volunteers who are very busy in their own lives, and volunteers may be spread out all over the country, meeting by conference call is one possible option.

Large national campaigns find it useful to develop several tiers of volunteer structures based on region, area of responsibility, and affiliation. A university or a national organization, for instance, might want to identify regional campaign chairs, create regional committees, and even provide regional staff to support the work of regional volunteers.

A smaller nonprofit operating in one region should keep the structure simple, with one committee leading all the campaign activity. The chief advancement staff officer should be present at committee meetings and often the executive director/CEO joins the meetings also.

The *campaign steering committee* can also be a helpful addition to the campaign volunteer structure. A steering committee is composed of the top four or five people who have roles in the campaign leadership. This group could include the campaign chair or co-chairs, the board chair, the executive director/CEO, the campaign consultant, and the chief advancement officer. This smaller group is sometimes more efficient than a large committee. It should meet regularly to set policy, plan activity, and assign prospects to a larger group of campaign volunteers.

For medium sized nonprofits, here is a model that integrates the work of the two committees. Bring the campaign steering committee together for a meeting every two or three weeks to direct the activity of the campaign and to focus on leadership prospects. Have the full campaign committee meet less often, once a month or once a quarter, to review their progress with prospects and receive campaign updates. Prospect assignments and prospect activity can still continue without interruption, as the committee members should be staffed individually through calls and e-mails from the staff.

TALES FROM THE BOARDROOM

The elderly past chairman of the board was the lead donor to a building that carried his family's name. He spent a lot of time checking things out once the building was open and running. He moved the furniture around, supervised the janitorial staff, picked up trash, and adjusted the lighting. The executive director was finally forced to intervene when security found him "borrowing" computers from the staff offices.

When the executive director politely confronted the donor, he looked hurt and replied, "Well, you know, it IS my building."

Campaign Chairs and Co-Chairs

The leadership qualities of your chair or chairs will help to determine the course of your campaign. See the nearby *Tips and Techniques* for important qualities to look for in selecting a campaign chair. Usually recruiting the chair or chairs is done by the executive director/CEO and the chair of the board. Selecting the campaign leadership is an important decision and should not be entered into lightly.

Rather than identifying one campaign chair, consider a model with three co-chairs, selecting one co-chair who is in charge of corporate prospects, one who concentrates on wealthy individuals, and one who is focused on foundation activity. In general, recruit enough chairs and committee members to reach the prospects needed, although of course the committee size has to remain manageable.

Qualities to Look For in a Campaign Chair (or Co-Chairs)

- Loyalty and passion for the organization and its mission.
- Capacity to make a leadership gift.
- Ability to lead others.
- Time and energy to commit to the campaign.
- Experience asking for gifts.
- Highly respected in the community.

If you are involved in recruiting a campaign chair (or if you yourself are being asked to step up to this position), you should ask the staff to prepare a volunteer position description. In the sample description in Exhibit 9.4, you can see that the position is a demanding one time-wise. Be prepared to discuss how much time the chair or chairs will need to spend on the campaign and how long the chair position will last. Some campaigns set a term limit for chairs to avoid burnout. This might be a negotiating point when the chair is being recruited.

The individual being recruited may also ask how much they have to give. The answer depends on the nature and size of your campaign, but it is always better if the chair or co-chairs make a gift near the top of the gift table. Prepare an answer to this question about the gift size before making the recruitment call on a potential chair. Depending on the circumstances and how well developed the relationship is with the prospective chair, it may be appropriate to recruit the chair and ask for a leadership gift in the same meeting.

EXHIBIT 9.4

Sample Position Description: Campaign Chair or Co-Chair

1. Provide leadership for all campaign activities.
2. Plan your own gift commensurate with the resources available.
3. Chair meetings of the campaign committee (identify frequency).
4. Allow the use of your name and position in campaign materials.
5. Host and attend campaign events, such as the campaign kick-off.
6. Serve as a spokesperson for the campaign and for the organization's needs.
7. Identify and open the door to prospects for the campaign.
8. Assist with the cultivation and solicitation of top prospects.
9. Serve on the steering committee for the campaign.

Recruiting campaign volunteers can be done by the CEO, the staff, or by the campaign chair. If you are asked to be a co-chair or a member of the campaign committee, be sure that you understand what you are being asked to do, whom you will work with, and how your work fits into the bigger scheme of the campaign. Request a job description that outlines the position, the duties, the term of service, and the expectations. See the sample in Exhibit 9.5.

EXHIBIT 9.5

Sample Position Description: Campaign Committee Member

Term: from January 2010 through December 2012.

1. Support the campaign through your personal efforts.

   - Support the goal of 100 percent participation in gifts for the campaign from members of the board and the campaign committee.

   - Make your own gift to the campaign commensurate with your means.

- Contribute to the campaign in other nonfinancial ways, such as hosting an event, contributing professional services, or committing time.

2. Serve as an ambassador for the organization.

- Allow your name to be listed as a committee member in printed materials.

- Attend meetings of the campaign committee (specify frequency).

- Serve on the host committee for campaign events and attend when possible.

- Assist with public relations outreach and related communication efforts.

3. Assist with the identification, cultivation, and solicitation of prospects.

- Help identify potential prospects whom you know or can reach.

- Assist in determining the best way to approach the prospects you know and to bring them closer to the organization.

- Assist in opening the door for staff, volunteers, or board members to call on prospects whom you know.

- Make cultivation and solicitation calls as a member of a team representing the organization.

- Assist with thanking donors for their gifts.

Of course, the more that you as a campaign volunteer know about your organization and your campaign, the better you will be able to represent the organization's interests with prospects and donors. Participating in volunteer training is an imperative.

Some of the tasks that board members can do don't require additional training or staff support. For instance, board members can provide free or at-cost assistance to the campaign in their own areas of professional expertise, such as public relations, printing, communications, event planning, entertainment, tech support, video production, computer equipment, architectural planning, or catering.

YOUR ROLE AS A BOARD MEMBER

If you are asked to join the campaign committee, there are three rules to being an effective volunteer:

- You should ask for and be given meaningful work and trained to do it well.

- You should be well informed about the organization and its needs.

- You must make your own gift to the campaign.

Most campaigns involve their volunteers in the actual process of fundraising: that is, the identification, cultivation, and solicitation of prospects. The most productive way to use your time and expertise as a campaign volunteer is to tap into your knowledge of the prospective donor community. This might involve raiding your rolodex or contact list in order to create an invitation list for an event, or it could mean asking you to make calls as a member of the team to ask for a gift.

Many volunteers, even experienced campaigners, need support and training when it comes to asking for money. Organizations can provide formal training sessions for campaign volunteers. Such a session can help put volunteers at ease, shows the volunteers that the organization supports their efforts, and often creates bonds between members of the committee who will be working together over the course of the campaign. (See Exhibit 9.6.)

EXHIBIT 9.6

Options for Training Campaign Volunteers

- Hold a training session during the first or second meeting of the campaign committee; use your CAO or hire a consultant to run it.

- Use the sample scripts and the role-play exercise included in the Board Retreat section in the Appendix of this book and on the companion web site, www.wiley.com/go/boardfundraising.

- Hold a board retreat that focuses on fundraising; see the Board Retreat section in the Appendix of this book and companion materials on the web site. Download the PowerPoint, ''The 5 Elements of the Successful Ask,'' available at www.wiley.com/go/boardfundraising.

- Ask an experienced volunteer or board member to partner with less experienced campaign volunteers and make training calls together to learn the ropes.

An important outcome of such training is that the volunteers themselves start thinking about who they know and how they can be helpful to the organization. Training volunteers to ask can also be accomplished informally, simply by pairing an inexperienced board member with more experienced solicitors on prospect calls. See nearby **Tips and Techniques** on how to provide "on the call" training.

TIPS AND TECHNIQUES

Sample scenario for informal "on the call" training:

- Identify a prospect whom you know who you think might be interested in the organization's work and who has the capacity to give.

- "Open the door" to this prospect by calling to set the appointment with him or her.

- Arrange in advance to bring along an experienced partner—it could be a board member, the executive director/CEO, or a senior advancement staff member (tell the donor who is coming when you set up the appointment).

- Take on a specific role in advance for the call that you are comfortable with, such as explaining to the prospect why you support this organization, and review your role with your experienced partner before you go.

- Make the call and play your part, but watch and listen to learn how the rhythm of the call flows and how the ask is made.

- Follow up with the donor after the call and thank her when she makes a gift.

- As you observe the other members of the solicitation team, you will learn how to play other roles in future calls.

Making the Case

Making the case means being able to tell others why it's important to make a gift to this campaign, for this specific purpose, right now. Campaigns make it or break it on the strength of their case. As nonprofits have proliferated, donors have realized that they have more flexibility in selecting which organizations they invest in. Therefore, making a strong case has become a key component of the campaign repertoire.

The case for your campaign should be well thought out, with materials prepared in advance that you can share with the donor. For instance, for a capital campaign, you will not only want color renderings and site plans (see the nearby *Tips and Techniques*), but you will need to be able to explain why the building is needed, who will use it, and how it fits into the programs that your nonprofit already offers.

TIPS AND TECHNIQUES

Materials Needed for a Capital Campaign

Capital campaign materials require advance preparation. Your organization will want to have ready some or all of these materials:

- A color rendering of the new building.
- A site plan.
- A floor plan showing the basic rooms and layout.
- An estimate of costs.
- A list of recognition prices connected to the naming of each room or area.
- A color brochure with photos showing the people who will use the building.
- A campaign video or PowerPoint presentation highlighting the reasons the organization needs the building, who will use it, and how it will look.
- Campaign stationery and logo.
- Campaign gift table.
- Proposal template and sample letters to prospects.
- A color folder with pockets in which to put all these materials.

Your board and the campaign committee should review the case for the campaign together, selecting themes that you can highlight, and identifying key message points. Use stories and examples of people who have been helped by the organization to interest the donor in your project.

After you review the case in a group setting, make sure you are comfortable presenting it in your own words. Try it out on a friend or family member to see how persuasive your presentation of the case can be.

Consider developing a short version of the case (known in the business as the "elevator speech") for those occasions when you run into a prospective donor who might be interested in the grocery store or at another event.

Here are some questions to ask yourself when formulating your version of the case:

- What are you raising money for?
- Why is this project or building needed?
- Who will use the services provided, and how fast is the need growing?
- What has the organization done that makes you want to invest in it?
- Why is this project needed now?
- What is the plan for maintaining the building and supporting operations once it is opened?
- Are there other projects like this in your community, and if so, how does this one stand apart from the others?
- Why does this project, above all others, deserve your investment?

Making the case can be made through pretty brochures, campaign videos, PowerPoint presentations, and a variety of expensive materials. Or it can mean just going into a donor's living room and telling him or her why this campaign is so important, speaking from your heart. As long as you are committed to your project and have made your gift yourself, your passion and interest in the project will help to persuade others to join you.

The case for your organization should be linked with themes that are popular in your community. Themes that resonate with donors right now include economic development, education, and providing healthy lifestyles. Examples of these thematic elements and others that can be built into campaign messaging and materials:

- Broad-based community support: Show the projected use of the project by the entire community, especially those who are lower income.

- Education: Feature educational aspects of the project and how children and adults will learn from it.

- Economic development: Show financial aspects of the project (like construction dollars committed) and explain how the community will benefit from it.

- Work force development: Provide information on how the project will train workers and give them new skills for the marketplace.

- Visitor projections: Explain how the project will increase tourist visitation and spending across the region.

- Economic impact: Have a professional economist conduct an economic impact study to show the dollars the project will generate in the region.

- Innovation: Explain how the project encourages and supports innovation and creativity. Tie this to young families and their needs.

- Improving health and families: Highlight how the project will improve overall health and strengthen families across the community.

- Improving quality of life: Emphasize how this project improves quality of life for all residents.

IN THE REAL WORLD

Making the Case Personal

A small nonprofit that worked on low-income housing issues was running its first ever capital campaign. The CEO asked the chair of the local bank to chair the campaign. He held a cultivation meeting for a selected group of wealthy foundation trustees in his bank boardroom. They came because he asked them to come; none of them knew the organization or had donated to it in the past.

> The program included a personal testimonial from a disabled veteran, an articulate middle-aged man who had lost a limb in one of the recent wars. He rolled to the front of the boardroom and talked for five minutes about how the organization had turned his life around by helping him to buy a home and renovate it for his wheelchair.
>
> By the end of his comments, everyone in the room was wiping away tears. By the end of the meeting, everyone in the room was making a pledge.

Campaign Recognition and Pricing

Recognition is the term used for methods that organizations employ to give donors visibility and satisfaction in return for a gift. Because of IRS rules, charitable gifts cannot be traded for items of value. Nonprofits have thus had to become creative about what gift recognition they do offer. The type and style of recognition offered often is related to the amount that the donor has given.

As a campaign volunteer, your goal in working with prospects is not only to motivate them to make a gift, but to make a gift that is at the high end of their capacity. The decision by a donor to give to capacity, as opposed to making a smaller commitment, can be motivated by the size and visibility of the naming opportunities offered at each giving level. Not all donors are motivated by having their name on a building or a plaque, but enough are that this type of recognition has become commonplace in the nonprofit world.

Naming Opportunities in the Capital Campaign

Most campaigns prepare a list of naming opportunities for donor recognition, with prices attached, before the solicitations begin. This list becomes a key element of the solicitation process.

In campaigns that involve a building or a renovation, the advancement team will work with the architects to identify and price naming options that will be offered to donors. Prices are usually set by the level of visibility and importance of the space, rather than by the cost per square foot or size of the room. Thus, external naming options and highly visible areas, like conference rooms and lobbies, usually are priced higher than inside rooms.

Prices must also be set relative to the gift table. If the highest tier of giving on the gift table is $1 million, then it is not appropriate to set the highest level naming option at $3 million. Make sure that there are attractive naming options available at each tier of the gift table so that donors will find something to name at whatever size gift they can afford to make.

How to Set the Price for Naming a Building

In most campaigns the board, or at least the campaign committee, reviews and approves prices and naming recognition levels. Be sure that your campaign team identifies any external recognition possibilities in your project. In general, non-profit organizations can command a premium for external naming recognition. External names are those that go on the outside of a building, wing, or campus. These usually involve bigger, external signage that gives more visibility to the name of the donor.

Some states have legal requirements that affect naming rights. For example, in Louisiana, it is not legal to name a building owned by the state after a living donor (this law was imposed to halt graft and corruption). Make sure your board and staff are familiar with any local, state, or federal regulations that might affect your project.

TIPS AND TECHNIQUES

To determine the price for the external naming of a building, consider these three factors:

- The percentage of the total cost of the project that can be assigned to one donor.
- The going market price set by peers in your region for external naming of a building.
- The giving capacity of the prospects at the top of your gift table and how much can be raised from other donors after the naming price is established.

Most consultants recommend setting the external naming price of a building at 30 percent to 50 percent of the total project cost. In other words, if the project total is $10 million, the external naming option would be priced from $3 million to $5 million. Setting the percentage higher is preferable, because then there will need to be fewer gifts raised from other donors to reach the goal.

However, there are significant regional differences in the setting of naming prices, and this should be factored into your planning. Campaigns on the East Coast and the West Coast tend to have the edge in requiring a larger percentage of the total goal to name a building. This may be due to the number of campaigns, competition for big-name donors, or to the enhanced prestige of having your name on a building in a larger city.

Don't forget that your campaign must find a prospective donor who can afford the naming price! While you don't want to undersell the recognition opportunity, you must be realistic, or the campaign will end up in trouble.

If your organization's top gift to date has been $500,000 and your top prospect is rated at $1 million, then pricing your building's external naming option at $3 million is a risky strategy. Should you do it anyway, in the hopes that the campaign will attract a donor who will make a gift of that size? Perhaps, but if this risk is to pay off, you will need to help your organization identify and cultivate more high-capacity prospective donors.

A new reality of current major gift fundraising is that donors are taking longer to make up their minds about committing to large gifts. This delay may be due to uncertainty about the economic environment or there may be other, more personal factors at work. The age, circumstances, and family situation of the donor may all come into play. Don't make the assumption that your campaign can quickly close agreements for the largest gifts, even if the donors are inclined to support your efforts.

A sample list of recognition options and naming prices can be found in Exhibit 9.7.

In the campaign illustrated in Exhibit 9.7, the university has decided to ask for 50 percent of the total cost, or $5 million, for the external naming

EXHIBIT 9.7	

Sample List of Recognition Opportunities and Prices

Capital Campaign for a University Social Sciences Building
Total Campaign Goal: $10,000,000

External Name of the Building	$ 5,000,000
Internal Spaces:	
First Floor	$ 1,000,000
Entrance Lobby	$ 750,000
Auditorium	$ 750,000
Second Floor	$ 500,000
Exterior Courtyard	$ 500,000
Dean's Suite	$ 500,000
Conference Suite	$ 500,000
Classrooms (5 @ $100,000 each)	$ 500,000
Faculty Offices (5 @ $50,000 each)	$ 250,000
Interior Courtyard	$ 250,000
Computer Labs (4 @ $50,000 each)	$ 200,000
Student Lounge	$ 150,000
Faculty Lounge	$ 150,000
Total of Named Spaces	$11,000,000

Note: The naming options add up to 10% more than the goal in order to make up for options that might not get sold and to provide a cushion if the top gift of $5 million can't be reached. It is also possible to add 10% or 20% to the goal for the project in order to raise a maintenance endowment, a feature that has been getting more popular in recent campaigns.

recognition. Other spaces are priced according to their visibility and prominence, not according to their actual square footage.

Note that the total sum of the naming options is 10% more than the total goal for the campaign. This allows the campaign some leeway if some spaces remain unsold, or if their lead donor can only give $4 million instead of

$5 million. This institution may also want to use the additional 10%, if it can be raised, to start a maintenance endowment for the new building.

> **TALES FROM THE BOARDROOM**
>
> A certain wealthy donor wanted his name to be on the new building at his favorite public university. He ran up against a problem: In Louisiana, where he resided, there is a law against naming a public building for a living donor.
>
> After talking to the chair of the campaign, he met with his lawyers and created a new foundation carrying his name. Then he made the gift to the university from the foundation. The building was thereby named after the foundation, not an individual, but it ended up carrying his name, just as he wished.

Planning Donor Recognition

Donor recognition needs to be planned at the commencement of the capital campaign. Board members or campaign committee members should participate in these discussions. Think about the needs of all donors, from the very top all the way to the bottom of the gift table.

Many campaigns do a good job of recognition with the big donors, those who name buildings or create endowments, but they lose their focus as the gift sizes go down. Smaller donors are important too. Small donors build the base for your future campaigns, they talk to others in their community about your organization, and they may become big donors someday. So treat them right!

Donor recognition can include plaques, lists, web sites, publications, bricks, and donor walls—there are many options. There are artists and firms that specialize in creative recognition ideas, such as murals and sculptures.

It is wise to set the rules early for how your campaign will recognize gifts of all levels, and to educate all staff, volunteers, and board members so that everyone is clear about the policies. This is an area in which campaign committee members can provide good advice and input.

Here are some organizing principles to consider in donor recognition:

- Recognize gifts according to purpose. For instance, don't mix recognition of gifts for the annual fund with capital gifts.

- Determine which dollar levels of gifts will be recognized.

- Determine how and where each level of gift will be recognized.

- Create a policy for the use of signage, plaques, and naming recognition throughout the capital project and stick to your plan.

- Determine how (and whether) you will recognize gifts that are revocable, such as bequests and unrealized planned gifts from trusts or life insurance.

It may help to plan out donor recognition on a chart, with large gifts receiving the most recognition and small gifts getting less visibility (something like a gift table). A sample chart that links donor recognition to gift levels appears in Exhibit 9.8.

Note that the nonprofit makes use of many different types of donor recognition in this chart, including printed annual reports, web site donor lists, naming of spaces, external naming of a building, articles in newsletters, events, and donor walls.

Recognition for Gifts to Endowment

Recognition options for donors to endowed funds are usually handled differently from recognition given to capital campaign donors. Because endowed gifts are permanently invested with the aim of producing an annual income stream, they are different from gifts to capital projects, which are spent outright. An endowed gift is usually given to name something that is continuously funded, such as a faculty or staff position, or to support an ongoing program, while a capital campaign gift almost always is recognized with the naming of a tangible space.

As discussed above, capital projects often develop a list of recognition options comprised of named spaces within the area being constructed. Endowments can also be named, but usually the item being named is a fund that will

EXHIBIT 9.8

Sample Capital Campaign Donor Recognition Chart

Gift Level	Recognition Offered
Under $100	Listed in the campaign report and on the web site at the lowest giving level
$100 to $499	Listed in the campaign report and on the web site in the second-tier giving level
$500 to $999	Listed in the report and on the web site in the third-tier giving level
$1,000 to $9,999	Listed in the report and on the web site as a leadership donor
	Listed on a permanent donor wall in the new facility
$10,000 to $99,000	Listed in the report and on the web site in a higher category
	Given a selection of rooms to name
	Listed on permanent donor wall in larger typeface
$100,000 to $1,000,000	Listed in the report and on the web site by giving level
	Given a selection of more visible rooms to name
	Offered an individualized dedication ceremony for their space
	Listed on a permanent donor wall in largest typeface
$2,000,000	Receive all of the above
	Given external naming recognition with custom signage on the outside of the new facility
	Article written about the gift for local newspaper
	Special public dedication ceremony to honor donor
	Featured gift in campaign report

last "forever," a fund that is invested to contribute to the future of the organization on a permanent basis.

Endowing Positions

A common practice among schools and universities is the endowment of staff or faculty positions. In universities, these positions are called "endowed chairs," and they are often awarded to a well-known scholar. Positions can be fully or partially endowed, depending on how much money the donor gives for the position and how much salary must be expended annually to fill the position.

Leadership positions, such as the president's or the executive director's salary, can be endowed in any nonprofit. In most cases, the name of the donor (or of whomever they wish to honor) is then attached permanently to the president's title. This name can be used on stationery, in publications, and in formal introductions. The recognition for the endowed support of a nonprofit leadership position can grant the donor quite a bit of exposure if handled well by the organization.

Other Types of Endowed Funds

Nonprofits can seek gifts to endow programs, buildings, funds, and even operations. Remember that only 4 to 5 percent of the original gift principal will actually be available as an annual payout to spend on the purpose selected by the donor. That means that endowed gifts are often larger than other kinds of gifts, but they don't have as much immediate impact on the nonprofit's activities right away.

The power of endowed gifts comes in their ability to keep funding a program or fund year after year. If the principal is wisely invested and the endowment grows, then over time the institution has more financial stability with an endowment than its peers who are not similarly blessed.

Program endowments are donated funds that are specifically targeted to support a program or activity selected by the donor.

Examples of program endowments include:

- $50,000 to endow a literacy program for adults who can't read.
- $100,000 to endow a program for feeding the homeless.
- $250,000 to endow the education program of an art museum.

Usually the organization will identify the name of any endowed fund that is used to support a program when conducting program activities. Printed materials, announcements, press releases, signage, and program names can also be used to recognize the program endowment donor by name.

Endowments can be given at a range of dollar levels and can always be added to through additional gifts. Most organizations set a floor for endowed gifts at a level such as $25,000 or $100,000. This limitation is set because endowments require active fiscal management, including proper investment, accounting, and tracking of expenditures. It becomes unproductive for an organization to provide financial tracking and support for very small endowments that produce less than $1,000 per year.

A warning about endowment fundraising: It is generally more difficult to raise endowed gifts than to raise funds for capital or program needs.

Why? The majority of donors like to see their investment put to work for the organization right away, and endowments do their work over the long term. Buildings and programs are more popular with donors because they are more visible, more concrete, and can have a more immediate impact on the organization than endowments.

And finally, with the stock market volatility recently experienced, donors will want to be assured that their endowed gifts are invested with care. Be sure that your board has a policy and a plan for the investment of endowed funds before you start asking for these kinds of gifts.

YOUR ROLE AS A BOARD MEMBER

Board members are often the most passionate supporters of fundraising for endowments, because they understand the day-to-day pressures on the organization for resources. Endowments are the only sure way to provide sustained resources over the long run to keep the organization providing services to meet its mission.

As a board member you can champion the cause of endowment in your organization. Endowments can be raised in a campaign focused solely on endowed gifts, or they can be one component of a larger capital campaign. The majority of gifts to endowment are made through planned giving techniques because endowments, like planned gifts, are the result of long-term planning and consideration for the organization's future. Planned giving is discussed more in Chapter 10, but you can learn more about these tools and use them with donors to help grow your organization's endowment.

OVERCOMING COMMON BARRIERS TO SUCCESS

WHAT IF WE CAN'T FIND OUR LEAD GIFT?

First of all, it isn't wise to set your top naming price at $5 million (or whatever the top gift level is) if you have no prospects who can make a gift of this size. Your organization may have set the overall goal too high for your realistic fundraising potential. If this is the case, your board will need to revisit the needs and adjust the campaign goal.

In some campaigns, however, the problem boils down to how to engage a prospect who is capable of a gift of this size and get them interested in the project. The donor has to be totally engaged and committed to the success of the nonprofit to make a decision to invest $5 million in its future.

Make a short list of every prospect with a connection to your organization who has the capacity to make a gift of the size you need. Prioritize the names based on probability of success (a donor who is unhappy with the nonprofit is probably not going to be at the top of the list).

Pull your committee together and develop an individualized strategy to bring each donor closer to the organization. Set up personal visits with each of them, bring them to see your site, invite them to lunch, and introduce them to those who use your services—in other words, step up the cultivation. Continue cultivation for at least six months, or until one of these top prospects is ready to solicit. If he or she doesn't make the gift, then focus on the other names on your list.

In the event that after a significant period of time (measured in years) no donor comes forward to provide the key naming gift, consider dropping the price. Go back to earlier prospects who turned down the $5 million option to offer them the lower price if they expressed interest in the project.

Be careful about making private deals with donors who want to negotiate a lower price; usually this information comes out, it makes the board angry, and it makes the other donors more likely to demand a negotiated price. It's a slippery slope once you start cutting prices, since every donor would be pleased with a discount price.

WHAT IF THE LEAD DONOR WANTS TO SELECT THE ARCHITECT (OR THE CARPET)?

Donor engagement can take on a whole new meaning when the lead donor to a capital campaign begins to view this as "his building." His involvement may include choosing the architect, approving the building plans, managing the construction, and selecting the carpet color.

To keep things in perspective, this is a good problem to have: You have an eager donor who wants to make sure his investment is going well. This augurs well for his continued commitment to the organization and to the campaign.

These things can get out of hand, however. If your donor makes choices that increase the price of the project, for instance, or add six months to the construction timetable, it's time to intervene. Bring in someone he will listen to: The board chair, the executive director, and the architect can all help to work things through with the donor face to face. You don't want to anger your donor or make him walk away. But you do need to preserve organizational control over the basic building costs, functions, and timetable.

Some organizations turn to their building contractor, project director, or another experienced construction professional to manage these relationships. It might be worth spending money on a project director if it keeps the donor involved in a positive way. If your board views this level of donor involvement as absolutely unacceptable, make sure your lead donor doesn't expect to be so heavily involved—it can be ugly to see a donor pull out of a project.

Summary

Board leadership in fundraising campaigns is critical to the campaign's success. Learning the appropriate campaign roles for board members, volunteers, executive directors, and the advancement staff can help everyone form a strong team. Select and recruit chairs, co-chairs, and members to your campaign committee who will be active and contributing volunteers. A good chair should be able to make a leadership gift as well as solicit others for their gifts.

The ability to make a strong case for the campaign is a skill you will need to sharpen in order to convince donors to make their gifts. Practice making the case with other board members and develop a version in your own words before making your first call on a prospect. Develop short and long versions of your case so that you will be ready if you happen to meet a prospect on the street.

There are a variety of strategies and techniques that enter into decisions about naming options and pricing. Make sure the campaign gift table and the prices of recognition options are aligned, and that you have identified recognition items for every tier of giving on the gift table. Endowment donors require a different set of recognition options from capital donors because their gifts are used to provide permanent support for an ongoing position, fund, or program. Keep your focus on providing consistent and appropriate recognition to help motivate donors to make their very best gift possible.

CHAPTER 10

Additional Sources of Giving
Foundations, Corporations, and Planned Giving

I have found that among its other benefits, giving liberates the soul of the giver.

—Maya Angelou

After reading this chapter, you will be able to:

- Raise money from foundations and corporations.
- Know how to use planned giving tools.
- Conduct good stewardship to keep your donors giving.

The past chapters have focused on board involvement in individual giving, mostly from fellow trustees and peers in the donor community. It is appropriate to focus first on individual giving, because on a national basis over 75 percent of the total charitable giving, which reached $290 billion in 2010, came from individuals (giving totals reported from the *Giving USA 2011 Report*).

Now we will look at some special topics: how you can be helpful in raising money from foundations and corporations, how to use planned giving as a tool, and how to keep your donors giving through good stewardship programs.

Giving from Foundations

There are over 100,000 private foundations making gifts in the United States today. Foundation grant making by private, community, and operating foundations fell by 8.9 percent in 2010, according to the Foundation Center (down 8.6 percent adjusted for inflation). This reported drop is most likely due to changes in foundations' asset values experienced from the losses and volatility experienced in the stock markets over the past several years.

Giving USA had a more positive report, measured using a different set of parameters from the Foundation Center. According to the *Giving USA 2011 Report*, foundation giving held steady, with only a slight drop of 0.2 percent for 2010. The report was based on giving by two main types of foundations, family foundations and professionally run national foundations. Family foundations accounted for $19.5 billion in total giving, or almost half of the $41 billion donated by all foundations in 2010.

Most family foundations have a smaller asset base than the big nationally known foundations like Ford, Carnegie, and Rockefeller, so many board members of nonprofits think they should concentrate on the big players in the field. This might be a mistake, because there are more family foundations than national foundations, their number is growing, and they are easier to develop a relationship with than the more formal and established national foundations.

Foundation fundraisers need specialized information to prepare an effective approach. Foundation profiles from sources such as the Foundation Center supply critical information, such as areas of giving, application deadlines and requirements, names of trustees, and size of prior gifts. The online version of the Foundation Directory also allows the user to search for valuable information in the foundation's 990 filing and to search the entire database using key words. See the nearby *Tips and Techniques* for several foundation resources.

Foundation Resources

There are several good foundation guides available.

- *Foundation Directory Online* from the Foundation Center (http://fconline.foundationcenter.org),
- *GrantStation* (www.grantstation.com), and
- GuideStar (http://www2.guidestar.org/).

While these resources cost money, the information they offer is invaluable if your organization wants to tap this key source of funding. Many foundations do maintain their own web sites, for further information, and *The Chronicle of Philanthropy* profiles giving from a number of national foundations in each issue.

Some community foundations and other community giving resource centers will provide these resources free of charge, so ask your staff to check out what's available in your community. Many larger nonprofits have a staff member who has expertise in foundation giving. Find out what resources are already on hand in your nonprofit and your community before dipping your toe in these waters.

TALES FROM THE BOARDROOM

A prominent billionaire real estate developer was invited to lunch with several members of the board to discuss a potential seven-figure gift. His lovely (third) wife was seated next to one of them.

"And what do you do?" asked the wife politely.

"I am the chair of the development committee," responded the board member.

"Development!" exclaimed the wife happily. "Why that's what my husband does, too."

Family Foundations

If you are approaching a family foundation, start with ones that are located in your region, since the majority of family foundations support local and regional interests. Look up the names of the foundation trustees for all the foundations in your geographic or metro area using one of the foundation guides listed here. Then circulate the list of trustees for each foundation to your board members for their review.

Ask board members to answer these questions when reviewing the list of foundation trustees: Do you have any connections to any of the names on the list? Whom do you know well enough to open the door to? Does their foundation give in our area of service? Do you know what their giving interests are?

The advantage to using an online foundation data service will quickly become apparent. Online research allows for a keyword search, so you can search for a word related to your fundraising cause, such as "dogs" or "housing" or "history." There are also search capabilities by trustee name, zip code, interest areas, and foundation name.

Once you develop a list of potential foundations and find out if your board has any connections to foundation trustees, you are ready to start making contact (see Exhibit 10.1).

EXHIBIT 10.1

Steps for Approaching Family Foundations

- Find a foundation trustee whom you or one of your board members knows or is acquainted with.

- Visit the friendly trustee with your team and try to have the person become your advocate with the rest of the foundation's board.

- Ask the trustee for advice and help on whom in the family to see, what they like to give to, and how much to ask for.

- Ask if the foundation's trustees would like to hold their next board meeting at your organization, and offer a tour of your site.

- Ask if the foundation will allow you and your team to make a presentation about your proposal to them at their next meeting.

- Write a strong proposal and ask the trustee whom you know if he or she will read a draft of it and give you advice.

- Make sure you touch base with all the family members who need to be courted before you make your application.

- Research and follow the guidelines for submitting a proposal to the foundation by the appropriate deadline.

- Recognize all the members of the family in subsequent events and printed materials to avoid making anyone angry.

For family foundations, personal contacts are very important, and many times the prospect you know can be treated like an individual donor. Make contact using someone the foundation trustee knows, make a call using your team approach, and ask whether the foundation would consider a proposal from your organization. Follow the basic elements of the solicitation process described in Chapter 7, but gear your questions and comments toward what the foundation would prefer to support.

Foundation trustees who are convinced of the worthiness of your cause will often give you good advice on key strategic points, such as who else in the family you will need to talk to, which item from the table of needs to ask for, and how much to ask for. Some trustees become so involved with helping the ask along that they offer to read a preliminary proposal. Don't hesitate to accept whatever assistance is offered! Help from the inside is always welcome.

Foundations usually require a written proposal or letter that meets specific guidelines. Find out when the applications are due (deadlines are listed in the *Foundation Directory Online* and on the foundation's web site, or you can call them) and make sure you are using the right format.

If you have staff in your organization who are used to working with foundations, ask them to help you put together a proposal. Sometimes in small organizations the executive director writes foundation proposals. Proposal writing is a skill, and it tends to get better with experience. There are proposal writers for hire in every community who can help your organization put together a strong proposal if you don't have access to someone with this skill on staff.

National Foundations

The approach to national foundations is fundamentally different from the approach to individuals and family foundations. The large national foundations like Ford, Carnegie, Gates, and Rockefeller are run by foundation professionals, people who are trained to give away money to meet specific foundation goals.

The goals set by national foundations may be authentically philanthropic, but they are often very focused on solving specific problems. Giving to support the widespread use of inoculations against disease in Africa, for instance, might be one foundation's goal. This goal may or may not be very closely related to the work that your organization undertakes. Many national foundations prefer giving to program support, rather than capital or endowment. Once again, good research is required to identify those foundations that give in ways that meet your organization's needs.

Don't waste your time writing proposals to national foundations that are not going to give in your area of interest. Even if the Gates Foundation is the wealthiest foundation in the world, if they don't focus on your organization's cause and field of endeavor, they aren't going to give to your nonprofit.

Table 10.1 shows the top five U.S. foundations and the total dollars they give away in a year.

TABLE 10.1

The Five Largest National Foundations by Giving (2010)	
Bill and Melinda Gates Foundation	**$3.055 billion**
Ford Foundation	$468.3 million
Buffett Foundation	$407.9 million
Walton Family Foundation	$360.4 million
Hewlett Foundation	$358.1 million
Source: Foundation Directory Online	

Once you have identified a national foundation that gives in your field of interest, see the foundation's own web site for details on programs, contacts, and application information. Then call the program director. The program director will often work directly with you (or your staff member) if they think your project would be of interest to the foundation. You may also get some help from your local community foundation in making contact with program directors at national foundations that support your cause.

National foundations are less approachable and less interested in personal connections than other kinds of giving entities, but this doesn't mean they are immune from the personal touch. Consider making a visit if encouraged to do so. Some foundation program managers make a visit to your site before approving proposals. Look around and learn which foundations are active in your region; sometimes foundations take a regional approach to a problem (e.g., the homeless or access to affordable housing) and are looking for local and regional partners.

IN THE REAL WORLD

Foundation Giving Post-Katrina

National foundations and even foreign governments have played an active role in disaster recovery and rebuilding. Many of the leading national foundations were very active in New Orleans after Katrina. Several sent personal representatives down to survey the situation on the ground and invested millions of dollars in recovery projects.

In their response to the disaster, the foundations made their giving and application requirements more flexible, and they supported a broad range of needs, from building homes to rebuilding the city's famous arts and culture infrastructure. The outpouring of generosity from private sources, mostly individuals and foundations, was in direct contrast to the slow and bureaucratic response of most government entities.

What did this giving look like? The government of France made a generous grant and loaned the artwork to support the first major art exhibit to open post-Katrina, an exhibition of French Impressionist and contemporary

(continued)

> **IN THE REAL WORLD (CONTINUED)**
>
> portraits of women at the New Orleans Museum of Art. The Rockefeller
> Foundation helped to fund the creation of a citywide recovery plan with
> neighborhood input. The Ford Foundation and the Getty Foundation provided
> grants in the arts to a number of organizations. Several national foundations
> supported school reform in New Orleans by funding new charter schools, re-
> sulting in dramatic changes to public education in the post-Katrina
> landscape.

Corporate Philanthropy

Corporate giving has changed dramatically over the past few decades. At one
time, the top corporate executives made mostly personal choices about charitable support, directing large charitable gifts to areas where the CEO maintained
a personal interest, such as his alma mater or a nonprofit where he served on the
board. Smaller corporate giving was often ad hoc, local, and mostly separate
from the company's business and marketing needs.

That personal model has become less common as corporate philanthropy is
now more aligned with the values, mission, and goals selected by the company
as a focus for their community outreach. Philanthropy has turned into one aspect of big business; the identification of large corporations with specific causes
has become an important part of corporate marketing and image enhancement.

Giving USA 2011 reports that corporate giving rose 10.6 percent in 2010 to
a total of $15 billion. Note that this is still only a little more than one-third of
the total giving by foundations, which was $41 billion. Corporate giving, while
important to many nonprofits, represents only a small piece of the total charitable giving pie ($15 billion out of $290 billion in total giving for 2010, which
amounts to about 5 percent of all donations).

Today, corporate giving is often managed by a community affairs director or
gifts are made through a separate corporate foundation with its own board.
Many public companies now have to answer to their shareholders for the distribution of philanthropic dollars. This doesn't mean that corporate philanthropy
is dead—far from it; but company leaders now target their gifts to communities

where their presence will make an impact on workers, their communities, and selected causes that will make them "look good." These causes are selected with care to match the company's desired values.

Some companies have chosen to target their giving in sectors that match their business interests, such as housing, or children's health issues, or animal welfare. Others give their money to a specific cause, like "solving hunger," or "curing cancer," that they feel will improve the company's image or appeal to the companies' customers.

Many companies now make sure that they get as much "bang for their buck" as is possible, making demands on nonprofits for enhanced visibility, marketing, and benefits in return for financial support. Contracts between non-profits and corporate donors are now more common, spelling out exactly what advertising, PR, naming rights, and benefits are expected. An increased emphasis on cause marketing and co-branding has stepped up the number of tie-ins between nonprofits and their business partners.

In short, corporate giving has become more corporate—more like a business decision and less like a philanthropic decision.

Corporate philanthropy has also become more global as the American economy has expanded globally. The non-American boards of huge international companies like Shell Oil are beginning to become more involved in setting giving policy. Much more corporate and foundation money is being directed to global needs such as health and education in the underdeveloped countries where international companies work, hire, develop natural resources, and sell their products. Those nonprofits that work and deliver services in a global environment may find their potential for corporate support expanding and their recognition needs becoming tied to the international marketplace.

Review the web sites of national companies to see what kinds of community support they provide. Many national firms now have community funds or corporate foundations to distribute funds in regions where they do business. Find out how to tap these funds through research on the company's web site and make a visit to the local site manager or community giving coordinator.

Most of these funds are small, under $5,000, but they can come in handy when your organization needs additional support.

TALES FROM THE BOARDROOM

A small nonprofit received a gift from a very generous donor who ran a restaurant supply company that counted several local restaurants among its customers. The chair of the board invited the donor out to dinner at a well-regarded local restaurant to celebrate the gift. The chair ordered what he thought was a great appetizer for the table.

"I can't eat this," the donor said, making a face when the food arrived. "This isn't made from one of the brands we carry."

YOUR ROLE AS A BOARD MEMBER

Start your search for viable corporate prospects with a list of local and regional companies that operate in your community. Such lists are readily available from regional business publications or your local chamber. Research is important to determine which companies are making a profit (especially in times of economic uncertainty) and which ones have local ownership (they are more likely to invest in the local community).

Then identify those whom your board knows. Compile and circulate a list of local corporate and business leaders to all the members of your board. CEOs, corporate managers, corporate board members, and owners of private businesses are more likely to have the clout to make a giving decision than mere employees. You can approach the community giving officer of your local bank, for instance, but if you or another board member can set up a meeting with the bank president, your organization is more likely to get the gift.

RULES OF THE ROAD

Don't accept a gift from a corporation that you wouldn't be proud to see publicly aligned with your nonprofit. Your organization's reputation is worth more in the long run than the money they can give.

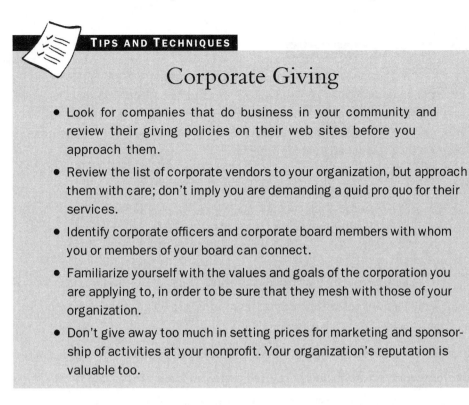

TIPS AND TECHNIQUES

Corporate Giving

- Look for companies that do business in your community and review their giving policies on their web sites before you approach them.

- Review the list of corporate vendors to your organization, but approach them with care; don't imply you are demanding a quid pro quo for their services.

- Identify corporate officers and corporate board members with whom you or members of your board can connect.

- Familiarize yourself with the values and goals of the corporation you are applying to, in order to be sure that they mesh with those of your organization.

- Don't give away too much in setting prices for marketing and sponsorship of activities at your nonprofit. Your organization's reputation is valuable too.

Planned Giving: Add to Your Fundraising Toolbox

Many of the largest major gifts actually arrive as planned gifts. All board fundraising volunteers should be trained and updated on planned giving tools in order to make the best of opportunities that may arise with donors. And if your organization is conducting an endowment campaign, think planned gifts—many endowment donors make their gifts by using planned giving techniques.

A major gift donor will often make more than one gift during his or her lifetime of involvement with an organization, but in some cases the "ultimate" gift will be a planned gift. It should be a long-term goal of donor engagement to bring a donor to the point where the feasibility of a planned gift can be discussed.

Planned gifts can also be a method of increasing the size of a major gift, especially in cases where a gift made from income, rather than one made from assets, might result in a smaller dollar amount. Most endowment gifts, for instance, come to nonprofits through planned gifts, especially from bequests.

Fundraising through planned giving does not have to be conducted solely by a professional who specializes in trusts and estate planning. Board members and volunteers who are properly trained and who keep up-to-date on the various elements of planned giving can begin the process by introducing the topic to potential donors.

Acting as the donor's financial or legal advisor can become the basis for a conflict of interest lawsuit if relatives feel that the nonprofit has taken advantage of the donor. So can asking people for money if they are no longer legally considered of sound mind. The IRS and the SEC (the United States Securities and Exchange Commission) have taken a dim view of charitable organizations acting as estate planners or investment and tax advisers. So keep the conversation on the types of gifts available and why the donor should support your nonprofit's cause.

Planned giving is just a tool for giving. What counts most is the donor's intent to give. The gift will be moved forward by the quality of the relationship between the donor, you and your team making the call, and the nonprofit. If the intent to give is there, the use of planned giving is just one tool that you have available to make the gift work for the donor and for your organization.

YOUR ROLE AS A BOARD MEMBER

When talking about planned gifts, you do have to be careful not to offer specific legal or financial advice to the donor. It is appropriate for you to familiarize the donor with various types of planned giving options, including trusts, bequests, and charitable annuities. You can also help the donor learn the benefits and limits of each different type of giving arrangement. In some cases, learning about new giving tools might help the donor to support the nonprofit in a different manner than he or she is contemplating, and could actually bring benefits to the donor.

Most sophisticated donors will have their own legal, financial, and estate planning experts to attend to their needs. Your role should focus on encouraging the donor to make a gift, educating the donor about the options available, offering to supply information, and supporting the intent of the donor. Do not offer to write trusts or wills, or work on tax returns! This is a clear conflict of interest.

RULES OF THE ROAD

Do not act as the donor's legal or financial advisor, even if the donor asks you to take on this role. It could be viewed as a conflict of interest because of your position on the board of the nonprofit where the donor is making a contribution.

How to Recognize a Planned Giving Prospect

Planned giving prospects are surprisingly easy to find—they exist all over, even among potential donors who might not consider themselves wealthy. And planned gifts are not just for seniors. Research shows that planned giving donors are likely to add charitable causes to their estate plans in their 50s and 60s, especially when they are planning for their retirement. (See *Discovering the Secret Giver*, a report available at stelter.com. The Stelter Company supplies planned giving products and advice for a fee.)

Planned gifts are usually gifts made from assets, not gifts from income or cash reserves. Thus it is superficial, and ultimately foolhardy, to assume that people who don't look wealthy can't make planned gifts. Often, those who spend the least have the most money saved up somewhere.

Astonishing stories have emerged as part of development lore of people who left huge bequests to charity who had no apparent means. A few years ago, there was the famous example of the Mississippi laundress who had saved hundreds of thousands of dollars over a lifetime of manual labor. It all went to charity. Recently in New Orleans an older Jewish man left over one million dollars when he died to restore his synagogue. His fellow congregants thought he was indigent.

IN THE REAL WORLD

Where There Is a Will (or an Insurance Policy), There Is a Way

Two professors, married to each other for 40 years, worked at the same institution. After the husband passed away, the wife wanted to create an endowed chair, both to memorialize her husband and to assure that work would go on in his field of research.

Neither had any wealth beyond the usual faculty retirement funds, but both were passionately committed to furthering research in their field of study. Madame Professor knew that she could never save enough to make a gift or a bequest to fund a chair, which required an endowment of $1,000,000. Although she was approaching late middle age, she was in good health, so she shopped around and bought two life insurance policies and dedicated them to underwriting the chair.

Within a few years Madame suffered a massive heart attack and passed away. The insurance policies paid to fund the chair almost immediately. Her husband's name lives on and so does his area of research, just as she desired.

Due to the wide array of vehicles and options in the planned gift arena, planned giving donors come in all shapes and sizes. Retirees with substantial savings in their retirement plans make wonderful planned giving donors. Entrepreneurs who have taken their company public make wonderful planned giving donors. Couples who have tired of their second home and want to get tax advantages for giving away the property make wonderful planned giving donors. And anyone who has made—or plans to make—a will is a wonderful planned giving donor.

TIPS AND TECHNIQUES

Helpful Hints to Find Planned Giving Donors

If you hear a donor say:

- I am planning to retire soon.
- I am working on my estate plans.
- I need my money to support my children.
- I want to make sure my wife is taken care of after I'm gone.

He is a potential planned giving donor.

If you know that she has:

- A second home she no longer uses regularly.
- A company she started about to go public.
- An income stream from rental property.
- A 401(k) or other tax-deferred retirement account.
- A primary residence that will not be needed by her heirs.

She is a potential planned giving donor.

Types of Planned Gifts

Sometimes nonprofits, as well as donors, think of planned giving as only providing a long-term benefit to the organization through bequests and charitable trusts. While such gifts can be very valuable to the organization, they are often underrated because organizations have pressing needs now and want gifts that can be used now.

Some planned gifts can be structured for use immediately and can provide current cash for projects underway. These gifts include gifts of real estate (as

EXHIBIT 10.2

Types of Planned Gifts

I. Gifts That Provide Funds for Current Use
- Charitable lead trust—provides a stream of income over a period of years to the nonprofit, then the assets revert to the beneficiaries at the end of the trust period.
- Real estate—gifted, then sold by the nonprofit.
- Gifts of marketable securities—stocks or bonds.
- Dedicated income stream from royalties or rental income.
- Donated art or other real property—gifted, then sold by the nonprofit.

II. Gifts That Provide Funds on a Deferred Basis
- Charitable remainder trust—provides a stream of income over a period of years to the income beneficiary, then the assets go to the nonprofit at the end of the trust period.
- Charitable gift annuity—donor makes a gift; nonprofit agrees to pay an income stream to the donor for life; nonprofit invests the gift.
- Bequest or other estate gifts.
- Most gifts of life insurance.
- Gifts of tax-deferred retirement plans.

long as the organization can sell it), stocks, bonds, gifts assigning a stream of royalties to the nonprofit, and donated works of art or other real property (if the nonprofit is able to sell them). See Exhibit 10.2 for types of planned gifts that can be used to meet current uses and those that are better matched with deferred needs.

Consider Charitable Trusts

Charitable gift annuities and charitable remainder trusts are popular vehicles for donors, because they provide income over the lifetime of the donor to him or his beneficiaries.

You may already be familiar with charitable remainder trusts, which are useful for providing for a spouse or child who needs ongoing support. These vehicles, which are commonly known as life income plans, do have some cost for the non-profit, which must pay the annuity or, in the case of the trust, won't receive the money until after the beneficiaries have passed away. If well invested, however, these instruments can earn money in the long term for the nonprofit.

Some charitable trusts, such as charitable lead trusts, can provide income for the nonprofit right away. The charitable lead trust is the mirror image of the more common charitable remainder trust. In the lead trust, the donor transfers assets to a trust that pays income to the nonprofit for a set number of years, and then the assets go to the donor's beneficiaries at the end of the trust period.

The charitable lead trust is even more bankable than a pledge, since it is a legally binding document that assures an income stream to the nonprofit over the life of the trust. For this reason, charitable lead trusts are especially valuable in capital campaigns, where cash flows need to be assured. (This vehicle is complex to create and administer and requires outside legal advice, so it is most useful for donors of seven-figure gifts.)

Bequests: The Most Popular Form of Planned Giving

Other planned gifts are focused on deferred giving. Working with these gifts can bring powerful resources down the road to the nonprofit, because the largest philanthropic gifts are often made through bequests and trusts. Bequests produced over $22 billion (8 percent of total charitable giving) for nonprofits in 2010 (as reported in Giving USA 2011).

Bequests are probably the easiest planned giving vehicle to understand. (See Exhibit 10.3.) The donor, if she has a will, can add a codicil making a gift to the nonprofit. If she doesn't have a will, encouraging her to do so is of lasting benefit to her entire family.

The main advantage of a bequest is that the donor has the full use of her assets during her lifetime. Many older women, who often outlive their husbands, are most comfortable with bequest giving, because it is a vehicle that allows them to be certain that their money will take care of them throughout their life, and if necessary, provide for their final care and medical costs. See Exhibit 10.3 for more on giving through bequests.

Because bequests and wills are subject to change by the donor at any time, most organizations do not announce or grant recognition to this type of gift until it is actually received, meaning that the donor has passed away. See the nearby *Tips and Techniques* for ways to thank bequest donors through recognition and active stewardship. Since bequests can be changed at any time during the donor's lifetime, it is important for the nonprofit to keep these donors in the fold through ongoing attention and active involvement in the work of the organization.

TIPS AND TECHNIQUES

Recognition for Donors of Planned Gifts

- Most gifts made through bequests are not recognized during the donor's lifetime, that is, until the donor has passed away and the gift is received.

- Talk to donors directly about making a major gift while they are still alive, when they can see the impact that their gift makes on the organization.

- Ask the donor if he or she is willing to enter into an irrevocable giving arrangement, such as a charitable trust.

- Work with endowment donors to set up the endowed account with a smaller gift while the donor is alive, and then ask the donors to fully endow the project through a gift in their will. Family members can continue to make contributions to endowed funds after the original donor has passed away.

- Identify future donors of bequests (known as "bequest intentions" in development circles) and other planned gift donors and recognize them through the establishment of a planned giving society.

- Offer annual recognition to the members of the planned giving society in the annual report, list them on a special donor wall, and invite them to annual events to keep them abreast of the organization's activities.

TALES FROM THE BOARDROOM

The executive director of the nonprofit asked a prominent attorney for $2 million. The next week the attorney was indicted in a plot to steal money from his clients. The director went to his board for advice. "Don't you think we should drop the gift discussion?" he asked his board members.

"Well, let's not be hasty here," a board member responded. "Can't we wait and see what happens when he's convicted? All that money he stole has to go somewhere."

EXHIBIT 10.3

All about Bequests

Advantages of Giving through a Bequest:

- A gift through a bequest can be made in any amount.

- Bequests can be added by codicil to a will already drawn up.

- Bequests allow the donor the use of the funds during her lifetime.

- Bequests are gifts that are relatively easy to make and to honor.

- Bequests can make a very large impact on an institution.

Types of Bequests:

- A specific dollar amount can be identified.

- A percentage of the estate can be named.

- The gift can be a residual interest in the estate.

- The gift can be real property or real estate named in the will.

Uses of Bequests:

- Unrestricted (for general use).

- Restricted, for uses such as program support, equipment, facility mainte-nance, or capital projects.

- Establish a named endowed fund in perpetuity.

- Add to an existing endowed fund.

Gifts of insurance and tax-deferred retirement plans are also popular forms of delayed, or deferred, giving. Insurance and retirement plan gifts have the advantage of requiring less legal advice than trusts. The donor can just sign over a policy or make the nonprofit the beneficiary of his or her retirement plan.

How to Talk About Planned Giving

While the tools of the planned giving trade—trusts, bequests, insurance, real estate, annuities—are often complex, the actual concept of giving away something that the donor owns other than cash or pledges is not difficult to grasp, and it can be explained easily to even financially unsophisticated donors.

Often the most difficult issue for you as a board member is how to bring up the concept of planned giving in a conversation with a donor. Certainly one would not wish to be crude or to pry too much into a donor's personal estate plans. And in our society, many people find talk about or inference of death to be inappropriate. There are some key indications, however, that a donor might find it helpful to consider a planned gift (see "Helpful Hints to Find Planned Giving Donors" in *the Tips and Techniques* above).

A good way to introduce the topic of planned giving is to bring up an example of a planned gift that another donor has made. This can be done without naming the donor if permission hasn't specifically been granted to use her name, but it is often more powerful with a name attached, especially if the donor's name is well known. Then, using this other gift as an example, you can offer information on planned giving options.

 TIPS AND TECHNIQUES

How to Talk About Planned Giving

For example, if the donor is concerned about providing for his wife or child after he is deceased, bring up the charitable remainder trust in the following manner:

Many of our donors have found that planned gift options have helped them to resolve the same kind of issue you are facing. I know that Suzie Jones and

> *her husband have recently made a gift like that. Do you know how the charitable remainder trust works?*
>
> Follow up by talking about the advantages and disadvantages of the type of planned giving arrangement that might work for this donor. Knowing the benefits and advantages of each type of planned gift arrangement should be part of your training in planned gifts.

Another way to bring planned giving to the attention of a donor is to offer to forward information as a follow-up to a visit:

I would like to send you something on charitable remainder trusts that might help you to think about how to provide for your wife and daughters.

Your own sense of tact, your training and familiarity with the tools, and your knowledge of the donor will all enter into the decision about how and when to bring up planned giving in the conversation.

Be sure to ask your organization to provide training on planned giving as part of your fundraising preparation. Such training should be provided by a consultant, attorney, or staff member who is professionally trained as a specialist in planned giving. All board members who are acting as fundraising volunteers should be trained in planned gifts and be prepared to step in when the situation makes one of these tools an appropriate option for the donor to consider.

Marketing of Planned Gifts

Planned gifts can be made in response to marketing materials produced by the nonprofit. Several high-quality for-profit companies now offer an extensive array of brochures, pamphlets, web sites, and newsletters that cover planned gifts. Donor stories, examples, and information are all offered in layman's language. See Exhibit 10.4 for advice.

Your organization can personalize these materials to the extent that they look as if they were created in-house. With the help of these sophisticated marketing materials, you can produce a planned giving program without actually having the technical support of a lawyer or planned giving specialist on your staff.

EXHIBIT 10.4

Where to Go to Get Help with Planned Giving

See offerings from the Stelter Company, at stelter.com, and the Sharpe Group, at sharpenet.com. Both are for-profit firms that offer research, consulting, materials, and seminars on planned gifts and planned giving. One of the latest products offered by Stelter, for instance, is an interactive planned giving web site that connects seamlessly with your own organization's web site. It not only provides information and donor stories, but it has an online planned gift calculator so that your donors can plan their own gifts.

TIPS AND TECHNIQUES

Gifts of Retirement Plan Assets*

A nonprofit can be named as a beneficiary of a donor's IRA, tax-sheltered annuity, Keogh plan, 401(k), or other qualified pension and profit-sharing plans.

Advantages of Giving through Retirement Plan Assets

- It is easy to execute: Simply name the nonprofit as a beneficiary of the plan.
- The funds pass to the nonprofit outside of probate and free of all taxes.
- Gets both estate and income tax savings.
- May be better for heirs than giving through a bequest because of the tax advantages.

* This area of estate planning is subject to change in legislation enacted by Congress. Check with an attorney or tax expert before giving this advice to donors.

Interactive planned giving web sites, like those offered by Stelter, have the capability to show the donor what tax advantages and benefits might accrue to him given certain financial parameters that he enters himself. These web sites can be linked to an institutional web site in a seamless manner. Web sites can be coordinated with newsletters to create a continuous array of planned giving information.

Another effective marketing tool is to find real-life examples of planned gifts that have been made to your institution and profile those donors in newsletters, mailings, and on web sites. Use donors who have made planned gifts to help explain the advantages that accrued to them in their own words.

Remember that bequests and wills can be changed at any time by the donor before he or she passes away. Most deferred gifts are not irrevocable. Therefore good stewardship and donor relations are important elements of creating an ongoing relationship with bequest donors.

Creating a planned giving donor society that recognizes those who have made gifts to your organization through their estate plans is a good option for developing a bequest donor stewardship program. Offer benefits such as events, newsletters, donor honor rolls, and membership certificates.

Consider asking all board members to commit to including the organization in their estate plans. As we have discussed in other aspects of fundraising, board leadership can set the pace for others in the community.

Finally, make sure that all inquiries are followed up on personally by a volunteer or staff member. Properly constructed, your organization's planned giving program can provide ongoing assets for years to come.

Stewardship Programs

Stewardship is the overall term for the array of activities that are undertaken to keep donors happy with their giving to an organization and to make sure that all donor-driven agreements and legal requirements regarding the gifts are met. At its simplest level, stewardship involves thanking donors in a genuine and personal manner for their commitment.

Stewardship activities can be much more sophisticated, however, and involve elements such as personalized reports that show how the donor's money has been put to use, having the donor meet with beneficiaries of the nonprofit's services, and creating events to celebrate high-level gifts.

Good stewardship is the key to bringing donors back to make additional gifts. Whether the gift is for annual giving, a campaign, or endowment, donors want to be kept informed, treated right, and have their intentions honored.

Major gift experts now talk about building "lifetime relationships" with donors, from the first gift to the final bequest. Good stewardship is the basic currency of this relationship.

What are the components of good stewardship programs? Donor stewardship starts with the receipt of the gift and continues throughout the pledge payment period, and in the case of endowed gifts, may continue throughout the donor's lifetime.

Basic stewardship requires that the donor receive a gift receipt and a thank-you, that the money is spent in the way the donor intended, and that any recognition promised is delivered. Good stewardship should also involve ongoing communication so that the donor is aware of how his or her gift has been used, the result of the giving for the organization, and the effect on the services it provides.

See Exhibit 10.5 for the main elements of a good stewardship program.

EXHIBIT 10.5

The Basic Components of a Stewardship Program

- Send out a receipt right away with the correct information.

- Send a personal thank-you letter in addition to the gift receipt.

- Arrange a thank-you call from a board member for a very special gift.

- Confirm with the donor, in writing, the basic terms of the gift; this will include: the naming rights being offered, the full gift amount, the pledge period with payment dates, how the donor wants his name listed (or not listed), and the specified purpose of the gift.

- Keep the terms of the gift on file so that when the staff changes the gift will still be handled correctly.

- Adhere to the terms of the gift and make sure that the relevant staff understand and observe the terms of the gift.

- Keep the donor informed about the use of the gift on at least an annual basis.

- For donors of endowed gifts, supply annual reports on the endowment's growth, payout, and use.

Your Role as a Board Member

You can help provide good stewardship to your organization's donors. Thank those donors whom you see for their giving. Write handwritten notes when people you know make a gift. Talk about the good work that is being done with their money. Attend donor recognition events and campaign events, such as dedication ceremonies, where you can thank donors personally for their support.

The key point to remember about stewardship is that satisfied and informed donors are more likely to say good things about your organization and to give again. It is much less expensive to keep getting gifts from the same donors than it is to identify, cultivate, and solicit new donors. Providing good stewardship is a cost-effective way to keep donors giving and to improve fundraising results for the long term. Good stewardship makes your job as a fundraiser easier!

In the Real World

Homemade Stewardship

At a nonprofit that serves the needs of the aging in a small town in Texas, there are two elderly board members who give $10,000 to the annual fund, year in and year out. These two donors literally keep the program running with their generous annual support.

How to thank them? The creative development committee chair took a bag of locally sourced pecans she bought at a farmer's market and baked the donors a homemade pecan pie. Those two will keep giving as long as they know they are appreciated (and they don't have to declare their pies to the IRS, either).

Overcoming Common Barriers to Success
Why Talk About Planned Giving?
We Won't See Any Results for Years.

Planned giving is like a hidden advantage—it can provide resources that your organization never even knew were coming. Those people who fundraise for your nonprofit 20 to 30 years from now will thank you for your work today.

Planned gifts offer these advantages to the donor:

- Planned gifts allow the donor to make a larger gift than might be possible during his lifetime.
- Planned gifts allow the donor the use of her funds during her lifetime for unforeseeable needs.
- Planned gifts often allow the donor to realize tax advantages.
- Planned gifts can increase retirement income, depending on the vehicle selected.
- Planned gifts can be used to establish an endowed fund to honor a loved one in perpetuity.
- Planned gifts can allow the donor to pass assets to his heirs at a lower transfer tax cost.

All of these advantages can be useful in helping you close a gift from a donor who might not otherwise be willing to make a gift at all.

Planned gifts offer a number of advantages for your organization, too. They can increase the donor's gift level; they can bring long-term financial stability to the organization by providing a future cash flow; they can provide valuable funding for endowments; and they are a sign that people support the long-term health and welfare of your organization. They are the "ultimate gift" from someone who cares about your cause.

CONFRONTING POSSIBLE ETHICAL PROBLEMS FROM A CORPORATE GIFT

This is a scenario that has become more likely with the advent of corporate malfeasance (think Enron), so it's important for your development committee to set policies ahead of time for the review and acceptance of corporate gifts and partnerships. Some nonprofits have learned to their dismay that certain corporations are not above using their community giving to clean up a bad corporate image.

Environmental polluters, for instance, have used this tactic for years, making offers to support a number of environmentally focused groups in an effort to "clean up" their name. Or companies that do animal research may try to give money to animal welfare groups to buy off their opposition. Some boards feel that it's acceptable to take money from a source with opposing values because the nonprofit will be using the money to correct past wrongs.

You and your board will have to decide what the right thing to do is in each situation. It's clear that taking money crosses the line and becomes unethical if your organization is being asked to "sell out" by dropping opposition to or endorsing a specific product that repudiates your values. But these issues can become murky, and the need for the money is a strong motivating force.

The bottom line: Your organization has many opportunities to raise money, but making one big mistake can sully the organization's reputation for years. Be responsible, be careful, and set policy ahead of time to protect your organization over the long term.

Summary

Giving by individuals can be augmented by gifts from corporations and foundations. Approaching these groups, however, may require different skills and special training. Review foundation guidelines to find a good source of support for community needs. Make sure that your organization is willing to offer corporate sponsorships and marketing tie-ins before you promise them to a corporate donor.

Planned giving techniques are good tools for all volunteer fundraisers to have in their back pocket. Focus on the donor's needs and beware of going over the line in providing financial or legal advice—this can get you and your organization into hot water. Planned gifts are not just for seniors, and they can be very helpful in increasing the size of the gift that a donor can make.

And finally, pay attention to the stewardship of donors who give to your organization. Good stewardship includes thanking donors properly, keeping them informed about the use of their gifts, and taking the time to keep them engaged in the work of your organization. Keep your current donors happy so that you can go back to them for future gifts, making your role as a board fundraiser that much easier.

Appendix

Note: This book has a companion web site at www.wiley.com/go/board fundraising, where readers can go to download all of the materials that appear in this Appendix for use in a board retreat or in a board training session. The materials are available on the web site for you or your staff to download and edit to personalize in order to meet your organization's needs. Included exclusively on the web site is the PowerPoint presentation, "The 5 Elements of the Successful Ask," which can used as one segment of a training session for board members.

Materials for a Board Retreat on Fundraising

Preparation

1. Board Retreat basics:

- Invite all board members, the executive director/CEO, the CFO, the chief advancement officer (CAO), and any advancement staff whose role is to support board members with their fundraising.

- Make certain that the chairman of the board, the development committee chair, and the campaign chair or co-chairs (if the nonprofit is in a campaign) can all attend when setting the date.

- Set a four- to five-hour time frame.

- Hold at a site away from the nonprofit, such as a boardroom, hotel room, or conference center.

- Provide food: breakfast items, a light lunch, and some healthy snack items, as well as coffee and cold drinks (nonalcoholic, unless you really want people to be creative!).

- Ask attendees to dress casually and to turn off their phones.

- Set up the room in a U-shape or casual conference style around a table and avoid stiff rows of chairs and formal settings.

2. **Select a meeting leader/facilitator:**

   The selection of the right meeting leader or facilitator is important to your Retreat's success. If you select someone in-house, identify an experienced leader who is respected by all who attend. Make sure he or she is prepared to listen to and coach others as well as present information. The chief advancement officer (CAO), the executive director/CEO, or an experienced volunteer could be the right person to lead the group if he or she brings fundraising experience and the appropriate communication skills.

   Many boards hire a consultant to conduct their Board Retreat. A consultant provides several advantages over an in-house facilitator:

   - The consultant provides a fresh voice that may shed new light on a familiar topic.

   - The consultant usually brings a high skill level.

   - The consultant may bring in other examples from a broader array of nonprofits that could be helpful to your group.

   - The consultant is sometimes more respected than an in-house session leader.

   - More board members will show up to hear what the consultant has to say (provides variety and interest as a new voice).

   Not every fundraising consultant is skilled at this kind of board training. If possible, check to see if the consultant you hire has done board training before, get recommendations, and check references. Be sure to meet with the consultant ahead of time to discuss specific issues relevant to your board. A consultant who has worked in your community or one who has helped to fundraise for the cause your organization works on might be best suited to your needs.

3. **Create a small planning group to prepare for the retreat:**

   Create a small planning group, including most or all of the following: The executive director (CEO), the chief financial officer (CFO), the chief advancement officer (CAO), the consultant or facilitator, the board chair, the campaign chair, and the development committee chair. This is the work of the planning group:

   - Review sample agenda for Board Retreat and adjust for your own organization's needs (see Attachment 1).

   - Establish primary Board Retreat goals (see Attachment 2).

   - Review all other materials (Attachments 3 through 10) with the planning group in advance and adjust for your organization's needs. Make sure everyone in the planning group is in agreement on key points, such as fundraising goals and areas of need.

   - Prepare the top prospect list (NOT PROVIDED) for review by the board with the help of advancement staff or development committee members.

   - Assign roles for presentation and review discussion points with each presenter (see Sample Retreat Agenda with discussion points). Provide talking points for discussion leaders if desired.

   - Make sure the facilitator understands the goals, needs, and history of the fundraising efforts in your nonprofit before the Retreat.

4. **Materials needed for a Board Retreat and where to find them:**

   Note: all sample materials noted here are provided in this Appendix and on the companion web site to this book at www.wiley.com/go/boardfundraising. Downloading the materials from the web site allows you to personalize them to meet the needs of your organization.

Attachment 1. Board Retreat Agenda

A sample is provided in this Appendix and on the web site. Edit the presentation content, presenters, goals, and timetable to meet the needs of your organization.

Attachment 2. Board Retreat Goals

A sample is provided in this Appendix and on the web site. Edit the goals to meet the needs of your board and your nonprofit.

Attachment 3. Table of Needs

A sample is provided in this Appendix and on the web site. This is the list of the areas the organization has determined it needs to raise funds for, with costs if they are available; e.g., operating funds, a new building, program support, and endowment. This list should be developed through a strategic planning process held prior to the retreat.

Note: If no prior planning session has occurred, use the retreat to develop a table of needs and allot more time for this discussion.

Attachment 4. Fundraising Goals and Timetable

A sample is provided in this Appendix and on the web site. This is a one-page summary of all fundraising goals, annual and capital, with a timetable, provided by the CEO, CFO, and/or CAO.

Note: If no prior planning has occurred, use the retreat to develop goals and timetable and allot more time for this discussion.

Attachment 5. Case Statement Summary

A sample is provided in this Appendix and on the web site. This is a one-page summary of messages and themes focused on why a donor should make a gift to this organization at this time for the needs identified.

A draft of the case statement summary can be prepared in advance by the CEO and/or the CAO, or it can be the focus of a retreat discussion led by the meeting facilitator.

Note: If the facilitator is starting without a case statement draft, allot more time to this discussion.

Attachment 6. Board Policy on Giving

A sample is provided in this Appendix and on the web site; use the policy of your own board if one has been established.

Attachment 7. Charge to the Development Committee

A sample is provided in this Appendix and on the web site; use the charge to your own development committee if one has been established.

Attachment 8. Role of the Board and the Staff in Fundraising

A sample is provided in this Appendix and on the web site; edit to meet the needs of your organization and staffing levels.

Attachment 9. PowerPoint presentation on "5 Elements of the Successful Ask" (not available in the Appendix)

Visit companion web site www.wiley.com/go/boardfundraising to download; edit to meet the needs and experience level of your board.

Attachment 10. Three Sample Scripts for Role-Playing Calls

Three sample scripts for calls are provided in this Appendix and on the web site; edit to meet the needs of your organization or provide your own script.

List of Potential Prospects for Gifts

NOT PROVIDED. Make a list of the organization's top 50 to 100 prospects for review by the board; to be provided by the CAO or development committee chair.

Note: Bring backup info on each prospect, e.g., giving summaries and any prospect research available. Have this information available for reference, but do not copy or circulate to the board members; to be provided by the advancement staff.

Sample Board Retreat Agenda

Arrival—Light Breakfast Served   *8:30 am*

Section I: Creating the Fundraising Plan   *9:00 am*

1. Welcome and opening comments—Board Chair

   - Introduce Facilitator

   - Review agenda for the day

   - Review goals for the Retreat

2. What are we fundraising for?—Facilitator with CEO

   - Review or establish table of needs

3. How much do we need to raise?—Facilitator with Development Committee Chair and CAO

   - Review or establish fundraising goals and timeline

4. How can we make our best case (why should someone give)?—Facilitator

   - Discussion: What attracted each board member to the cause?

   - Review or establish key messages and themes

Short Break   ***10:30 am***

Section II: Getting Organized for Fundraising

1. What is our Board Giving Policy?—Facilitator with Board Chair

   - Review or establish a Board giving policy

2. Who is on the Team?—Facilitator, Development Committee Chair, CAO

   - Review or establish the charge to the Development Committee

   - Discussion of roles of Board, the CEO, and advancement staff

Section III: How to Ask for and Close a Gift   ***11:15 am***

1. PowerPoint: The 5 Elements of the Successful Ask— Facilitator

2. Role Play Exercise and Discussion—Facilitator with volunteers

Short Break   ***12:15 pm***

Section IV: Prospect Identification   ***12:30 pm***

—Development Committee Chair, CAO, Facilitator
(This section can be combined with a working lunch)

- Review top prospect list

- Discussion about how to identify new prospects

- Discussion about cultivation: how to engage prospects with the organization and its cause

Section V: Next Steps—Facilitator, Board Chair, CEO   *1:15 pm*

- Review retreat goals met and key decisions made

- Identify specific next steps for Board and staff

- Closing remarks—Board Chair

Adjourn   *1:30 pm*

Sample Board Retreat Agenda with Discussion Points

Note: All times are estimated. Some groups may take more or less time at certain points in the agenda than the time indicated here. If the morning discussion runs longer than indicated, consider deferring the Prospect Identification activity (Section IV) to another time. Either meet with individual board members to review lists or use part of a separate board meeting for group review of prospect names.

Participants Arrive; Serve a Light Breakfast and Coffee   *8:30 am*

Section I: Creating the Fundraising Plan   *9:00 am*

1. Welcome and Opening Comments (5 minutes)

Board Chair

- Welcome and introduce the facilitator to everyone.

- Review agenda for the day (refer to Attachment 1).

- Thank everyone for coming and giving their time for this important cause.

2. Review Key Retreat Goals (5 minutes)

Board Chair or Development Committee Chair

Review the key goals for board retreat (refer to Attachment 2):

- Unite the board in taking a leadership role in fundraising.

- Provide education on needs and goals.

- Secure advice and input from board members.

- Establish roles for board and staff.

- Develop skills and practice fundraising techniques.

- Identify top prospects.

- Define next steps for board and staff activities.

- Turn program over to the facilitator

3. What are we fundraising for? (30 minutes)

Facilitator with CEO

Review the table of needs (refer to Attachment 3):

- Explain why these needs are on the list.

- Tie to strategic plan for the nonprofit.

- Review cost of programs and needs in each funding area.

- Explain costs and opportunities to the organization of meeting or note meeting these needs.

- Identify needs in each funding area: operations, capital, program, and endowment

- Build board consensus for meeting fundraising needs.

4. Fundraising Goals and Timeline (20 minutes)

CEO or Development Committee Chair

Lead discussion on fundraising goals and timeline (refer to Attachment 4).

- Discuss the goal for each funding area and how goal was derived.

- Explain fundraising priorities and establish timelines.

- Discuss inclusion or exclusion of annual fund with other goals.

- Discuss types of campaigns and campaign goals and timelines if a campaign is under consideration.

- Discuss the "marketability" of each goal area.

- Build board consensus for fundraising goals and timeline.

5. **Making the Case (30 minutes)**

Facilitator with full board

Review case summary (refer to Attachment 5).

Facilitator leads discussion on case, asks questions like:

- What is important to you about this organization?
- Why do you give to this nonprofit?
- Why do you think other people give to this organization?
- What are the key messages we should be communicating to our donors?
- Why would people want to give for the needs we have identified?
- How can we talk about the people who benefit from our services?
- How can we communicate the urgency of our needs?
- Build board consensus for case themes and messages.

Short Break   *10:30 am*

6. **Board Giving Policy (10 minutes)**

Board Chair: Review board giving policy (refer to Attachment 6)

Facilitator leads discussion, asks questions such as:

- How can we set the pace to enhance overall giving?
- Do we want to set a 100 pecent board giving goal?
- Do we want to set a minimum dollar amount each board member is expected to give?
- Who will organize the effort and ask the board for their gifts?
- Reach consensus on board giving policy and process for solicitation.

7. **Creating the Team (10 minutes)**

Review Charge to the Development Committee (Attachment 7).

Discussion led by Facilitator and Development Committee chair—

- What should the development committee's tasks be?

- Should we consider the "development committee as a whole" concept for this board?

- How can we encourage all the members of the board to become active in fundraising?

- Reach consensus on development committee charge and fundraising activities of whole board.

8. **Review board vs. staff roles (10 minutes)**

Facilitator, development committee chair, and CAO lead discussion—Refer to Attachment 8.
Ask questions like these:

- What staff do we have, and how much time does staff have to support board activity in fundraising?

- What is the role of the CEO in fundraising?

- What information and support can board members expect when they prepare for a call?

- How can we work together as a team to improve our results?

- Do we have the ability to manage and track everyone's activity with prospects?

- Reach consensus on staff role vs. board role.

Section III: How to Ask for and Close a Gift   *11:15 am*

9. **PowerPoint, The 5 Elements of the Successful Ask (30 minutes)**

Facilitator presents the PowerPoint, use about 1 minute for each slide.

- Introduces each element of the ask with examples

- Highlights special techniques

- Encourages audience questions and discussion

10. **Conduct role-playing: Facilitator and volunteers (30 minutes)**

Identify three board volunteers in advance to help with this portion of the meeting and share the scripts with them.

- **Use the sample scripts in Attachment 10 to structure the role-play exercise.** This section contains scripts for 3 different asks, one for annual gift (leadership level), one for capital, and one for endowment. Select one or use all three, depending on the time available and the type of funds being raised.

Take questions and open discussion, encourage participation.

Short Break   *12:15 pm*

Section IV: Prospect Identification   *12:30 pm*

11. **Review top 50 to 100 names on prospect list (45 minutes)**

Lists to be developed and provided by staff and/or development committee. **Discussion led by Development chair or CAO and facilitator.**

Review names, discuss each name one by one, ask the following questions:

- Does anyone know this prospect?

- Do you know them well enough to open the door?

- How much could they give (if they were interested in our nonprofit)?

- What would interest them on our table of needs?

- How can we get this person interested in our nonprofit?

Ask the board to help identify any new names of prospects not on the list.

- Let the board suggest additional ways to identify prospects.

- Ask the board to suggest cultivation activities and events that could be used for some of these prospects.

Make sure all information is recorded but don't make final prospect assignments at this meeting. This is better handled as an action step after the meeting, when the planning group or development committee has had time to process the information and can match prospects with the appropriate board member.

Note: In some cases board members are uncomfortable with this kind of information being shared, even in a small group. Be sensitive to the needs and styles of your board and make plans for individual follow-up to gather information where needed.

Section V: Next Steps (15 minutes)   *1:15 pm*

Facilitator, Board chair

- Thank participants.

- Discuss achievement of retreat goals.

- Summarize consensus points, review areas of agreement and disagreement, and assign responsibility for next steps.

- Set timetable for actions.

Adjourn   *1:30 pm*

Next Steps: After the Meeting

Good staffing is fundamental to a strong volunteer fundraising effort. Having staff or the development committee chair provide consistent, reliable follow-up information is crucial to the success of board and volunteer fundraising activity. Identify a central contact point for all information and reporting on calls—whether it is a board member, advancement staff member, or consultant. Next steps include:

1. Assess board retreat and determine whether goals were reached (consider an anonymous assessment survey of all board members).

2. Adjust drafts of all the materials used during the retreat based on the board's discussion: the table of needs, the fundraising goals and timelines, the case, the role of board and staff, and the charge to the development committee.

3. Meet with development chair, identify and recruit development committee members, hold development committee meeting.

4. Determine with development committee how to implement the board policy on giving; who will ask board members, timetable for board giving, and how gifts will be announced to the board.

5. Summarize results of prospect list review, make prospect assignments and send out to all board members in an easily accessible format, such as an Excel spreadsheet.

6. Provide cultivation opportunities for board volunteers for each of their prospects and assist with cultivation activities.

7. Provide background information on each prospect for the board volunteer assigned, including suggested ask amount, area of interest, fellow team members on the call, and past giving summary.

8. Prepare a basic information package personalized for each prospect: Include case materials, pledge card, return envelope, proposal (if appropriate), naming opportunities, list of fundraising committee names, list of full board, and contact information for someone at the organization who can answer questions.

9. Report all activity with prospects back to the development committee or staff. Develop a tracking system to manage board contacts with prospects.

10. Keep the entire board updated on fundraising progress. Make regular e-mail updates on fundraising activity and results a regular feature of board communication.

Keep up the momentum until goals are met!

Attachments to Use in Board Retreat on Fundraising

Note: These materials will need to be adjusted for your organization's individual needs and goals. Feel free to make any changes or use your own materials in place of these where appropriate. These are meant to provide you with a sample or a guideline so that you are familiar with what content to include in each section of the presentation.

Attachment 1. Board Retreat Agenda

The sample Board Retreat Agenda is included in the materials previously. There is one main version of the Agenda, without timing and discussion points, for handing out to all the board members, and one version with timing and discussion points added for use by the presenters. It might be useful to prepare a packet or folder with all the materials in advance for each board member with his or her name on it, to help distinguish between presenters and non-presenters.

Attachment 2. Board Retreat Goals

Sample Goals for the Board Retreat

- Unite the board in taking a leadership role in fundraising.
- Provide education about the table of needs (what the organization needs to raise money for).
- Establish goals and timeline for fundraising efforts.
- Secure input from the board on making the case (how to talk about the organization with prospective donors).
- Establish a board giving policy and consider recommended giving levels.
- Review the role of the development committee and identify ways for all board members to take part in fundraising activities.
- Identify board and staff roles in fundraising.
- Develop skills for making fundraising calls and learn fundraising techniques.
- Review a top prospect list and identify potential board assignments.
- Establish next steps for active board involvement in fundraising.

Attachment 3. Table of Needs

This sample, derived from the five-year strategic plan for a community art center, combines annual, capital, program, and endowment needs. You will want to identify and build your table of needs around the areas your organization will be fundraising for. Most organizations derive their own table of needs from conducting a strategic planning exercise with board input and involvement.

Sample Table of Needs: Community Art Center

1. Annual Fund   **$ 300,000/year for 5 years**

Use: for current operations; includes salaries and overhead.

Goal: $300,000 per year; include 4% annual increase each year in future years.

2. Program Support $ **110,000 over 4 years**

   Use: for a new program to develop an Internet-based curriculum for
   children about the visual arts.

   Cost: $110,000 total; $50,000 for the first year, includes curriculum preparation costs; $20,000 each year for the following three years to update
   materials and circulate to schools.

3. Capital Support $ **500,000 over 2 years**

   Use: renovation and expansion of current facility to establish more space
   for educational programs and online program development.

   Cost: architect has estimated a cost of $450,000; add 10% to cover contin-
   gencies and cost increases.

4. Endowment support   **$1,000,000 over 5 years**

   Use: endow the Program Director's salary.

   Cost: $1,000,000 endowment invested to produce a payout of 5%, or
   $50,000 per year; this will not cover the entire salary, but it will cover about
   80% of it, relieving the current budget of that amount.

5. Summary of Needs: Year 1 $ 800,000

                          Year 2 $ 782,000

                          Year 3 $ 545,000

                          Year 4 $ 558,000

                          Year 5 $ 550,000

   Grand total of needs: **$ 3,235,000**

Attachment 4. Fundraising Goals and Timeline

Note: This set of fundraising goals was derived by a small nonprofit that has
just held a Board Retreat to focus on fundraising efforts. The dollar goals are
modest and the goal for board giving is for 100 percent participation. This is a
good starting point; the nonprofit can move its goals up in future years.

Sample Fundraising Goals and Timeline

Prepared in September for Fiscal Year that Ends on December 31.

Fundraising Goals for Last Three Months of Fiscal Year (FY):

- **Goal # 1:** $100 percent participation in the Annual Fund by all Board members. Board members will make a gift by the end of December.

- **Goal # 2:** Raise an additional $30,000 in operating funds by calendar year-end as a result of enhanced Board fundraising efforts.

Goals and Activity for next FY:

- **Goal # 1:** $100 percent participation in the Annual Fund by all Board members. All Board members will be asked to make a new gift to the Annual Fund in the new FY.

- **Goal #2:** Raise $300,000 for a special project as a result of Board efforts.

- Review projects to be funded and determine highest need (Development Committee will recommend a project to the full Board by December).

- Approve project to be funded and finalize goal by January.

- Development Committee takes the lead on identification of prospects and assignment of prospects to Board members in January.

- All Board members participate in fundraising activities.

- All Board members participate in meeting the goals!

Attachment 5. Case Statement Summary

Note: This sample includes suggestions for making the case for each type of funds needed for an animal welfare organization. You should develop your own case and messages based on your organizational needs.

Sample Case for Annual Fund:

1. Focus on increased need for services: Demands for our services rose 15 percent last year alone. Annual fund gifts provide us with the capacity to offer services to any animal in need.

2. Explain the gap in revenues: Our "gap" this year between revenues and the cost of services is $200,000. Annual fund gifts fill this gap.

3. Give specific examples of how the money will be used: This is how your annual fund dollars are spent:

   - $100 spays or neuters a shelter pet.

   - $250 can supply five elevated beds for our adoptable animals.

   - $500 offers heartworm treatment for a shelter dog.

Sample Case for Capital Campaign:

1. Develop attractive materials to show the donor: Use materials such as floor plans, color renderings, or drawings showing animals in the new facility.

2. Show need for a new facility: Demand for our services has grown by 10 percent in each of the last three years. We are turning away animals that we could save if we had more space.

3. Emphasize features of a new facility: The new shelter will provide state-of-the-art facilities for animals. This includes a new clinic for spay-neutering and a new exchange air system in the kennels so infections aren't passed from one animal to the next.

Sample Case for Endowment:

1. Focus on long-term provision of need: Endowed funds provide us with a permanent base of support so that animal welfare work will continue beyond your lifetime.

2. Explain how an endowed gift works: Your endowed gift will be invested, with only 5 percent paid out each year, so that your gift will continue giving forever.

3. Discuss investments results: Our endowment fared well, even in volatile markets; we have averaged an 8 percent growth rate over the past five years.

4. Suggest a giving area appropriate for endowment: Endowing a staff position allows us to attract and keep talented professionals who will serve us well and stay over the long term.

Attachment 6. Board Policy on Giving

Example of Board Policy on Giving and Fundraising

All board members are expected to support the institution financially to the best of their ability, first through an annual gift, and if the organization is in a capital campaign, through a gift to the campaign. (*Note: Some nonprofits set a minimum gift level—this will depend on each board's culture and membership constituencies.*)

All board members are expected to assist in identifying potential sources of financial support, opening the door to introduce the institution to these prospective donors, and assisting with the solicitation of those sources to the extent that they are able.

All board members are expected to support the organization's fundraising efforts by attending fundraising events, participating in fundraising programs, and assisting with community outreach to broaden the base of support for the organization across the community.

Attachment 7. Charge to the Development Committee

Sample Charge to the Development Committee

1. Lead by example and make your own gift first. Take responsibility for the solicitation of all board members for their annual gift as established by board rules and procedures.

2. Create and review policy related to the solicitation and acceptance of gifts to ensure that donors and their gifts are treated in an ethical and legal manner.

3. Recommend fundraising goals for approval to the full board; set achievable goals and develop accountability measures to ensure that goals are being met in a timely manner.

4. Advocate for development staffing and appropriate program support to meet budgeted goals. Review cost of funds raised in order to ensure that this cost is within peer and industry standards.

5. Provide input in the hiring of key development staff, especially the Development Director.

6. Review major fundraising materials that present the fundraising case; not to design by committee, but to ensure that the organization, its mission, and goals are fairly and accurately represented to potential donors.

7. Oversee standards for gift accounting, gift receipts, thank yous, and donor stewardship to ensure that donors are being treated fairly and that funds are deposited efficiently and meet the wishes of the donor.

8. Provide opportunities for training for all board members so that fundraising leadership can be exercised by each member of the board.

9. Actively lead the board in identifying prospects, opening doors, asking for money, and expanding the reach of the organization to develop new resources.

10. Provide appropriate and timely reporting to the full board on all fundraising goals, progress towards goals, and challenges encountered.

Attachment 8. Role of the Board and the Staff in Fundraising

Example of Board and Staff Roles

Your Role as a Board Member

It is very important to see the staff fundraiser as a professional supporting your efforts, not as a professional replacing your efforts.

The best way to think of the professional fundraiser is as a team member who can organize and provide support for your own fundraising work as a board member. The staff person is best suited to provide the structure, planning, integration with other efforts, and back office work to make the fundraising program more efficient and effective. These are all areas where staff is more efficient than board.

Your role as a board member is to do those things for which the staff is least well-suited. These areas include:

- Make your own gift first.
- Identify potential donors through reviewing lists of prospects.
- Make phone calls and emails to past donors to "bump up" their giving to a new higher level (up to $1,000).

- Take assignments for personal visits to donors capable of giving $1000 or more.

- Use social networking to increase the number of young supporters.

- Assist with development of an email communication strategy for all prospects, forward emails of prospects you may know.

- Review ease of on-line giving and improve on-line experience for donors.

- Help to develop strategy for major gift prospects ($10,000 and up) by identifying their interests, rating them for a gift, and creating a cultivation plan.

- Bring potential donors to the site for a visit.

- Host a small group cultivation event for major donor prospects at your home.

- Sign letters and proposals to donors with a personal note.

- Assist with stewardship— thank donors personally.

Role of the Development Staff (Small Development Office)

The Development Director should be ready and able to make calls on prospects, ask for money, and close gifts. However, many prospects make their best gift when approached by a volunteer or Board member, so the Board should not expect all the funds to be raised by the Development staff alone. The Development staff should be viewed as team members in the drive to secure funds.

Here are some of the activities that the Development staff members can provide to support the work of the Board and other fundraising volunteers.

- Assist in the development and presentation of fundraising goals to the board.

- Create a timetable for all development activities.

- Provide training and support for board fundraising activities.

- Develop and implement a plan to engage the board in fundraising activities.

- Prospect identification: review names, lists, giving history, and background information on potential prospects with board volunteers.

- Prospect rating: work with the board to determine who can give, at what level, and where the donor's interests lie.

- Assign prospects to board and volunteers in an organized fashion.

- Provide appropriate materials to use for calls on prospects.

- Support calls made by board members: this might include appointment setting, research, script preparation for the call, and joining the team making the call.

- Follow-up activity after calls: produce proposals, letters, pledge forms, gift agreements, and track follow-up activity.

- Oversee or conduct gift recording and gift accounting.

- Provide thank you letters and gift receipts in a timely fashion.

Attachment 9. PowerPoint presentation on "5 Elements of the Successful Ask" (not available in the Appendix)

Visit companion web site www.wiley.com/go/boardfundraising to download; edit to meet the needs and experience level of your board.

Attachment 10. Use Materials for a Board Training Exercise on Fundraising in next section.

Materials for a Board Training Exercise on Fundraising

Role-Play Exercise

Note to the facilitator: While it's important that everyone at the retreat learn how to ask for money, not everyone will feel comfortable engaging in a role-playing exercise in front of others. Our recommendation is to select three volunteers in advance of the retreat, give them these materials, and ask them to take on the different roles identified in each scenario.

We have included three sample scripts that you can edit to meet the needs of your organization in order to provide each of the three volunteers with an opportunity to take on each role. Please use your own creativity to develop a script for your organization; these are meant merely as samples or a guideline.

The scripts include solicitations for a leadership annual fund ask, a capital ask, and an endowment ask. Use one or all of the scripts depending on the time available and the fundraising needs of your nonprofit.

Encourage your volunteers to be creative and have fun with the role-playing—this is a good time for the board to relax and laugh after a morning of hard work. Ask the "donor" to make up different objections, and have the "solicitor" try to respond with an appropriate answer. Keep things informal and relaxed, and the lessons will be learned!

Introducing the Role-Play Exercise: Development Chair

Review Goals for the training exercise:

- To practice using the components of a solicitation call.
- To demystify the process of asking for a gift.
- To see the different roles that members of the solicitation team can play.

Three Sample Role-Playing Scripts

Sample Script #1

Ask for a $1,000 leadership annual gift

- Volunteer #1: Take the Opening, Making the Case, Making the Ask
- Volunteer #2: Lead the Active Listening and Response, Close the Gift
- Volunteer #3: Play the donor

1. **Opening (who you are, what your relationship is with the non-profit and with this donor)**

   Hi, I'm Jane, and this is Bobby. We serve on the board at the Neighborhood Day School. I know that your son is a student there; mine is, too. Didn't we meet at the soccer game last month?

   First, let me thank you for your past generous gifts to the Neighborhood Day School. We appreciate your loyalty and your continued support, which is so important to maintaining the quality of our program.

2. Making the Case

We are here to talk to you about our annual appeal, which we launch in the spring, and about a special giving opportunity that is new for us this year, our new Founders Circle.

The Founders Circle is our new giving society to honor our most important annual donors, those who give $1,000 or more. We will recognize donors to this important group by listing their names on a donor plaque in the school lobby, in our annual newsletter, and on our web site. We will also honor all of our Founders Circle donors at a special annual event.

(Pause and let the donor make a comment or ask a question.)

It's important that we have additional funds to meet our operational needs this year. As you know, each family does pay tuition for their student, but the amount we receive per student doesn't cover everything we provide.

This is what your money will be used for:

- To maintain excellent teacher/student ratios.
- Provide new equipment in the computer labs.
- To update the campus and keep our facilities top notch.

3. Making the Ask

John (my husband) and I have decided to give $1,000. We hope that you will consider doing the same. It's important to us to keep Neighborhood Day School going strong, and we know we are going to have to help meet some of the additional costs.

I hope we can count on your making a gift of $1,000 to join the Founders Circle.

(Pause and let the donor respond.)

4. Active Listening and Response

The donor might use one of these objections:

- The gift level is too high for us.
- It's too much for me to give on top of tuition.
- I already give to the athletic program.

- We are unhappy with Neighborhood Day over Johnny's having been sent home last week for hitting another child. Don't they have supervision on the playground?

  (You can ad lib questions and responses, but bring the conversation back to the ask at hand.)

5. **Closing the Ask**

Can we count on you to join us as a member of the Founder's Circle?

We appreciate your commitment to joining us in this new program.

Let me give you a pledge card with a reply envelope. Gifts must be received by the end of the fiscal year, which is in June.

Or—propose a solution to objections the donor has raised:

Let me suggest that we get back to you with that financial information. Can I call you next week? What would be a good day for you?

Thank you for seeing us!

What you are doing means a lot for keeping Neighborhood Day School strong for our own kids and for future members of our community.

Sample Script #2

Ask for a $25,000 gift to name a room in a new wing for a museum's capital campaign

- Volunteer #1: Play the donor

- Volunteer #2: Take the Opening, Making the Case, and Making the Ask

- Volunteer #3: Lead the Active Listening and Response, Close the Gift

1. **Opening (who you are, what your relationship is with the nonprofit and with this donor)**

Thanks for seeing us today. I'm John and this is Mary. We are both on the board at the Art Museum and we appreciate your time and interest in the arts.

First, let me thank you for your past support of the museum. Didn't we meet at the opening for the Matisse show?

2. Making the Case

We are here to talk about our new photography wing. Have you been over to see the construction site yet?

(Pause and let the donor make a comment or ask a question.)

It's important that we finish the fundraising before the building opens next May. The new photography wing will showcase the collection of Mr. Adams, which was given to the museum through a bequest. It will also provide a new space for educational activities for our school outreach program.

(Pull out the rendering and the site plans and share with the donor.)

This is where the new classrooms will be located. As you can see, there will be three of them, each one fully equipped with computers, smart boards, and the latest in technology.

3. Making the Ask

Susan (my wife) and I have decided to give $25,000 to the campaign. We hope that you will consider doing the same.

We would like to ask you to consider making a gift of $25,000 to the museum's capital campaign to name one of the new classrooms.

(Pause and let the donor respond.)

4. Active Listening and Response

The donor might use one of these objections:

- $25,000 is too much for me.

- Can I make a pledge?

- I already give to the Museum at the donor's circle level.

- We are unhappy with the museum over the Adams bequest. Those photographs should be displayed in the current galleries. Why are you building this new wing?

(You can ad lib questions and responses)

5. Closing the Ask

Can we count on your gift to the capital campaign?

Why don't you and your wife come over to the construction site to learn more about the project?

Or—propose a solution to objections the donor has raised.

Let me suggest that we get back to you with a written proposal outlining some giving options other than the classroom. Can I deliver it to you next week?

Maybe we can meet for lunch to discuss the project again at the end of the month, after you have time to review the possibilities.

Thank you for seeing us!

The gift that you are considering is very important to the success of our capital campaign. We appreciate your time and interest and look forward to discussing the project further with you.

Sample Script #3

Ask for a $500,000 gift to endow a scholarship at a university

- Volunteer #1: Lead the Active Listening and Response, Close the Gift
- Volunteer #2: Play the donor
- Volunteer #3: Take the Opening, Making the Case, and Making the Ask

1. Opening (who you are, what your relationship is with the non-profit and with this donor)

Good morning. This is Brady and I am Serena. We are both members of the board of Scholar U. Thanks for agreeing to see us today.

Let me ask you a little about your own experiences at Scholar U—you graduated in 1975, just a few years before I did. Who was your favorite professor?

2. Making the Case

We are here to talk about the need for building the endowment at Scholar U. You probably know that tuition is rising at levels that make the U hard to afford for many middle-class families. Building an endowment will help us to provide scholarships for many of these kids, so they can have the same wonderful experience that you and I had.

(Pause and let the donor make a comment or ask a question.)

With endowment gifts, the principal is invested, and only the interest or income is spent on the project you designate as the donor. Our endowment is currently valued around $40 million, which is small for an institution of our high caliber. Our board has established an annual endowment payout of 5 percent, which amounts to $2 million per year on a base of $40 million. However, we currently need to budget over $5 million per year on scholarships. This is the area of our greatest need.

3. Making the Ask

We would like to ask you to consider endowing a scholarship fund with a gift of $500,000. A gift at this level would allow us to offer two full scholarships each year in your family's name. A $500,000 endowment would produce $25,000 per year, providing a significant level of annual support for our scholarship budget. This fund would bear your family's name in perpetuity.

(Pause and let the donor respond.)

4. Active Listening and Response

The donor might use one of these objections:

- $500,000 is too much for me.

- How is the endowment invested and how has it fared in the market over the past five years?

- We already give to my wife's university.

- We are unhappy with the university over their inviting Howard Stern to be the graduation speaker. How could they do that?

  (You can ad lib questions and responses.)

5. Closing the Ask

Can we count on you to endow a scholarship for deserving students?

We appreciate your interest in providing scholarships. This scholarship will honor your parents for generations to come. I'll ask our staff to send you a pledge letter.

Or—propose a solution to objections the donor has raised:

Why don't we bring you some information on the current endowment investment policies and results from the past five years? Could we meet again next week after you have time to look it over?

Let me suggest that we do some research on the endowments of comparable universities and share it with you. I think you will find that we have used the limited funds we have very well.

Thank you for seeing us!

The gift that you are considering is crucial to our ability to attract new scholars to Scholar U. We appreciate your interest in our long-term financial health. We want Scholar U to be there for our kids, and building the endowment is a great way to ensure that will happen.

Glossary of Basic Fundraising Terms

F undraisers have their own unique vocabulary. Here are the definitions of some commonly used fundraising terms, so that you will be able to understand and use basic development terminology.

Development terminology is explicit and is often tied to the sources and uses of gifts. Most nonprofits use similar terms to mean the same things, but some organizations may use different definitions of certain types of funds based on their own internal accounting or board requirements.

Annual Fund The name commonly associated with a nonprofit's annual drive to raise operating funds. Often the goal of the annual fund is to fill the gap, the term used to describe the balance left after adding up all annual revenues and subtracting them from the total of annual expenditures.

Annual Gifts Those gifts, usually at smaller dollar levels, that are made by cash, check, or through the transfer of securities on an annual basis in support of operations.

Campaign Goal The total dollar amount needed to meet the campaign objectives. The goal may be subdivided to include phases, interim objectives, or components of a larger campaign.

Campaign Timetable The total time (in months or years) that the campaign will take before the goal is reached. Campaign timetables can be broken down into phases or interim periods of activity focused on a set of objectives.

Capital Campaign   A set of fundraising and related outreach activities that are focused on reaching a set dollar goal for a defined capital need (or set of needs) within a specific time frame. Most capital campaigns are conducted to build or renovate a building or facility, but capital campaigns can also raise funds to pay staff, support programs, buy equipment, and cover ongoing maintenance costs for a new facility. In recent years many campaigns have started to include an endowment component to help secure the long-term financial health of the organization. A comprehensive campaign is a fundraising campaign that combines all of the nonprofit's funding needs into one large, multipronged fundraising drive. The comprehensive campaign usually includes component goals for annual fund, capital, endowment, and program needs, and will usually be a multiyear effort.

Capital Funds   Funds targeted for an expenditure of a nonrecurring nature, such as money spent on physical plant, equipment, or property.

Challenge   Some donors make their gift as a challenge to invoke gifts from other donors as a match for their efforts. Challenges can be used in both annual and capital campaigns. Challenge donors often stipulate the ratio at which they want their gifts matched (1:1, 2:1, and 3:1 are all common) and to whom their challenge is directed (such as new donors, increased donors, or capital donors).

Donor   An individual, corporation, or foundation that has made a gift to a nonprofit. The gift may take various forms, including cash, pledges, stock, gifts of property, or planned giving vehicles such as trusts and bequests.

Endowment   Endowed funds are assets that are put aside and invested, with a set percentage of payout determined annually to be spent on predetermined expenses. Usually the donor indicates that a specific gift should be endowed, although a nonprofit's board can choose to place assets they receive from any source into their endowment.

Gift Counting   In most nonprofits, philanthropy from private sources is counted and reported separately from grants made by public entities, such as federal, state, and local governments. While there are standard rules set by national professional organizations associated with counting the funds raised, especially in campaigns, an organization can set any counting rules it wants as long as the board approves them. These rules can cover such areas as how to count trusts, bequest promises from living donors, and other planned gifts; pledge periods; purposes of the gifts made; and sources of funds (e.g., private vs. public).

LYBUNTS and SYBUNTS   These terms derive from annual fund campaigns and refer to the giving history of past donors. LYBUNT stands for "last year but not this year" and refers to a donor who is being asked to renew his or her annual gift. SYBUNT, which means "some year but not this year," refers to a donor who for some reason has omitted an annual gift in the previous year or years (most organizations track donors for at least three to five years) but who is still considered a potential annual donor due to past gifts.

Matching Gifts   Many corporations in America offer their employees the benefit of matching their individual employees' gifts to a nonprofit with a charitable contribution from the corporation to the same charity. These contributions are usually made for annual fund gifts up to some annual dollar cap per employee. The process must be initiated by the employee with his or her own employer, although many nonprofits send reminders to their donors to encourage these types of gifts.

Nevers   This one is self-explanatory. A never is a member of an identified group of potential donors, such as alumni or parents of students at a school, who has never made a gift to the organization. Nevers are the hardest prospects to solicit but can be the focus of a special campaign, challenge, or targeted fundraising effort.

Operating Funds   Money used to cover the basic costs of staying open and doing the work of the organization. Operating funds include budgeted items like salaries, benefits, rent, supplies, travel expenses, printing, and mailing.

Planned Gifts   Charitable gifts that are structured over a long period of time or that entail a giving method other than cash or a check are known as planned gifts. Some of the largest gifts to organizations come as planned gifts. Planned gifts usually provide some tax advantages to the donor or his or her heirs.

Typical types of planned gifts include bequests, trusts, gifts made from an IRA or other retirement account, insurance gifts, gifts of art or other valuables, gifts of real estate, and gifts of stock or negotiable securities. Attorneys, planned giving experts, and financial advisers often get involved in these gifts, making them more complex to solicit, close, provide stewardship for, and administer than a gift of cash or a pledge.

Pledge   A promise of a gift or a gift agreement, usually made in writing, paid out over a series of years. Most annual fund gifts are pledged over a one-year period (including the use of monthly electronic transfers), while campaign pledges are written for three to five years. Most pledges are structured so that an equal amount is paid out each year, but exceptions can be made to fit a donor's needs. It is important to get pledges in writing to make sure that all parties agree to the terms and the payout period.

Pledge Reminders   Letters or reminders sent by the nonprofit to remind the donor of his or her commitment. These reminders can be sent ahead of the expected payment period, or they can be used as a collection tool if the pledge payment is not made promptly according to the timetable agreed upon.

Program Funds   Money raised to underwrite specific activities or programs of the organization. Donors often select which programs they want to support.

Prospect   An individual who has the potential to make a gift to the organization. Usually prospects are identified based on certain factors that make them more likely to give, including previous ties to the nonprofit, interest in the cause or work of the organization, previous giving, future giving potential, relationship to a volunteer, or other visible ties to the organization.

Corporate prospects and foundation prospects can be annual fund or campaign prospects, but usually they are identified separately from individual prospects. Corporate prospects are identified by the company's name, and then linked to a contact person who works at the company. Foundation prospects are usually listed by the name of the charitable foundation, followed by the names of contacts at the foundation, which may include program officers, staff, foundation trustees, or family members connected to the foundation. Since the entire universe of corporations and foundations is so large, development professionals attempt to identify those prospects most likely to support their organization.

Public Phase   A later component of the campaign timetable, the public phase is a defined period of time (in months or years) toward the middle and the end of the campaign when the solicitation of lower-level gifts from donors who might be less familiar with the nonprofit takes place. This is also the time for a larger outreach effort aimed at broadening the base of support for the nonprofit across the community.

Quiet Phase   Usually the first component of the capital campaign timetable, the quiet phase is a defined period of time (in months or years) at the beginning of the campaign, when the solicitation of larger gifts from donors who are closer to the nonprofit takes place. Also, the period of time in which the campaign goals and objectives are tested quietly with leadership donors, helping to determine whether the campaign is feasible.

Restricted Funds   Donors can designate, or restrict, a gift for a specific purpose at the time they make their gift. Legally, the donor can demand or even sue the nonprofit to ensure that the gift is used for the stated purpose. This stated purpose can be for capital, operating, endowment, or program. An organization or its board can apply a restriction to a gift once it has been made, but this is not legally binding and can later be changed.

Unrestricted Funds   Unrestricted funds can be used for general purposes by the nonprofit and carry no restrictions from the donor. Most donors give unrestricted funds for annual operating purposes. Unrestricted gifts are often smaller than restricted gifts, but because they can be used for any purpose, they are highly sought after by nonprofits.

Index